from the depths i call

from the depths i call

Lea Fuchs Chayen

TARGUM/FELDHEIM

Published by:
Targum Press, Inc.
22700 W. Eleven Mile Rd.
Southfield, MI 48034
Fax toll free: 888-298-992 or Israel (02) 651-0432
e-mail: targum@elronet.co.il

Distributed by:
Feldheim Publishers
200 Airport Executive Park
Nanuet, NY 10954
www.feldheim.com

Printed in Israel

DUE TO THE SENSITIVE AND DISTURBING
NATURE OF SOME OF THE MATERIAL
IN THIS WORK,
PARENTAL GUIDANCE AND
SUPERVISION IS SUGGESTED.

Dedication

*This book is dedicated to
the memory of my parents and
family, who were murdered and whose ashes were
strewn in the Valley of Death in Birkenau.*

My parents, Salamon Fuchs and Minna Klein Fuchs

My grandfather David Klein

My sister Rachel Gili Fuchs Kohn
Meir Kohn, aged 10
Neomi Kohn, aged 5

My brother-in-law David Deitel
Yaacov Deitel, aged 11
Benjamin Deitel, aged 10

My sister Miriam Fuchs Sternberg
Moshe Sternberg, aged 7
Samuel Sternberg, aged 3

My sister and her husband,
Chanah Fuchs Schenk and Yisrael Schenk

My brother, Moshe Zwi Fuchs

May the Almighty avenge their blood.

To my aunts, uncles, cousins, friends, school-
mates, teachers, and to the rest of my nation,
whose ashes are all over Europe: in Belzec,
Maidanek, Bergen-Belsen, Auschwitz, Birkenau,
Theresien, Drancy, Gross Rosen, and many
other camps, and in the woods of Germany,
Poland, Ukraine, Russia, Lithuania, Rumania,
and many other countries.
May the Almighty avenge their blood.

To all those who suffered in body and soul and
by a miracle stayed alive.

To those of my brethren who lived through
the miseries of the camps, and on arrival in
Israel joined the army and fought and fell during the war of liberation, many of them buried
without a name, the last survivors of their
families.

May you all rest in peace.

Acknowledgments

My thanks to Judy Montagu, chief copy editor of the *Jerusalem Post*, for her support and encouragement.

To my children, their spouses, and my grandchildren, my love and thanks for guarding and carrying on our tradition.

My everlasting love and thanks to my friend, partner, and husband, Prof. M.S. Chayen, MC, for having taught me to live and laugh again.

My humblest thanks to the Almighty for giving me all this.

Introduction

In writing this book, I was trying to do my minimal duty as a survivor, to the past, present, and future generations of my nation. We speak of six million of our people murdered, but this is merely a number, which no human mind can grasp. We have to think of six million individuals, with names, faces, personalities, and talents or lack of them; of the million and a half Jewish children, whose lives were cut short before they even started — we know how a small baby has its own personality and is a whole world in itself.

Therefore I am writing my own personal story and that of those who were near me. As I write, I relive everything. I am there again, feeling the cold and desperation — even the smell of Birkenau is with me every now and then. I try to describe things as accurately as I can.

If I manage to convey to my readers even a small part of that unbelievable personal tragedy of each and every person of the six million murdered, and of the survivors, too, I should be grateful for it.

שיר המעלות,
ממעמקים קראתיך ה'.
אד-ני שמעה בקולי,
תהיינה אזניך קשבות
לקול תחנוני.

A song of ascents:
From the depths I called
Thee, God.
O Lord, hear my voice:
May Your ears be attentive
to the voice of my
supplications.

(Psalms 130)

Journey to Hell

*I*t was a most beautiful and sunny day in May, when the grass, the trees, and the flowers send messages of renewal of life. On days like these one gets out of bed hearing the birds singing, feels strong, and thinks how good it is to be alive.

But not on that lovely day in May.

It was 1944, the second day of Shavuot, and our part of the ghetto was getting ready to be taken for annihilation by the order of the German SS and the Hungarian gendarmerie.

On that beautiful morning, our lovely garden, laden with roses and other flowers which had not been tended to for some time, was witness to heartbreaking prayers and Torah reading. About a hundred people took part in the service, and for the vast majority of them it was the last time ever. It is difficult to say when we started the prayer, for we had no watches anymore. All jewelry, even wedding rings, had been taken weeks before.

We rose at daybreak, as soon as there was enough light to

dress by, and prepared for our last journey. We did not have electricity, of course, because we were Jews and therefore we did not need it. Even if most of us could not sleep on our last night at home, we lay there not moving, perhaps afraid to think, just waiting for the sun to come up. Even the Germans could not deny daylight in the ghetto.

I was born on December 6, 1923, to a well-respected family, the youngest of six children. My late grandfather on my father's side was the chief rabbi of our town, and after him my uncle was chosen to be the spiritual leader. On my father's side there were *dayanim* and rabbis going back several generations. My father was a *talmid chacham* both in Talmud and in worldly knowledge.

My mother was a lovely, elegant person of regal appearance. We had several good drawings of hers hanging on our walls, but she did them all when she was a girl. In later years I never saw her drawing, although she did give me advice on drawing and painting when I asked for help.

Nagyvárad, where I was born, is called Oradea today. It had a population of a hundred and thirty thousand. In our town and the surrounding area there were thirty-seven thousand Jews. The town itself was pleasant, with a wide and fast-flowing river and several bridges. The main language was Hungarian, although Transylvania, where my town was situated, had been annexed to Rumania. The Jewish population spoke Hungarian, as well as German, which was considered the language of culture, and most of them spoke English as well.

At the age of three and a half I started learning to read Hebrew for the prayers and after that, Hungarian and German. At about the age of eight I started to learn English. At home we spoke either Hungarian or German. Life was pleasant and comfortable, with many branches of our family living in the town.

Two of my sisters were married and lived in Kolozsvár, today Cluj, with their husbands and children. My eldest sister, Rivkah (Rici) and her husband, David Deitel, had two children, Yaacov (Yankele), aged eleven, and Benjamin, aged ten. My second sister's name was Rachel (Gili), and she and her husband Moshe Jaacov Kohn had a son, Meir, aged ten, and a little girl, Neomi, aged five. My third sister, Miriam, was married to Samson Sternberg, with two boys, seven-year-old Moshe, and Samuel, aged three and a half. They lived in our town, not far from us. My youngest sister, Chanah, was married to Yisrael Schenk, and they also lived in our town. They had no children, and as her husband was an Austrian citizen who had run away from Vienna, on many occasions they needed to hide from the Hungarian anti-Semites. After my four sisters came my brother, and then me.

For the first fifteen years of my life, until the outbreak of World War II, it was an accepted thing for the better-off families to have a live-in Jewish cook, and of course a full-time maid. I simply cannot remember having seen my mother carry shopping from the market, the butcher, or the grocer. It simply was not done.

We had happy holidays together with the family, and during the summer our house was full of children and youngsters. In our large garden we had two big chestnut trees. In spring, when they were in bloom, one could see from far away masses of red and pink flowers. Under these chestnut trees we used to play table tennis with our friends. In the afternoons, when the table was put away, we had a hammock hanging between the trees. How pleasant it was, on a hot afternoon, to go to sleep in the hammock, swinging gently and listening to the lullaby of the birds.

Further down the garden, we had a small pagoda. Going up a few steps, there was a room with only one meter of trelliswork around it; it was open to catch the breeze. Two sides of the roof were covered with wild vine and black grapes. In autumn it looked like a painting with different colored bronze, brown, and green leaves. There was a table with chairs, where we played chess, or the girls did needlework, crocheting, knitting, and tatting (lacemaking). Here, in summer, we used to eat Shabbat lunch and our *seudah shelishit*, the third meal of Shabbat in the late afternoon.

Next to the pagoda there were rose bushes, and further away there was a circular flower bed with flowers of the season. Near the house we had a large walnut tree, so in autumn, when the nuts were ripening, we had many helping hands to pick them and, of course, to stuff their pockets and the little sacks that were specially prepared as a reward for their shouting and noise.

Nearby was a large weeping willow which almost curtained off the garden from the house. I loved sitting and hiding under the tree. I sat in the shadow, where I could observe the comings and goings of the household, and yet I could not be seen.

This was the house where I grew up.

When they set up the ghetto our house was included, and there were seventy-six persons pushed into our home. People coming into the ghetto from outside could only take a minimum of personal belongings with them. Ours was the first ghetto in Hungary. I did not realize at the time that there was yet another ghetto in our town. It was at the brick factory, under the open sky, and their conditions were far worse than ours.

I do not know much about life at home during the few weeks that the ghetto lasted. How did my parents manage with all those people? What and with what did they cook? There were many children among the families put into our house, but most of them did not behave as children — they were too depressed.

As soon as the ghetto started, we had to improvise hospitals. Our own Jewish hospital was not inside the ghetto, and of course Jewish patients were thrown out of all hospitals, including our own. As far as I know, we were not allowed to take out any equipment or medicine and certainly no beds.

We had, of course, many Jewish doctors but only one fully trained nurse. Together with other girls, I volunteered and tried to ease the misery of the sick people. We took a large synagogue, removed all the furnishings, and tried to obtain as many folding beds or mattresses as we could. (The synagogues had not been in use for some time, as more than three people was supposedly an illegal gathering.) In the ladies' gallery, upstairs, was the obstetrics section. How many babies stayed alive amongst those who were born there?

The Great Synagogue was turned into a mental hospital. A number of people preferred to commit suicide before leaving their homes, choosing to die in their own beds rather than go through the horrors awaiting them.

We worked, I do not know how many hours, as long as we could, and then curled up in a corner, fully dressed, slept a little while, and then continued to work.

As soon as the ghetto was set up, all fences were taken down so that escape or hiding would be more difficult. People were not allowed to walk about in the ghetto unless they had a pass. Doctors, nurses, some public workers, and the new curse called the "ghetto police" were allowed to move around inside the ghetto. The ghetto police were Jewish boys. I do not know what they got for it or why they wanted to be bosses, but it was very sad to see young boys I knew "keeping order."

Every few days I went home to see my family and change my clothes. Did they wash the clothes? And if they did, how did they do it? I do not know, nor was I home to see. At the hospital, there were no sheets for changing unless the family of the patient could supply them, but since moving around in the ghetto was becoming more difficult every day, they could visit their loved ones less and less. When patients died, the burial society was allowed to take them out of the ghetto to the Jewish cemetery. I cannot remember if anyone from the family was allowed to leave the ghetto in order to participate in the funeral.

If I think back, when I was home, there should have been a lot of noise with so many people in the house and garden. There were also a fair number of children, about fifteen, yet there was no shouting or noise, certainly no laughter. What I witnessed was the silence of the grave, the grave which none of them was lucky enough to achieve. To be brought to *kever Yisrael*, to be buried according to the Jewish ritual, was a luxury, and I envied every person who died in the ghetto and was buried in the Jewish cemetery.

I found this waiting in the ghetto terrible. Day followed day, and the only difference between one day and the next were the tortured people we picked up off the street outside the brewery, which was near the synagogue hospital. Each day there were more people brought in. One night we heard very loud and fast dance music coming from the brewery, but we had no idea what was happening there. In the morning we picked up rich respected people who could hardly breathe or move. Each night some more people were taken to the brewery and tortured in order to find out where they had hidden their fortunes. If they broke under torture and told them about their hidden treasure, the torture went on in order to find out more. If they could not break them, or if the unfortunates had already given up everything, they continued the torture anyway.

I remember seeing my parents' friends being brought in, in shocking condition. The tortures were varied. They started by pulling off nails, burning eyelids, burning and beating the most sensitive parts of the body, and dancing in boots with heated nails sticking into them. The poor Jews had to dance fast, and in order not to hear their screams, the music was very loud. After a few nights, we became experts in differentiating between the screams and the music.

I also worked with the Polish Jewish refugees in a sort of underground, where we had to supply them with false papers, or take them from one hiding place to another, or sometimes if they could not get out, bring them food. None of them spoke Hungarian, which of course complicated matters considerably. For about three years, I heard about the ghettos in Poland, the hunger, and the transports from the ghettos for annihilation. At the beginning of 1943, a year before our ghetto was established, there were refugees who came to us and described the gas chambers and crematoria, although the names Auschwitz and Birkenau were unknown to me until my arrival there.

They told us about the killings in the woods, where people had to dig their own mass graves in order to be machine-gunned into them. They told us about the selections, where children under sixteen years of age and adults from about thirty-five and up were gassed and cremated. They told us that some of the strong young people were taken for work until they themselves became weak and dispensable and were murdered, too. We heard of the camps, of Dachau, Buchenwald, Maidanek, and a few others. I believed every single word they told me, but unfortunately the majority of the people would not believe it. The refugees insisted that the only way to survive was with Christian papers, blond hair, and praying that the war would finish soon. Unfortunately, most of these refugees were subsequently taken to Birkenau. How many of them survived, I do not know.

One morning I was hurrying home from the hospital to see my family; I was almost running, because there was not a single soul in the streets. A ghetto policeman, a young boy I knew, stopped me and started screaming at me, "How dare you break the curfew!" and "Don't you dare try any friendship on me!" Without uttering a word, I showed him my pass and went on my way, terribly depressed to see how fast some people had changed.

A few days before Shavuot the first transport left the ghetto. People started to worry because we were told and assured many times that we would not leave the ghetto, but after the first transport, the ghetto was divided up into several areas, and each area was told on which day it was to be ready to leave.

Each person could take twenty kilograms of luggage, but not in suitcases. Therefore, we started making sacks. We sewed sacks from any available material, starting with our heavy Gobelin curtains, and including tablecloths, which were doubled up so as to be strong enough. What a terrible thing it is to decide what you will take with you.

We were assured by the liaison of the community that we

would stay in Hungary, the families would stay together, the old people would look after the children, and the young people would work. We were assured by the liaison time and time again that the destination had been looked at by him and that he was in direct communication with the Hungarian and the SS authorities, including Eichman. Nevertheless, we were told by the same source, before the transports started, that we would stay in the ghetto. Now we were told again and again that the families would stay together in a place called Kenyér Mezö, which was in Hungary. No one had ever heard of this specially prepared place for the Jews, because it did not exist. The tragedy, of course, was how readily people were willing to believe in anything good or less bad than the tragic reality. That is how it happened that we were sold down the river, literally as slaves, or as fodder for the gas chambers and the crematoria.

Once the transports started, people who were working at the hospital were sent home, and only a small number of doctors and nurses stayed with the patients. I went home on the eve of Shavuot, because on the second day of the festival it was our turn to leave our home forever. As I had not lived at home since the ghetto had started, I found I had nowhere to sleep. My father had a very large mahogany desk, with a green leather top, and it was moved out onto the closed sun porch in order to make room for those families who had been put into the library. I looked at it — and made my bed on top of that desk. I was sure that never again would I have such a lovely, civilized bed.

As I walked home from the hospital, I wandered about a little, knowing that I should never see this place again. It was already dead, the place had become a ghost town. How quiet the streets and houses were! I was walking down the street called "Fuchs Moses St." after my grandfather, with the name still up on the street corner near the synagogue and the Jewish quarter. I thought how strange it was that I had always felt that I didn't belong to this place, always knew that I was an unwelcome outsider. We were constantly told, "You stinking Jew, go to Palestine." Each school had its own uniform, with its own initials, so that walking to school I had lots of stones thrown at me. I never did what I was told: to make myself small and never answer back anti-Semitic outbursts. For each stone I received, I sent back two, and I had stones prepared in my pockets, just in case. My parents were shocked at my behavior, because it was undignified and dangerous.

Walking home from the hospital, I went through the dead streets and past the houses near the synagogues and the Jewish schools. All the homes were empty of people. They had been taken away, either the same day or the previous day. Doors were open everywhere. I went into an apartment where one of our *dayanim* lived. There was not a soul, dear God — everything had been left behind, and it was certain that no one would ever come back again. How terrible it was when I thought of the good looking, dignified family. The name was still on the door: Dayan Blum. I walked out, not wanting to see any more. I felt a strange relief that our turn to leave the ghetto was already set for the following morning. I knew that all of us would be killed, but the waiting, the misery of the ghetto, and seeing how fast people disintegrated and changed was too painful to watch.

It was the first day of Shavuot. I was twenty years old. My cousin, Lea Normand, who was two years my senior, came to say good-bye, as she was to stay on, working at the hospital. She was the daughter of my mother's only sister, whose husband, a doctor, had recently died. Lea also had a brother,

Aharon Ari. Lea managed to arrange for her mother to go with the last transport, which was the hospital one. Some people still believed in the "civilized" Germans. They were sure that the hospital transport would be treated in a privileged way.

During that last day I also looked in on my grandmother's younger sister, who lived in a corner house not far from us. Aunt Rivkah, as we called her, was pleased to see me and consulted me as to what would be the most appropriate outfit for the journey. I looked in her wardrobe and suggested a plain dress. She told me that that particular dress was only nice with a large brooch (real of course) which she had had to give up with her other jewelry. She also asked me if she should take a hat with her. I felt like screaming, for I realized that she had no idea at all of what was awaiting her.

In the evening the ladies had to light candles for the second night of Shavuot. Some people had a tiny piece of candle, others took a few drops of oil and a wick in order to light up and make the appropriate blessings. I remember my father, mother, sisters, and brother, and possibly others, standing around the desk (the desk I slept on) in almost total darkness listening to my father pronouncing the Kiddush, the blessing which was usually made on wine in normal circumstances, over a large silver goblet reserved for Friday nights and the evenings of festivals. That evening my father made the blessing on cold imitation coffee. There was not even any real coffee! It was the last time my father ever recited Kiddush.

I often try to recall our lovely large dining room on Friday evenings, the table laid for dinner with our best china and silver, ten large candlesticks with candles burning, the family standing around the table dressed for the Shabbat, and my father holding one of the large silver goblets in his hand and reciting the Kiddush in his lovely melodious voice.

Of that last evening at home my memory recalls my broken parents standing in semi-darkness and my father saying the Kiddush in a hushed, choked voice. Did my father know that this was the last time?

We had saved some of our daily bread ration for the evening so as to have something to eat. After that we all went to sleep. I buried my face in my sheet and through it I smelt the leather which covered the desk. Lord, how quiet it was! Every now and then I dropped off to sleep. Once, I awoke, and perhaps because of the hardness of the desk and the wall next to me, I thought or dreamt I was in a grave. My heart was racing as I started breathing again. When I realized how ridiculous this dream was, I almost laughed out loud. Did I think I could get the luxury of a grave?

At the crack of dawn I rose, putting on two sets of underwear and two dresses, which, of course proved a big mistake because of the tightly packed boxcars where we were headed were excruciatingly hot.

All of a sudden everybody was up. Children did not have to be coaxed to get ready. They understood the serious position we were in. A short time after rising, people started to assemble in the garden around the pagoda for the morning prayers. More people joined us from the neighboring houses. What a sight it was, the lovely garden, the beginning of a warm sunny day: the trees still had that lovely light green tint of new leaves and tens of people were standing in their white tallitot (prayer shawls) praying.

I am trying to remember if mothers gave their children anything to eat, or if the adults ate or drank anything.

How long did the service last? It seemed forever. After the special prayers for the festival, we said the prayers of penance, which are recited on Yom Kippur.

The service was over, and people were taking off their tallitot, which they had to pack to take with them. I am there now — my mother comes out carrying a pale pink damask tablecloth, meant for twenty-four people. We used it for special occasions. This is a very special occasion. The tablecloth is going to be the shroud for the Torah scroll, which will be buried in it. We know that we are not allowed to take the Torah with us and we also know that if we leave it, it will be desecrated. According to Jewish law, one has to bury a Torah scroll or parts of it rather than have it desecrated. The ritual for the burial of the Torah is the same as for any Jew.

A few days previously, we built a double wall in the attic of the washhouse, which stood in a corner of the garden, near the house. For some reason we thought that in the attic of the washhouse, the Torah would be less likely to be discovered.

The tablecloth is placed on the table. The Torah scroll is wrapped in it again and again. One small part is still visible, it is left open because it will go from hand to hand to be hugged and kissed. Then it is covered completely, very carefully, and taken up into the attic for burial. We all seem to hold our breath. Did it take only a few minutes? Is it possible to bury our holy scripture, the code by which our forefathers, we, and all those Jews who will come after us, have lived and will live by? We are burying it and with it ourselves, our past, and our future. How can one do something so final in so short a time?

It seemed that it took hours or days; it seems to me now that everything was done in the slowest possible motion, and I see so clearly, even now, the pain, sorrow, anguish, and mourning. Did we hope to come back and retrieve the Torah? Or was this our own funeral procession — from the pagoda, through the garden and the flowers, to the washhouse, saying farewell to ourselves, our lives, and our hopes.

It was a large Torah, with a wine-colored mantle made of velvet with gold embroidered lettering and a large silver filigree crown.

The Torah was never found. I do not know what happened to it.

The gendarmes were coming into the houses, shouting and cursing, "Hurry up, stand five in a row, in the street!"

In the middle of people hurrying to take their sacks and belongings, a tragicomic thing happened. One of the people who had been placed in our house when the ghetto was established was an elderly lawyer, all alone, assimilated, not observing any religious practice, yet suffering for being a Jew. He had been acting rather strangely, and all of a sudden he walked up to one of the gendarmes, stood to attention, and said, "Beg to report, sir, I have lice." The response was a large blow on his head with the butt of a rifle.

The house was empty. I ran back just for one last look at the places I had particularly loved. My own room was a large square room, with two large windows and cheerful white furniture, with powder pink upholstery and rugs to match. The room was unrecognizable. There had been three families together with two old aunts crowded into it.

The next room I ran to see was the library. What a lovely room that used to be! The walls up to the ceiling had been covered with books, most of which were now gone, thrown down into the cellar so that people would have somewhere to put their belongings. The desk had been put out onto the sun porch — I had slept on it. The curtains and the round table with small armchairs around it were also gone. This room had seen many varied people, as my father would not lend out books but people were invited to come at any time and read in our library. I do not know how many families were put into that room, but I remember three families with children managing to make their home in different corners of the room, on the floor.

Amongst them was a young rabbi, Rabbi Levy, head of the yeshivah, together with his wife and their three small children, the eldest girl either five or six years old. What dignity and correct behavior right to the last moment of our arrival in Auschwitz! We were in the same boxcar.

I ran toward the garden just for a last look and good-bye. My parents were calling for me and getting nervous because they could not see me. So I did not say my farewell to what was once a lovely garden. I picked up my sack and walked away from my life, my security, the place where in the past we had even laughed, and walked toward what I thought was death. It certainly was for the vast majority of the people.

I can only imagine what my parents must have felt, walking away from what they had built up, from the happy times they had had with their children and grandchildren.

I stood in a row with my sister, mother, and grandfather, and we started moving. We had no idea where we were going. In spite of the cursing of the guards, we could not move faster. There were several thousand people, old, young, and children, dragging themselves and their twenty kilogram sacks.

It was getting hot. The sun was up and with all the clothes we were wearing, it was hard going. At the corner of the first street, we turned left and passed many homes I knew so well. We came to the end of this street, where our doctor had a large corner house, next to which was the wall of the ghetto. Part of the wall was taken down. We turned left into the deserted street outside the ghetto, with all the homes shuttered up and no people or traffic. We understood that they were taking us to a branch railway in a park nearby. The rails had been left there, although they were very rarely used except for bringing up supplies, every few weeks, to the nearby army barracks.

The gendarmes were growing nervous — they had to get us off the streets and close the wall of the ghetto (with wooden planks) so that people outside the ghetto could open their shutters, go to work, and resume normal life as if nothing had happened.

My mother, who was not used to carrying twenty kilograms on her shoulders and hurrying with it, was pushed and fell, then was kicked several times by the guards. She kept rolling down the street. We were not allowed to help her to her feet. At first she whimpered, then managed to get up, pick up her sack, and with her head held high, she started walking again. Luckily we did not have to walk too far to the park, and to the rails.

We arrived at the park, which used to belong to the estate of Count Rédalyi and had been donated to the town. Here we used to walk down the long shady avenues with magnificent old trees, flower beds, and large bushes; here we played hide and seek, blind man's bluff, or just ran around.

There stood the boxcars, meant for transporting cattle or goods. Two to three thousand people had to climb up with their sacks into these high boxcars, without steps. Some of them had wooden planks leaning against them, which possibly made the struggle a little easier. Helping each other, or being helped by a kick or a shove from the "master race," sweating and breathless, we were glad to be inside the train. We were careful for our family to keep together.

Each of us deposited his sack but found it almost impossible to stand due to lack of space. A Hungarian and a German SS guard came in to count us and decided to push more people into our car. Finally the count was seventy-two people, and we were told that if anyone should be missing, all of us would be shot. They rolled the large door shut, leaving a very narrow strip open. High up in one corner, there was a small opening with bars across it.

Whether we wanted to or not, we had to sit down on our sacks for lack of room. We were also becoming exhausted. It was growing hotter and hotter inside the boxcar. We had several layers of clothes on and there was no ventilation. We started peeling off layers of clothes. Outside there was a lot of running around and shouting going on.

My sister Miriam's seven-year-old son Moishele said, "Behind the train, on the other side of the park, is our house — we used to live there. Who lives there now? Are there any non-Jewish children playing with my toys?" I did not hear what my sister answered.

The door was rolled open again. No more Hungarian gendarmes. From now on we had dealings with the German death's head SS. Two large buckets were thrown into the car. We were warned to be quiet and the door was shut again.

The elderly people started to feel faint. We discovered that we did not have enough water to drink. Some people had brought some thermos flasks, but that was nothing to what we should have had. We still did not move. We kept saying and hoping that the moment we started moving we could catch a little breeze through the narrow opening. Families and friends were trying to sit together and keep an eye on one another.

Some time later, the door opened again and an SS guard appeared in the opening, pointing his rifle at us. "We have received information that people have dollars and jewelry and gold hidden in baked bread. Give it up and nothing will happen to you. If we find it, you and your family will be shot. We are going to search you all." No one moved. He ordered a few people to open their sacks, taking homemade bread or biscuits amid curses and threats. He had a lot of experience, it seems, of transports. He knew that baking was almost impossible in the ghetto and I was sure that he had found before, and would find again, diamonds, gold, or other jewelry hidden in the bread and cookies.

People were more and more beaten down and were waiting for the train to start moving. We were hoping that the heat, which was becoming unbearable, would ease a little. Of course we did not realize that this was just the beginning of a three and a half days' journey, and that things would become worse by the hour.

We heard the engine letting out steam, then came a shrill whistle, and slowly we started moving.

It sounds crazy but I felt relieved that we were at last on the move. Through the narrow opening, we got very little air and saw no signs of life, as if life had stopped outside. The only reality was the train and what was happening to us in the boxcars.

If someone had dared to write a play describing what we were living through, people would have said that only a sick and sadistic mind could imagine a nightmare like this. I have learned that no fantasy can be as cruel and terrible as reality.

We were leaving the park, that much we could see, and were passing by a stream called Pece. A large number of gendarmes were standing nearby, waiting. That was very bad news. They were standing near the manhole where people tried to come up from the sewer. There were Christians who for a lot of money were willing to wait for people at the manhole with clean clothes and false papers, hide them for a few days, and then take them across the border to Rumania. It had worked a few times, but either inside the ghetto or outside, it must have been discovered.

I, too, had planned to go across the border to Rumania. In Rumania it was easier to hide and stay alive by bribing, waiting to join the partisans, or just waiting for the Russians. But somehow, by the time I obtained my false papers and my parents could be convinced that there was nothing to lose if I were caught, it was too late. The evening when our group was ready to go, we were met by a a peasant woman who introduced herself as the wife of the man who should have come to meet us. She told us that her husband did not dare to contact us; they suspected he was under surveillance, as were most people living right on the border. She also told us that the previous night there had been a lot of shooting and they thought that the route had been discovered. She assured us that as soon as things quieted down, she would once again come.

During that same night the ghetto was surrounded by gendarmes, and at four in the morning the planks of the ghetto walls were hammered into place. By seven to eight o'clock a gendarme, with a clerk from the town hall, was collecting the watches from people's wrists and wedding rings from their fingers. They came around with a large sack, already half full with their loot. We took off our watches; my mother, without showing any emotion, took off her watch and wedding ring, threw them into the sack, turned around, and walked away. Other jewelry had been taken previously.

The train for some reason did not pick up speed, and as we were traveling slowly through the outskirts of our town, there were a few non-Jewish people standing near the rails shouting out names and asking worriedly about certain people — if we had seen them or heard anything about them. Perhaps they were looking for intermarried relatives or friends. It could not have been so healthy for them to be known as

Jew-lovers. I remember a man with blond hair and a moustache running near the train and wiping away his tears.

It must have been already mid-day; no one seemed to be hungry, the little water we had was gone, and a new serious problem arose. The biological needs of the people had to be looked after. We looked for the two buckets the SS had thrown into our car, and found two people sitting on them in a corner. At first they would not give them up. It seemed impossible that some people were already looking for small advantages and comforts. After a lot of argument, and only after the SS guard (there was an SS guard outside each boxcar) banged several times on the wall, did they give up the buckets. We had to get something to curtain off a small area near the door and narrow opening. People had to move even closer to each other and those who were sitting in the vicinity of the door started objecting to having a lavatory set up near them.

Only after some serious thumping on the wall by the SS did we manage to set up this luxurious lavatory.

For the ladies two girls held up a sheet, donated by my mother, and when men needed to use the buckets, men held up the so-called curtain. With seventy-two people, even though we had no water and were sweating, the two buckets filled up very fast, and the only way to get rid of the contents was to try and force it out through the narrow opening. I think it is fairly obvious what happens when one has a nearly full bucket and tries to pour out the contents, even if the wind is not coming from the opposite direction. It soon became clear that few people were public minded enough to do the work in these circumstances, and we had difficulty in smoothing things over. How fast people disintegrated and showed their more selfish sides. Not all, of course, and those who stayed dignified and polite in these circumstances saved our sanity.

It was difficult, even for young people like myself, to be constantly on the go. People started complaining and jealously guarding every centimeter of floor space where they sat. One could not stretch one's legs without the cooperation of the people sitting opposite. It was very difficult to get anyone to help at being a "lavatory attendant."

An elderly couple, who had been put into our house in the ghetto, asked for help. They were at the far corner of the car, and as I was the "nurse" (not that I knew much), I had to get to them somehow. They were both heart cases, and the gentleman had passed out. I had to push people in order to lay him on the floor to make him comfortable. I took off as many of his clothes as I could. I was sure he was going to die, and I had no idea of what to do, nor had anyone else. I remember saying to myself, "For Thy salvation I hope, O Lord." My mother sent across, from where she sat, a flask of cognac. I wiped his face, forehead, and neck with it and forced a few drops into his mouth. Slowly, perhaps in spite of my ministrations, he opened his eyes. We left him lying on the floor, but he took up a lot of floor space. He was the first of many more who felt faint or fainted later on during the journey.

The children were sitting quietly and undemanding. Perhaps they were getting extra attention from their mothers and I did not notice it. Among the adults, arguing started and went on almost non-stop, most of the time by the same people. A few of us who were lavatory attendants, nurses, and general dogsbodies tried to soothe nerves and to convince people to conserve their energies. Why did we, a few youngsters, take charge and do a thankless filthy job instead of sitting quietly and stewing in our misery? Was it pure public mindedness or was it selfishness, too, that time should go faster? *Many times, even today, I think about it and, honestly, I have no answer.*

Hour to hour, and later minute to minute, new problems arose. Sitting was very difficult for hours and days at a time, without anything to lean on. Only few people had the luxury of the wall of the boxcar. Soon requests were heard, at first politely, "Please do not lean on me, I can hardly sit upright, my back is breaking." For some time apologies could be heard but when people had to stretch their legs, they simply did, and then chaos reigned. There were more and more arguments, and more warning bangs on the walls by the SS.

The children were far better behaved. They needed less room, and it was easier for them to sit low without backaches, but they had to be protected not to be trampled on. Every now and then, we took turns picking up the wilting smaller children and holding them up to the tiny window near the top of the car; it gave them a breath of fresh air and some relief from the monotony of the journey. The amazing thing was that nobody cried, neither the children nor the grown-ups. We were beyond crying.

Late in the afternoon, we stopped in the outskirts of a town called Debrecen. As we passed through the station we saw the name written on top. This gave the people some hope that soon we would be arriving at the camp, which had been looked over by one of the Jewish representatives who had assured us that our families would stay together and work in Hungary. We started to feel the heat and lack of water, even more than before. There were boxcars with German soldiers in them right next to our train, so that any breath of air we might have had was stopped by them. We asked people if it was possible not to use the buckets, as here we could not empty them.

Opposite our car there was a German soldier, sitting with the door wide open, dangling his legs. I thought, should I ask him for water? I felt terrible asking a German for a favor. Would he do it? How could I get a container out? In the end we found a small saucepan, and through the crack I asked if he could get us a little water for people who were not feeling well. He looked carefully right and left, and nodded. I thanked him and said I would hand him a small container through the high window. I could not believe it — he brought the water and handed it up to me. At least half of it was spilt by the time I got it through the bars of the window. There must have been about two glasses of water left. We tried to moisten people's lips with it and the very old received a few more drops of water. I was ashamed of myself for having asked a German for water, but I think I was right. I also asked the soldier, through the crack, if he knew where we were going. He did not answer directly, but just pointed his thumb downwards.

As dusk fell and evening followed, we were still standing in the same spot, and the bucket problem became acute. From sheer exhaustion, people started to fall asleep and drop onto one another. A lot later, when it was completely dark, the train started moving again. The poor people started making tracks for the buckets, in total darkness, to the accompaniment of requests not to be trodden on; others just pushed people aside. I was expecting the children to start crying in the darkness, but no one did.

As soon as there was enough light, we tried to orientate ourselves, to determine in what part of Hungary we were traveling and where we were heading to. The men took out their tallitot and tefillin to pray. They wanted to be ready early because soon we were supposed to be arriving at Kenyér Mezö, the place which we had been told had been prepared for Hungarian Jewry for "resettlement" within Hungary.

A new day started with old and new problems, and with

nerves wearing rather thin. For some reason it was obvious to everyone that we should be arriving soon and that was why we were not being given any water. The poor doomed people in the boxcars were even encouraging each other to be more patient, in anticipation of soon getting out, stretching their limbs, and drinking as much water as they wanted.

The sun was up and it looked like another hot day. For what we could observe of the scenery rushing past, we had to admit that it was not the totally flat countryside of Hungary. Therefore, the people said we were making a detour to our destination, though they could not say why. We were all very lethargic and we tried to make light of the fact that because of the lack of water we did not eat, and so we saved our food. A discussion started about the type of work we would be doing in Kenyér Mezö. Would we be working in the fields or in factories? Were there any factories nearby? And so on.

About the middle of the day, the train started to slow down. We passed the station and were shocked to read the name "Kassa." Kassa was in one of the Hungarian-speaking parts of Slovakia, which had been given by Hitler to Hungary.[1] This could mean only one thing. We were heading for Poland! Even the biggest optimist amongst us realized that this meant the terrible camps, and who knows what else. It was dead quiet — we were all in shock. Although I knew all the time that our destination was Poland and death, when one is proven right, it is still a great shock.

The train comes to a halt. The doors are rolled open. The ramp is full of SS officers and guards with dogs. There is a lot of coming and going. We do not see any more Hungarian gendarmes. We are completely in the hands of the SS. We are told to send two people from each boxcar to collect water in buckets, which they supply. We all drink and drink and wipe our faces with a damp cloth, and meanwhile a high ranking SS officer, speaking fairly fluent Hungarian with a heavy German accent, goes from one boxcar to another and tells us, "You are going to Poland for resettlement. The families will stay together, the old people amongst you will look after the children and cook, and the young people will work, and as long as you work honestly, you will be treated in a fair way and will be fed."

We look at each other. We have been told we are being taken to Poland. We still go on drinking as if we know that after this there will be no more water. The sweat starts pouring out of us, we feel terrible, distended, sick, and in shock. I start crying — crying bitterly for all the things I wanted to do but

---

1 Kassa was on the Slovak border and used to belong to Czechoslovakia; its Slovak name was Kosicze. The language spoken by the population was mainly Hungarian and Slovak. The part of Czechoslovakia where the *Volksdeutsche* (Germans) lived was called Sudetenland, which was annexed by Germany in 1938, only seven months after the annexation of Austria (known as the *Anschluss*).

The rest of Slovakia received autonomy and two days later, on October 8th, the Hlinka guard was established. These were local thugs, like the SS in Germany. They were instrumental in rounding up the Jewish population, robbing them, and doing any filthy work against them, and doing it with great relish.

In 1940 Hitler started taking areas from different countries and giving them to his allies. He took part of autonomous Slovakia, part of Serbia, and the northern part of Transylvania from Rumania and had them annexed to Hungary. All these areas and a lot more used to belong to the Austro-Hungarian Empire before World War I.

shall never be able to do, for our lives and for all the Jewish people. More than anything else, I am crying for the last bit of dignity which all of us lost during the last few days. If only for this, may the Germans be damned forever and ever. Oh why do I have to spend the last few days of my young life in a boxcar, with my clothes soaked in other people's urine and excrement?

We are taking deep breaths of fresh air — soon they are going to shut the door again. We are told that if one person is missing on arrival, everyone in the boxcar will be shot. My mother talks to me quietly and begs me to jump off the train and run away. How can I do it? I have no false papers with me, and at this stage I do not want to leave my family and survive alone. I want to die with them.

The SS start shutting the doors. They leave a narrow crack open, put an iron bar across the door, and put a padlock on it. This is it.

My mother talks to me again in the presence of my two sisters, my brother-in-law, my brother, and my father, and says a very strange thing. She says it with utter conviction. "I do not know what will happen to us, but of one thing I am absolutely certain: you will be all right." I am shocked. How can she single me out and say this?

As far as I know, I am the only survivor of the seventy-two people in the boxcar. Later, when I found myself the survivor of my family, the one who could be the spark, which developed into a flame, to carry on our family's tradition, I realized that what my mother said to me in the boxcar was her last will and testament. To lead a serious dedicated life was what she meant by "all right."

The engine starts puffing again, outside the sun shines, and the train, carrying the several thousand condemned people, starts gathering speed.

Several thousand people, six million people, it does not mean anything. One has to think of the individuals, the children, the mothers, grandparents, fathers, beloved friends, good and bad people — we were all speeding to our deaths.

Recently, a friend who had not been in the camps asked me what was the point when I felt most dehumanized. I thought and answered, "Honestly, never. I felt hungry, sick, hopelessly weak and dirty, but never dehumanized." Strict adherence to my normal behavior, religious observance, and prayers, whatever I could remember by heart, gave me a feeling of superiority over the German barbarians. I looked down on the same people who committed mass murders and the most terrible experiments in the name of medicine and science, and listened to Mozart and Beethoven, and thought of themselves as superior human beings. I looked down on them then, and I look down on them now.

As I am writing now, I think that the nearest I came to feeling dehumanized, or rather stripped of my dignity, was in the train. Perhaps because I had to see my family going through all the humiliations. Somehow the train journey stayed in our minds as one of the biggest traumas.

After drinking a lot, we start eating a little, and so the buckets are in great demand again. It seems that now, crossing the border from Hungary into Slovakia, we are traveling faster. Less and less people behave as they used to at home. Who would have imagined it possible? I am grateful to the Almighty that my family and a number of other people pass the test with flying colors.

Conditions are deteriorating and more and more quarrels start up every minute. I am sitting on my sack for I feel I cannot climb over people and argue non-stop. I look around me and see that some people do not even open their mouths. I do not think they are in the boxcar. They are somewhere far away, thinking how they could have saved their families and also themselves. Thank God they will not have to live long with these thoughts. I doze a bit, get kicked, and doze off again, trying not to think. Oh, that cry was so good. Now I am just waiting with the others for the end.

Dusk is falling. Others are sitting and I take over the buckets, trying to smooth things out. What for? The train is beginning to climb. It is dark. What is the time? I sit again near my father, near my mother, near my family, my sisters, brother, and grandfather behind us, so that we can lean on each other. My grandfather, the epitome of an elegant and dignified gentleman, has not said a word for several hours and is clinging to his dignity with all his might.

I drop off to sleep. All of a sudden I wake up with a start. Opposite me sits a man with his wife and two teenage children, and he chooses to put his legs on my shoulders, so as to stretch them. I think he is asleep, I take his legs off my shoulders without remonstrating with him. He kicks me in the face and I fall back onto my grandfather, who falls forward onto some people opposite him, and so on. An outcry starts. The man opposite me starts kicking me in the stomach and tells me that if he wants to put his legs on me, then that is where they will stay. It is dark and one cannot see, only hear what is happening. My brother wants to know what has happened, and my father starts, politely, asking the man to stop. I get up and make my way toward the buckets, to work, or do anything that is needed. Dear God, why cannot we die now? Why go on with these tortures?

I look out, and through the crack I see the lovely hills of the Tatra. *People used to go skiing there and do so even today. How strange that Jewish youngsters ski there, laugh, and have happy times, not even thinking of the speeding trains going from all over Europe to Auschwitz, Birkenau, and other camps, only fifty-some years ago.* The hills, full of trees, rush by. My parents and grandparents know the Tatra — they used to come for holidays to Karlsbad and Marienbad.

I cannot understand why it takes so long to get to Poland. The misery, stench, nerves, and the hopelessness...I observe that even the quarrels are done with less strength now and not as loud. We are very dehydrated, some people feel giddy, and others do not care what happens around them, or what the future holds. They only want the train to stop so that they can stretch their legs. And now there is a new thing: a few people are saying the same thing over and over again, almost as if they are talking to themselves in a psychotic way. It is no use talking to them; they do not understand, nor do they hear me or just plain do not want to hear.

I do not go back to my sack to sit down, as the man opposite me still has his feet on my sack. His wife sees me and tells him to remove his feet; however, he turns on her and tells her to mind her own business. I sit down for a while with my brother and sisters, away from the man. We lean on each other and sleep a little. We are all so tired.

We are already used to the noise. The steam engine has a special message, a message of death and misery, going all the time, "chu, chu, chu." Thank God there are no longer any steam engines today! I went to see Landsman's film, Shoah, and as I was sitting there with my husband, the large steam engine appeared on the screen and I heard the noise, that "chu, chu" sound, which recurs in my nightmares. I almost ran out — I was back in the train, with all its misery. After an hour I got up with my husband and walked outside, into the reality of life in Tel-Aviv, with the sun shining, children laughing and talking Hebrew, and myself, not in the train, but a free citizen in my own Jewish country. Thank you, dear God.

As soon as there is enough light, people organize them-selves to pray, with their tallit and their tefillin — people are praying with hardly any strength left in them. *They were pray-ing, and now I know it was the last time in their lives.* I cannot un-derstand why the children do not cry. Why are they so quiet?

We can see more of the lovely scenery, but I think we are leaving the Tatra behind us. Now everybody realizes that we were sold down the river as slaves and carcasses. I wonder how many people still hope to stay together with their families, work, eat, and stay alive.

Another sunny day. I think we are in Poland, on Polish soil, soaked with Jewish blood. I pick up my sister Miriam's younger boy and hold him up to the window. He holds onto the bars and gets a little fresh air. The boy sees some children playing in the fields and he says in a sad tone, "I would also like to play outside with the other children." I promise him that soon the train will stop and then he will be able to play. I take him down back to his place, and the poor little boy keeps saying, "I am so thirsty, so very thirsty." I tell him soon, soon, we will drink water. I feel like screaming, "Why am I telling this lovely little boy all these lies?" Moishele would also like to drink, and I promise him as well. Dear God, forgive me.

How much longer? I look at my grandfather. How can he sit up all this time? He does not say anything. I look at my mother and father — they do not say a word either. I cannot see my brother, my sister Miriam is talking to her little boys. Her husband is not here, he is in the Hungarian forced labor service. My sister Chanah and her husband are sitting, just looking at each other. My heart breaks for her, now she will never have any children, this is the end.

The train goes slower. The "chu, chu" is driving me crazy,

the constant puffing, the quarreling, the SS banging on the wall. The buckets have to be emptied now, it is my turn to empty them. I stink already. Why do I have to die like this?

We pass a station, Krakow, or are we imagining it? The train has slowed down, where are we? This is our third day in the train. Why does it take so long to get to the place, to where they are taking us? How much longer can we stay sane in these circumstances? Or are we all mad already without our realizing it? There are many fantastic people in the boxcar, toward the end of the third day, who have managed to hold onto their dignity.

Nowadays I wonder why we did not talk to each other about important things. Perhaps there was nothing to talk about. We only said the most necessary things, the urgent things, like "I must get to the bucket."

It is getting dark and people are saying the evening prayers. We are hardly alive and the boxcar is becoming more and more quiet. There is no strength to argue, what does anything matter anyway?

I go and sit down near my father. We hold onto each other. The train is playing tricks. It stops and starts suddenly, or is it us who cannot sit up any longer? I can see my father is in pain. He has a hernia which was incarcerated in the ghetto, but who could even think of an operation? There was no possibility. I ask him and he only shakes his head. I kiss him and hug him. I drop off to sleep. My feet are terribly swollen, so I take my shoes off. I wake up and ask my mother how she is. I ask her to lean on me, so that the three of us clutch each other, on this very last journey. I must have dropped off to sleep again, for how long I have no idea.

I awake with a start. The train has stopped with a big jolt.

There is a lot of terrible shouting going on outside. Some light is coming through the crack. The door is violently slammed open and several men in striped suits with caps jump up and shout in Yiddish, "*Yidden* (fellow Jews), leave everything and get down quickly!" I am looking for my shoes and cannot find them, when suddenly I tread on them. The men hurry me. I turn to my grandfather, who stands dazed. He wants to take his tefillin but I hear one of the men telling him in Yiddish, "Old gentleman, here you will not need tefillin." I step up to my grandfather, wanting to kiss him for the last time. Someone picks me up and throws me onto the ramp, into the madhouse, into hell. I fly out and fall on top of the people on the ramp. At first I think it is daylight, but it is only a wall of reflectors, so that we cannot see what is behind them. The place is full of SS with thick sticks and dogs, and several hundred, or so it seems, prisoners in striped clothes, and several thousand completely dazed tottering people.

I pick myself up and look into the boxcar — I cannot see my grandfather anymore. I see my brother and father — and then they are gone, pushed on by the throng. I am also pushed in the opposite direction. I see my sister Chanah — is she saying good-bye to her husband? Am I imagining that she says, "Never mind, we will be together anyway"? Do I hear that? It is a matter of seconds, and my brother-in-law is pushed on and they are separated forever. I am looking for my mother and sisters. Men and women are already separated, the children are with the women.

The noise is terrible, everybody is looking, asking for someone. Nobody cries, neither children nor adults. I see my mother standing with my sisters and their children. I go and stand with them. An SS man sees me running there, takes his thick stick, puts the hook around my neck, drags me out, and throws me into another group. We are being pushed but I manage to get back to my family again and stand holding Moishele's hand. A prisoner in striped clothes comes by, gets hold of me, drags me out, and throws me into another group. I am pushed on, there are so many people pushing, for they are pushed as well, and I cannot get back anymore. I try turning, to get out of the crowd. SS men with dogs are all over the place. We are supposed to stand five in a row. Who can count, who can walk? Who can think? I have moved away from my mother and sisters and now I shall never find them. I so much wanted to die with them.

There are ambulances on the ramp for the sick! For the people who cannot walk. Each of them has a large red cross. *The ambulances are mobile gas chambers. With nurses in red cross uniforms!*

All one hears all the time is, "Have you seen...? Have you seen...?" The men are all gone, now we are only girls, and in our group there are no children. SS and dogs, dogs are everywhere.

It is so difficult to walk. But we do not have to, we are being pushed. Five in a row, five in a row. I hardly know anyone near me. What does it matter, it is the end. Slowly I start seeing the chimneys belching smoke and flames. Yes, this is what our refugee friends told us about. Our feet barely touch the ground. I am completely light-headed, as if I were drunk. It is impossible to think. I did so much want to stay together with my family, but I know they are going to die and so am I. We only take different routes, but go to the same place.

We come before a small group of death's head SS officers, all in boots, shining boots, dogs and boots. I look up — a tall death's head plays God. *I did not know at the time what he was doing with his thumb. I did not know that this was Dr. Mengele.*

How easily he decides: this one to life and the majority to death or for torture experiments in the name of German science. We are split again, five in a row, five in a row. The dogs, the boots, and the SS. We still cannot see where we are because of the blinding reflectors. Why is everybody behaving as if they are doped? Why doesn't anyone cry? No children, only dogs and boots.

We are beginning to turn left, when all of a sudden a cousin, Valvi Weisz, steps out to ask me to look after his daughter, Jetta, who also turned left, the same way I am going. This spoiled adored daughter, who was only fifteen, was all alone; his wife had gone in a different direction and one of his sons had gone still a different way, and he was worried. I promise him that I will look after his daughter, although I know I cannot do so, since we are all going to die. I think, "Let the poor man die in peace."

We are turning away from the ramp, we have turned left and now we are with our backs to the trains. We are pushed on, I feel like I am hovering and am not sure that I am really here.

There is a terrible smell. What is it? I see enormous flames at a distance, reaching up to heaven. Boots, dogs, and SS. Now people are falling and are pushed into the ditch on either side of the road. Here I recognize people. There is a lady lying in the ditch who has just fallen down. I hear a girl saying that she took the poison too late. Her husband took it first and was dead on arrival. I know the lady, she used to have one of those elegant handbag and accessory shops in the High Street. What an end!

The smell is terrible. We are going to our deaths, in a more or less orderly fashion, five in a row, with dogs and boots. I am starting to say, "*Shema Yisrael*, the Lord is our God, the Lord is

One." I know that decent Jews die with that on their lips. I also say, "*Al chet she'chatanu...*" the prayer of penance, and then again, *Shema Yisrael*, and so on. I look up to the sky, it is red with flames. Then it comes to me: the smell, dear God, it is the smell of thousands of burning bodies, of my brothers and sisters. I look around, I cannot see anything but reflectors, dogs, boots, and the terrible flames. The flames and the smell. We are getting nearer the flames, we are walking toward them. I say my prayers and when I finish, I start again from the beginning.

I am completely calm and everybody else seems to be too. I accept inevitable death, this is our nation's fate. It is difficult to put one foot before the other, but we all go on doing so. One cannot fight against one's destiny. I wonder if my mother realizes that I am going to die just as they are, but they are only taking us along a different route.

We are turning left again. The sky is purple, and we are definitely going toward the flames. I feel a slight panic. I have accepted the idea of a gas chamber and the crematoria but, dear God, to be burned alive out here for the amusement of the Germans? Shall I be strong enough to die with dignity? Please, oh please, help me not to beg for my life — in any case it would not be granted. It is not losing my life that so disturbs me, but being burned to death! I did not know about that...

The smell is getting nearer. We can feel the heat of the flames. Now we can see a cluster of trees and near them is this open fire. I see the SS nearby with dogs and prisoners and pitchforks. Am I imagining that people are moving in the fire? They probably burn other things there, too, not only bodies. I am waiting, praying, and telling myself not to lose my dignity and self-respect — it would be terrible to die for the amusement of the Germans. I have to be strong. We reach the open fire. We are not stopping, the boots and the dogs go on as well and do not tell us to stop. The flames reach to heaven, I am sure, carrying the souls right up. Dear God, when will it end?

We are turning left again. We are walking so slowly, how long did it take us to get here? When was it that I still had a family? It seems more than a lifetime ago. Now we are stopping, just standing, thousands of girls. Dogs and boots are standing nearby, we just stand. There is a low-lying house about seventy meters away — is that the gas chamber? At least the Germans will not be able to see and laugh at our death throes. We are moving very slowly toward the house. Soon, soon. Many girls have gone in already. We wait. I do not want to see the dogs and the boots, but if I look up to the sky, it is full of smoke and painted red by the flames.

We move some more. I know, I heard from the refugees that the Germans cut the hair and take the gold fillings out of the teeth. They also look for diamonds concealed in teeth instead of fillings.

When do they do it, before or after? I have no gold or diamonds in my mouth, but they do not know that. I only want to be strong and proud. Of what? I cannot think very clearly. Oh, I remember a psalm, it was written for now and here. "Even though I walk in the valley of the shadow of death, I shall not be frightened, no evil shall befall me. I shall not be frightened because You are with me." We used to sing this psalm at our third meal on Shabbat afternoons. I am trying to remember the tune, I am trying but already cannot remember. It is so hard to think.

My father used to teach me Psalms with the commentaries. Early in the morning in summer, I used to sit with my father in the garden and he taught me. Afterwards he taught me to walk and stand straight. Each of us took a stick and linked it through our elbows behind our backs and walked up and down the garden, breathing the fresh air in and out.

We are moving again. Why is everybody so calm and dignified? Were we all trained from the moment we were born to know how to die with dignity? Thousands of girls, and we are all so calm. Soon my turn is coming. There was another psalm we used to sing at the end of each meal on Shabbat. We are moving, this is it. I wish I could remember the tune. "They that sow in tears, in joy, in joy..."

I am inside the house. Gas chamber I am sure. We are told by prisoner girls to undress and just leave our things. They start shaving us. Where are all those lovely, good looking girls? We cannot recognize each other. We are all very calm. I am very muddle-headed.

I am waiting for an injection. I am sure that they are going to give us an injection before the gas. Why an injection, I do not know. What about our teeth? No injection. We are pushed into a very large hall. The ceiling is full of faucets, just to fool us that water will come out instead of gas. I have heard about this as well. We are so many girls, more than a thousand, waiting for the gas. No SS, no dogs, no boots.

Suddenly hot water comes out of the faucets. We all drink and drink and wash ourselves. I know the Germans, they are trying to fool us. After the water will come the gas. It is so good to drink and feel the water. At least I will die clean.

The water stops. Now, now I shall have to breathe in deeply. It is much better. It goes faster this way.

Nothing happens.

Some girls start moving. There are SS women and prisoners who keep shouting orders. What do they want? I am being pushed again. We are coming to a door, opening at the opposite end from which we entered. No more water, no gas. Perhaps we are going to get the injection. We are in another hall. The prisoners hand out "clothes." One dress, a rag, with nothing under or over it. I have no shoes. Some still have their shoes; if the shoes were not so good they allowed them to be taken into the showers. I was told to leave my shoes outside — good heavy walking shoes. Now we are told to get dressed. It is difficult to describe what we look like.

I get a brown silk dress with a very small pattern, long, down to the floor. I am dazed. No gas, no injection. I am still waiting for it. They are saying something. Shouting and pushing. I am being pushed again and I have to push the others. I am coming to the door. Now, now it will happen. We are pushed out through the door, outside the house, to the back of the house.

It is just beginning to be light outside. I look around, and my heart misses a beat. I feel I am going crazy. It cannot be. Wherever I look there is only barbed wire, as far as I can see, only barbed wire and watchtowers, many, many watchtowers. Dear God, what have I done to deserve this punishment? Now I realize, I am going to stay "alive" for a little longer, just as long as I have the strength to work. Why could I not die with my family? It comes to me with a shock that I have not got a family anymore.

The sun is beginning to come up. Opposite us I see several young boys, possibly twelve to fourteen years old, it is difficult to say. They are in striped suits with striped caps. We did not get striped clothes. That would have been too good for us. The boys look — I wonder if they see us or just look. Poor children. How long have they been here? I see their eyes, eyes full of sorrow, eyes which speak of two thousand years of persecution. No one cries, we are all standing dazed. We seem to stand five in a row for a long time. More girls come out. Five in a row.

Hell

Long, so long. After what seems an eternity, the SS women with the dogs bark orders and a *Kapo* girl comes along with a metal stick. She screams at us and uses her stick freely. "This is just a taste of the future," she says. "You animals, if I say something, you do it at once." She is a Jewish Slovak girl. Poor girl, how long has she been here in Birkenau? She has a striped dress and her hair has grown. She looks totally mad.

We start moving. We have to concentrate on putting one foot in front of another. I am in agony, I have no shoes. We are walking on gravel and I am not used to walking without shoes. I keep telling myself to forget what I was used to. A girl tells me that after a week or two, we will not even think about shoes. She says it is healthier to walk without shoes. She also says that when our hair grows again, it will be much nicer and stronger than before. She whispers, we are not supposed to talk. I look at her and she looks at me and we do not recognize each other. The voice bothers me, and I know that I know that voice. It comes to me suddenly — "one and two, one and two..." — it is Babi Morgenstern. I used to go to her last year for gymnastic lessons. She also recognizes me and says not to worry, as long we walk straight and do not bend all will be well. *As far as I know, she never got to see her hair grow again, poor thing.*

We are beginning to turn right, several thousand girls. I see that we are heading for the open fire again. No injection, open fire, no gas. It is so difficult to walk. I leave blood marks behind me, but so does Babi and the other girls who have no shoes.

We are just passing the open fire on our left side. Formerly we had the fire on our right side. Where are they taking us? We are dragging ourselves along. We walk straight on and finally come to a gate. Many sentries. Many watch towers. A sentry opens the gate. Boots and dogs and death's heads. Electrified barbed wire fences with death's heads on them. Double fences. *We were in a camp within the large complex of camps that was known as Auschwitz-Birkenau.*

On the right hand side there is a small house with windows and one or more doors, and window boxes in the windows with red geraniums growing in the middle of this mad world. These are the SS offices full of barking SS women. Next to it there is a long, I think prefabricated, house, which is the kitchen. That also has normal windows. In front of these buildings, there is a largish empty space and we are supposed to stand here quietly in the sun, without moving and without talking. We have SS women and dogs watching over us. Camps, camps, wherever I look, chimneys belching smoke and the flames of the open fire, cloudy smoke. The smell, the dogs.

I see Tereza Weinstein, who used to be my math teacher.

She is trying to organize us and begs us to stand quietly. No one takes any notice of her. Where is Babi Morgenstern? I cannot see her. There are others I know, but no family, no real friends. This seems to be a very large camp. There is no food, no water. We just stand. How long? Who knows?

Next to us is another camp, just as big, but it looks strange. Electrified wire and a deep ditch divide the two camps. Families, whole families. There are some very old people, some children, young people, and even one or two babies, so the girls tell me. They are in their own old clothes, old, but their own. They have their hair and look very thin and sick. Some children even have toys. Later I hear that that is the Czech camp, the Theresien Camp. Ours is the Hungarian women's camp, Camp C. Ours is not a work camp, we are told, but an annihilation camp. There was not enough room in the gas chambers and crematoria to "process us" so we have been put into this camp until...

It is becoming very hot and we are standing, or sitting down, or crouching. However, when the *Kapo* comes near, we pull ourselves up, for we have already tasted her metal stick. We see some girls come up to the kitchen and get the bread ration for their hut.

It is getting hotter and many more girls have come since we arrived, all freshly shaved and in some odd looking dresses, belonging, who knows to whom?

Five in a row. *Achtung!* Attention! Who can stand straight? A Slovak girl comes and counts us. She looks like a young, old person, with lovely black hair, a striped dress, a large irregular number tattooed on her forearm, and thick pillars of legs with scars on them. She looks at us with large sad black eyes; she probably came from a good home and is not more than twenty-two or twenty-three. Only the Lord and she know what she has suffered, what she has been through. She speaks to us in Hungarian, with a Slovak accent, and tells us to try and listen and obey what we are told, because it will make life easier for us and for her, too. She says she will be our "*Blockalteste*" — head of our hut.

Five in a row, *Achtung!* She counts us and tells us not to move. Five in a row. The *Lageralteste*, the prisoner responsible for the whole camp, counts us as well. She also must have been from a good family and must have been a lovely girl. She has an intelligent face and also speaks Hungarian with a Slovak accent, but she speaks German to us. She tells us we must behave ourselves. She counts us, then she speaks Slovak to our *Blockalteste* and to the other girl prisoners who will head the huts.

"*Achtung!*" Even the heads of the blocks stand to attention, and Irma Graese arrives. A demon. What a beautiful young girl! Blond flaxen hair plaited around her head. Freshly ironed and starched uniform, shining boots, and a folded leather plaited whip in her hand — and, of course, her dog. She is the second in command of our camp, Camp C. This is our first encounter with her, and after this we see her every day and the entire time we are in Birkenau. *The last time that I saw her was at her trial in 1946 in Luneburg, where she was sentenced to death by hanging — may the Lord not have mercy on her soul, if she had one.*

She counts us, looking at us as if we were the most disgusting reptiles imaginable, barks out a few orders, and goes on. Five in a row, and we are moving toward our hut with our *Blockalteste.* Her name is Babi. She was engaged to a medical student who was killed by a German.

We finally arrive at our new home. All the blocks (huts) are the same size. There are thirty-two blocks; each block holds from a thousand to twelve hundred girls. Along the middle of the block there is a long brick funnel which is supposed to carry the heat through the hut, if and when they heat. On either side of this funnel there are three-tiered bunk beds made of wood, with twelve girls in each bunk, six cn either side, with feet meeting in the middle. We lie on wooden planks, and often they break and we fall onto the bunk below.

That first day, when we walked into our hut, number 22, there were no bunks at all. The day was drawing to a close, and at night we had to be quiet and were not allowed to go outside. We were allowed to go to the latrines, where about fifteen hundred to two thousand girls went in all at the same time. I found out the usefulness of my long dress. A small strip from the bottom of it served in lieu of toilet paper. We were chased and shouted at, and had to hurry to allow other girls to come in. We ran back to our hut. It was growing dark. There was no electricity and it was physically impossible for the thousand to twelve hundred girls to sit down, but we were not allowed to stand. We had to be quiet, no noise. As soon as the *Kapo* or the second in command to the *Blockalteste* or the many *Stubendienst* (these were girls whose job it was to wake us up in the morning, chase us out to be counted, clean the hut, and distribute the food) moved on, we simply had to stand up, although often we could find foothold for only one leg. We fell over each other all the time. We trod on each other, trying to get near a friend or a family member.

This was our fourth sleepless night. We had not had anything to eat or drink since the shower, when we drank warm water. Many of us were going out of our minds.

I simply had to stand up, but could hardly stand. I found near me a wooden upright and held it tightly. I must have dropped off to sleep and fallen over. I picked myself up some-how and then I saw my father pass by, turn around and smile at me, wave, and then he went on. I called after him. He did not hear me. I begged the girls to let me out after him, but it was impossible to move. I asked everyone if they saw him. He smiled and waved to me. Somehow I managed to reach the main door of the hut, falling over and treading on the other girls, although my father had gone in the opposite direction. I was desperate. I kept asking if anyone had seen him. Although we were not allowed to leave the hut, many girls were wander-ing around outside. I looked up to the sky, full of stars, with the chimneys and the open flames behind me. I started run-ning around, hoping to find my father. Someone got hold of my arm and asked me to find her street and house. She told me she did not have to stay here, she had a comfortable home and bed. "Please," she pleaded with me, "take me home." She looked mad, and I realized all of a sudden that I was also losing my mind and seeing my father pass by was pure hallucination. I tried to tell the woman we would have to wait for daylight.

Most of the night we were either trodden on, or trod or sat on someone. There was a terrible noise going on, with peo-ple asking each other in the dark, "Who is next to me?" "Have you seen so and so?" or "Do not tread on me, you are sitting on my head or stomach. You are killing me." We were lightheaded and many of us did not know where we were. Twice that night I heard, "Did you hear? They are taking us home." I tried to think about my mother, my sisters with the two little boys, go-ing into the gas chambers. I found I could not breathe, there was a smell of gas. It was still dark and the *Stubendienst* started chasing us out to the latrines. On the way we noticed a wash-room, a hut full of taps. If you were lucky and could push enough, you could drink and wash yourself a little.

After the latrines we ran to the washroom, but I gave it up as a bad job, as I did not feel up to pushing and jostling with a few thousand girls. Five in a row, five in a row. You must not go into your hut. Our hut, our new home. You have to stand five in a row, to be counted.

Lots of shouting, beating. "You animals, five in a row." When the *Kapo* arrived, somehow things were better and more quickly understood. It was getting light, a new day in Birkenau. Hell on earth.

I look at my fellow girls and cannot imagine that a short while ago they and I were individuals with a will and a mind of our own. "*Achtung!* Attention! The *Blockalteste* is coming to count you. Five in a row, you animals, and don't you move," screams a *Kapo*. We are counted. We go on standing, and standing.

"*Achtung!*" The *Lageralteste* is coming to count us. We stand some more. They count the inmates of each hut and then add up the numbers. *Achtung!* A death head is coming to count us, boots and dogs. When all the huts are counted, then *Achtung!* Irma Graese, shining boots, dog, starched shirt, and long plaited blond hair. *Lageralteste, Blockalteste*, all stand to attention. She counts us, barks a few times, kicks a few unfortunate girls, and, with a smile, moves on. Only after every hut in Birkenau and Auschwitz has been counted and the numbers totaled up (the total should come to between 100,000 and 150,000 prisoners), and they know that no precious prisoner is missing, are we allowed to disperse.

Now we are going to get something warm to drink — tea, or at least it looks a little like tea, and it is sweet. We drink it slowly and with each gulp I feel life and strength flowing into me. We get it in large saucepans or buckets and are told that half a bucket is for ten to fifteen girls.

Each of us is allowed to take no more than two gulps. We hand it on and wait, almost shaking with eagerness, to have a warm drink. We get a second round, but by that time the liquid is almost cold. It is horrible how we watch each other so that we should not be cheated out of a few drops. We do not get any bread yet, no solid food ration, but we feel so much better already. We can disperse and go back to our hut.

There is not enough room for all of us to sit on the floor, so some girls have to stand. But it is so much easier to manage in daylight.

My head is beginning to clear a bit, and I realize I shall have to pull myself together and be very strong so that I should live as a human being until they kill me — not as a raving lunatic, which is what the Germans would like to reduce us to. I realize that we have to start counting the days. I shall have to make some order in my day, so that there should be a difference between morning, noon, and evening.

The most important thing is not to lose count of the Jewish calendar, to know when is Rosh Chodesh so that, should we survive long enough, we should know when the Jewish holidays occur.

I know that I was taken away from home on the second day of Shavuot, which was the seventh day of Sivan, May 29. We arrived in Birkenau on the night of the 10th of Sivan, so today is the 11th of Sivan, June 2. I am going to tell the girls around me, several times a day, the day of the week and the dates, in case I should forget or be taken away. I am certain that there are other girls keeping a count of the days and weeks too, but we are not allowed to talk and there is no way of asking or meeting the other girls, except those around me. The times when we run to the latrines or try to get near a tap to wash are the times I see girls from the other huts, but the urgency of the moment does not make for much conversation.

"*Alles raus, Alles raus!*" We are chased outside and have to do it on the double — always and everything on the double. We have to sit on the ground, between the two huts. Good news: we are to be supplied with bunk beds.

Now, for the first time, sitting outside in the blazing sun, we can look around and see who the girls are in the hut.

I see, not far from me, an eighteen-year-old girl from my town, the daughter of a doctor, who suffers from severe diabetes. She looks very pale — she used to be such a spoiled and carefully looked after child. *I do not know if she survived, but I saw her a few months later, in August or thereabouts, and she was doing well on the starvation diet we received.*

There are one or two girls who, for the last twenty-four hours, keep telling us, "Have you heard the latest? They are going to take us home." Some of us tell the girls to stop spreading this stupid news because it will cause mass hysteria.

A few girls try slinking away toward the latrines, then a stampede starts, which immediately brings on us beatings, curses, and punishment. The punishment is kneeling, straight-backed, without moving. It is very hot. We have not eaten for several days and we still have a deficit in fluids.

The *Kapo* arrives like a hurricane, with her stick. I am most afraid of her when kneeling because then we are invariably hit on the head, with rather unpleasant after-effects. I am not talking or moving, perhaps the stick is not meant for me, but she comes from behind and perhaps I cringe, so she hits me with all her might on my shoulders and head. I fall sideways onto the girl next to me, and so all five of us topple over. This, of course, calls for, "I will teach you animals how to behave and kneel to attention." She goes on rampaging somewhere else and I start to vomit and sweat, but continue to kneel. Thank heavens that the earth is not static, and so we slowly start getting a little shade. I am giddy, thirsty, and sick of living, but then again who is not?

"*Achtung*, five in a row, five in a row. Stand to attention to be counted!" We stand for what seems ages, and of course we move because we are giddy and light-headed. Finally we are counted and counted again, and counted for the third time, and there are a few girls missing from our hut. They discovered friends and relatives in other huts, where they have bunk beds, and managed to run there. The numbers must stay as they were, so either the same girls or others are brought back to our hut. When the final count is done, we get our first ration of "bread" and soup with bits of vegetable swimming in it. It is a thick piece of bread, and we wonder how much flour and how much sawdust is in it.

The soup we receive is in different sized buckets and saucepans. We have no spoons or anything else to eat with, of course. Some girls try to fish out a piece of vegetable with their fingers, to the objection and shouting of their partners to the bucket. We count how many gulps each of us takes and hope for more vegetables and thicker soup on the second round. As I take my bread with shaking hands, I stop and make the blessing. What wonderful food, it puts life into us.

After eating, I say *Birkat HaMazon*, the blessing after food, and feel that I am taking charge of my existence in these new circumstances. We finish eating far too quickly and now we are allowed to go back into our hut, which has been fitted with three-tiered bunk beds. The girls start running and pushing to get to a place which they think would be advantageous for them. Twelve to a bunk, six this way and six that way. I climb up to the top bunk in the middle of the hut. I choose to be

My parents during World War I. My father was an officer in the Austro-Hungarian army.

My parents on the front, near Lemberg, erev Yom Kippur, 1917.

My father with four of his grandchildren. From left to right: Yankele Deitel, Father, Neomi Kohn, Benjamin Deitel, Meir Kohn.

My second sister, Gili, with two of her children, Neomi and Meir.

My oldest sister Rici's boys, Benjamin and Yaacov Deitel.

My sister Gili with her little girl, Neomi.

My sister Miriam, 1944.

From left to right: my brother Moshe, Lea Normand, Aron Normand, and myself.

My sisters Chana and Rici, with my brother Moshe and myself, outside our house.

My sister Chanah and her husband, Yisrael

My sister Chanah

with my head near the wall of the hut, which is made of wooden planks. I want to be far away from the happenings of the hut. Here, lying on my side, I say *minchah* and decide to say it on the following day earlier, after the middle of the day.

We stretch out, and although we are lying on hard wooden planks, we do not notice the hardness but enjoy the luxury of lying down, which we have not done since leaving the ghetto five days ago. Now we are allowed to go to the latrines; we run there and back because we have established a tiny place we call our own and we do not want anyone else to take it away. We come back, most of us get our places back, some of us cannot remember where we were so arguments and quarrels start up, which brings the inevitable "Quiet you animals!" along with beating and more curses, until we settle down.

At the end of the hut there is a small utility room with two or three buckets, to be used only in extreme emergency. (These buckets were the center of our existence during the nights all the time I was in Birkenau. A little later, when we were all suffering from dysentery or urinary infection, and had to run so often, we were given up to four or five buckets.) Of course it was not enough, but we were not allowed to take them for emptying to the latrines. We were not allowed to go outside the hut.

Most of the transports arrived during the night, and the platform with all its human tragedies could be seen from our camp. The latrine we called our own, or rather the one which was nearest to our hut, was at the bottom of our camp, and the ramp with the railways was no more than fifteen or twenty meters away.

The buckets would fill up very fast, and there were two or three *Stubendienst* standing there with sticks and not letting the girls anywhere near the full buckets. The buckets were constantly overflowing. In sheer desperation, girls tried to get out of the hut, if they could, and run to the latrines.

I know that sitting in a comfortable home and reading this detailed account of how many gulps of soup we all had, how many times a day we were allowed to go to the latrines, how many buckets we had for the night, and how we managed to exist, must sound rather exaggerated. Nevertheless the purpose of the Germans was to reduce us, before killing us, to something like animals, so that our lives and thoughts should revolve only around food, how to get to the latrines, and how to wash ourselves a little, without soap of course.

I was asked, "How could you live in such a terrible stench?" I said, "What stench?" The smell which drove me crazy was the smell of the burning of my fellow Jews. When I saw the chimneys, the open fires, and the unending number of trains arriving with Jewish people from all over Europe, I was afraid of the annihilation of my entire nation. The smell of Birkenau is definitely the smell of burning flesh.

Night fell and we were in darkness. We were exhausted but we still had to learn how to lie and sleep with eleven other girls on a bunk bed. At first we were content just to stretch ourselves, but we learnt that two tall girls with their feet meeting in the middle would be kicking each other all the time. The other thing we had to learn was "No lying on one's back." We lay on our sides and if we wanted to turn, which was often because of the hardness of the wood, we had to ask all the girls in our row to turn as well.

Later on, when we had painful spots from beatings or infected sores, it was a problem how to lie, and on which side. My daughter recently asked me, "What did you talk about?" I think the answer is "Nothing." Certainly at the beginning. It is interesting that I remember so many important details about the first few days, yet I have no idea who the girls were in my bunk. Not even one.

I started reciting to myself *maariv*, the evening prayer. It was a quieter night, and the great misery of the night buckets had not yet started. We slept from sheer exhaustion, and it seemed almost immediately that we were awoken with the shouting, "*Aufstehen, raus raus!*" and given encouragement by being pulled off the bunks together with beatings, for those who did not jump up for joy at the arrival of yet another day in Birkenau.

A new day in Birkenau, which starts with running to the latrines. I was not so lucky. As I got off my bunk, a *Stubendienst* grabbed me by the arm, while holding another girl with the other, and dragged us toward the other end of the hut. There were three full buckets, brimming over. She told us, "Each of you take one and one in the middle between you. Take them to the latrines, empty them, then wash them and bring them back shining." We tried lifting them but of course they spilled and we could hardly move them. She screamed at us and we started on our way. Both our legs were soaked with the contents of the buckets. My partner was taller than I, a nice girl, who kept apologizing that the bucket was tilted toward me because of her height. On the way we found a procession of buckets. Some poor girls were carrying two buckets each.

By the time we emptied, washed, and returned the buckets, we could not go anywhere because of the screams, "*Appel, Appel!* (counting parade)." Therefore, we had to be counted again. There was no chance of washing ourselves, so from necessity we learnt how one cleanses oneself with earth. We took a handful of earth, it was a pity it had so many small stones in it, but we rubbed our hands, legs, and feet with it and repeated. Were they clean?

The sun was coming up so I could say *Kriat Shema*, "Hear O Israel," with the morning prayers. This time I prayed in an upright position and watched the light getting stronger. We stood for ages before anyone came to count us, but every now and then someone came over to remind us that we were animals and *Schweinhunde*.

We felt that there was something frightening going to happen, it was in the air. Our *Blockalteste* came out and whispered to some of the girls to pass on to others, "Mengele is coming to do selections. He was on the platform when you arrived. He was the one who decided where you go. You have to look well and healthy, stand straight, and do not look tired or sick. If he asks for girls under sixteen who would like to go to their mothers where they will get better food, do not move, do not react to his promises. Pinch your faces, so that you do not look pale." Boots and dogs, many SS death's heads, mainly men, run around to see that all is ready and waiting.

The *Blockalteste* starts counting us. *Achtung*. The *Lageralteste* counts us. All in order. *Achtung*. The SS man counts us, all in order. We hear the roar of a motorcycle. Lots of shouting, "*Achtung! Achtung!*" We start rubbing our faces, sometimes we rub the faces of each other and try to look healthy. It takes a long time before the crowd of boots, death's heads, and dogs work their way down the camp toward us.

"*Achtung!*" *Blockalteste*, *Lageralteste*, and we, turn wooden. He does not count us, he never counts us. His job is more important. There must be about five or six people with him. We are standing, as always, five in a row in two columns. He works his way down slowly, with Irma Graese and another death's head, looking at us carefully and, in a fairly normal voice, in order not to frighten us, says that if anyone is not feeling well or has diarrhea she should come forward to get treatment and medication. They are leaving. We hear that three girls are being taken by him for "treatment." We do not know who they are. They are from another hut. Later on we hear that one girl was taken because she had one brown and one light gray eye. The other two, no one knows why.

We are soon going to get something to drink. The excitement dies down, we get a few gulps of tea and after that we go back to our hut, to our own place on our bunk bed. We learn that this is going to be our routine, if we are lucky and no major excitement befalls us. We doze, we whisper.

Some people start whispering what they will cook when they go home. They start reciting recipes for meat dishes, cakes, and delicacies. This was a sign of deterioration, and in many cases later on, we saw that the next stage after recipes and cooking was to slowly become a *muselman*. A *muselman*, an Auschwitz expression, was a person whose mental and physical state was galloping down and further down. They hardly looked alive, and although they walked, most of them were not compos mentis. Their skin was stuck onto their bones, their eyes and teeth were bulging, and they sat doubled up in a fetal position.

I tried thinking of something, something that would take me away from this unbelievable existence. I remembered a book I had read about autosuggestion. I cannot remember who the author was, but it taught me to step out of myself and be an onlooker of what was happening to me. I learned never to say I was hungry, thirsty, or cold. In any case it would not help, but only make the misery worse.

The main events of the day were getting up while it was still dark outside (at this time it was still summer), running to the latrines, somehow managing to get near a tap and wash ourselves a little, standing sometimes for hours to be counted and, if we were punished, kneeling and being beaten, selections by Mengele two or three times a week (on other days, sick girls would be sent off on a two-wheeled cart), and keeping quiet on the bunk bed. Toward evening, we would be counted again and receive our bread ration and soup. Sometimes after the morning count we would get a thin liquidy porridge instead of tea. It we were lucky, this would be our uneventful existence.

Two days after I arrived in Birkenau, I was going to the latrines when I came face to face with my eldest sister, Rici. She had heard from a girl that she had seen me, but I had no idea at all that she was in the camp. We decided that she would come over right away and we would ask one of the girls, if she did not have anyone special in our bunk, to let my sister take her place.

Thus it came about that my sister and I stayed together all the time in Birkenau.

When we were lying on our bunk, she said to me, "Tell me, why don't you ask where Yankele and Benjamin are?" Yankele was eleven and Benjamin ten. I replied, "I thought they went with their father." She said, "No, they came with me, and I was told to leave the children with a Mrs. Gans and that we should meet later, so I did. Do you think," she asked me, "that the children and our parents are getting better food and are living in better conditions?" I told her I was sure they were. Later on she asked me if I thought the children would be getting vitamins. She asked these questions every day and often several times a day. Sometimes I felt like screaming and I thought if she continued to talk about the condition of our grandfather, parents, and children all the time, I should go out of my mind.

Very soon we developed a new occupation: scratching, and trying to kill the lice in our clothes. We had no lice in our hair since we had no hair, but we had lice in our clothes in the tens of thousands and could not get rid of them. It drove us crazy and sucked our blood. They were also dangerous because they spread typhus. Not long after getting our lice we became infected with scabies. This was very infectious and caused sores all over the body, but mostly between the fingers. It came from lack of hygiene and cleanliness. It itched terribly and was an added misery on top of everything else. The treatment of it would have been to wash with soap and disinfect everything we touched.

As time went on more people became sick, lost a tremendous amount of weight, and were taken away during selections. Often people had to be put into the small hospital in our camp, where the doctor, an angel, tried to smuggle people back into their huts if she knew that Mengele or Graese were coming.

We also started infecting each other with carbuncles, which were very painful. They were often full of pus and before they started discharging, we had fever. We would go up to the window of the *Lazeret* (sick bay) and ask the doctor or one of the nurses for some icthiol: a thick black ointment, very smelly, which was supposed to draw the infection to a point.

We had girls with us from villages and their knowledge of primitive methods of dealing with sickness was invaluable. These girls looked for and collected spider webs, which were supposed to heal wounds. Girls who were good at "organizing" (Auschwitz slang for stealing) and were sent to bring bread or food from the kitchen, sometimes had the chance to steal a few geranium leaves from the window boxes of the SS offices. These leaves were used for treatment of septic lesions.

There were days of special excitement when we stood or kneeled for hours with lots of beatings. One time the rumor was that some prisoners had escaped from Auschwitz. There was a small plane hovering above the camp. It started to rain and it went on pouring and we stood there. *Achtung* all the time, and yet another SS came along in a raincoat to count us, and as we failed to stand to attention we had to kneel again.

The following day we heard that two or three prisoners were caught and hanged, and that one got away. Of course I do not know if it was true.

One morning the *Blockalteste* announced that after *Appel* we were going to have disinfection. This was done periodically and did not help us as far as the lice or scabies were concerned, but only added misery to our lives. There was no DDT; on the contrary the lice seemed to love the disinfection. We had to take off our dresses. A large drum was brought to our camp and two or three huts joined in this misery. After each disinfection there were at least twenty to thirty girls left without clothes. The clothes, which were old anyway, were put in a large drum with steam. I do not know what else they put in, perhaps some chemicals. Some of the clothes disintegrated and some of them were stolen.

The girls who were left without clothes were given a piece of blanket to cover their nakedness, and were usually taken away during the next selection.

We all got different clothes. My long silk dress, which had served me so well in lieu of toilet paper and by now was getting on to being a mini, was given to somebody else.

More and more people were selected by Mengele and taken away...

My cousin's daughter Yetta, whose father asked me to look after her, was in the children's hut. One afternoon on the way to the latrines, she came into my hut with another girl from my town. This friend of Yetta's was one of twin sisters. They used to have dark copper hair with blue eyes. Mengele must have been very interested in them.

When I saw the two girls, I had the shock of my life. They seemed to have changed somehow, their arms had become so long and they themselves had grown such a lot. I wonder if they had been given growth hormones. The girls were very happy to find me. Yetta told me that she had constant diarrhea (most of us did) and that she had heard that the best treatment was to eat jam. In the last two days we had been given a small blob of jam. Why? Who knows... She asked me if I could get her some, as she felt so weak. She also told me that she was often taken to the other camp, but did not tell me what Mengele did to her. She had decided, she told me, to tell Mengele that she was not feeling well. Mengele had promised them to reunite them with their mothers, where they would be given better food. I asked both girls not to do this, and not to believe what Mengele said. I also promised that if I got jam, I would give it to them. I never saw them again, these once lovely girls, these spoiled children... May God avenge their blood.

The Germans decided that what we really needed was a little culture. There was a camp orchestra in Auschwitz which gave "concerts" to the inmates. They also played near the gate when the prisoners left for work in the mornings. *There is an arch there, and on it is written* "Arbeit macht Frei" *(Work makes you free). I saw this for the first time in 1994, with my husband and children, when I led a large group of youths from Israeli schools. I should like to take that writing down and replace it with an epitaph for the German nation, taken from a poem by one of their great poets, Friedrich Schiller, and called* Das Lied von der Glocke: *"This*

is what makes up a person and this is why he was given his under-
standing, so that he should feel in the depths of his heart what he
has created with his hands."

After we were counted, we stood in the sun for what
seemed hours; then we sat on the ground, then we stood
again, but the orchestra had still not arrived. Almost all of us
suffered from diarrhea and we did not know what to do with
ourselves. There were girls who ran to the buckets and there
were girls who ran to the latrines, through the back of the
huts. They were all caught and beaten. I was amongst them. I
was trying to get to the buckets in the utility room, but was
caught before I got there. I received about twenty or thirty
lashes, I cannot remember the exact number. I know I was telling myself, "This is not happening to me. I am watching this
scene. This does not hurt me." I cannot remember who picked
me up and brought me a little water to moisten my lips. I
dragged myself outside to clean myself up. I could not climb
up to the top bunk for a day or two and had a bit of a problem
lying down or sitting.

The orchestra did not come that day, although we must
have waited for it and stood and been beaten at least eight or
nine times. Once, on a very hot day, it must have been noon,
the orchestra came, passed through the middle of the camp,
playing, and came back — and after that we were indeed cultured people. There was a girl in the orchestra from my town,
so it was pleasant to see her and I suppose it was pleasant for
her to discover people she knew.

As time went on there were more selections, more diarrhea, more *muselmen*, and more misery. Yet I did make some
new friends. One of them was a lovely girl called Graete, with
a lovely complexion, which in the end was her undoing. One
of the good things that happened to us was that about 95 per-

cent of us stopped menstruating. The other five percent were in much trouble, as there was no way of dealing with it.

One night I heard a terrible barking coming from the next hut. It went on all night. I heard that a girl from my town, a barber's daughter, thought she was an SS dog and kept barking and tried to attack and bite people. In the morning, the poor thing was taken away.

Although it was in the middle of the summer, we began to suffer from the cold in the nights. There was some bartering going on. For three portions of bread, one could buy a sweater, old and dirty, of course. For one to one-and-a-half portions of bread, one could buy a three-cornered piece of cloth to cover one's head. We all suffered terribly from the wind and the cold on our heads. When one is used to having hair and it is shaved off, one feels the lack of it very much.

There was another interesting phenomenon: only a few people committed suicide, although it was rather easy to do by just running up to the high tension fence — touch it and it was over. Every now and then we saw people near the fence, or we saw someone running up to it, but there were not many.

I am asked what made us carry on in such terrible misery. I can only speak for myself.

In the ghetto before we were taken away, I sat with my father and asked him to tell me at which point it is permissible to commit suicide. He said things would not come to that and that everything would be all right. I insisted on having a definite ruling, so we sat and discussed it with the head of the yeshivah. We had heard from the refugees that some girls had been taken for the soldiers in the early years of the war. The ruling was that should this happen, God forbid, I should be allowed to commit suicide. Thank God it never came to that.

There were rumors that German manufacturers came to look for workers, and if one could get out of Birkenau, it would be a very good thing. Many girls volunteered and some of them were taken away from Birkenau, but first their forearms were tattooed with a number. Other groups, who were supposed to go to work, were simply marched off to the gas chambers.

I met Babi Morgenstern, the girl I had spoken with when we were walking toward our new camp without shoes. I was shocked at what had happened to her, she looked like her own grandmother. Perhaps I looked no better than she, but somehow she was bent almost double. She told me she was not going to volunteer for work because they might tattoo her arm, and "imagine what a tattooed arm would look like in an elegant evening dress." Poor Babi, as far as I know she never made that evening dress.

One morning, there was a great deal of excitement. Light planes flew over Auschwitz-Birkenau. It had been raining heavily during the night and even when we started standing for *Appel* to be counted, it was still drizzling. The chimneys seemed to have been working overtime, as well as the open fire, and somehow we sensed a lot of nervousness among the Germans. We stood for hours, and many times we were counted and heard the barking of *"Achtung"* again and again. Mengele arrived and the *Blockalteste* said, "We have to be very careful, today he will take many people." It seemed to be a pay-off for something.

My sister complained she was cold and told me if Mengele came she would tell him that she was not feeling well, and she would like to go to her children where she would get better food. I told her she must not say a word to Mengele. But when Mengele came and told us nicely that anyone suffering from diarrhea or weakness should step out and would be taken to the children and parents, where of course they would get better food, my sister was standing at the end of the line. She stepped out in order to go to him. I grabbed her and gave her a terrible slap on the face, pushed her into the middle of the row, stood on one of her feet, twisted her arm, and asked a friend to do the same. She was pinned down, could not move, and was stunned by my violent behavior. I told her, "I swear I shall kill you myself if you try and say a word to Mengele, rather than let him kill you."

Mengele pulled out several girls from each hut. They had to stand separately, guarded by SS men and women, and dogs as well. There was one young girl who was desperate to get away; she knew what this meant. In the end she somehow escaped from the group, with the help of the other girls. There were so many girls who were selected standing separately, that I think the SS lost count of them.

A cart came by. It had two wheels and was used for transporting the sick and the dead to the gas chambers. As Jews were cheaper than horses or donkeys, two girls had to drag the cart. On it sat three *muselman* girls, in a fetal position, two of them not caring about anything or at least that is what they looked like. No clothes, but covered with a small piece of blanket. The third girl, in the front, with bulging eyes and teeth sticking out of a head where the skin was tight and stuck on to the bones, and holding in front of her two sticks which not long ago had been her arms, called to us as they passed, "Girls, do not forget us!"

I do not know who these girls were, or if there is anyone who mourns for them, but I do remember them and please, those of you who read this, remember and say a small prayer for these three young girls, who wanted to live, love, and be loved, but ended their lives in the gas chambers in Birkenau.

The SS seemed crazed with nervousness and all the time

there was something happening. Security was even stricter than usual. After a few days, some civilian Polish workers came to work together with a gang of prisoners under SS guard, and deliberately dropped a dirty screwed-up paper near some of the girls. It was in Polish, from the underground, and was about the unsuccessful attempt to kill Hitler. As most of us could not read or understand Polish, the rumor started that Hitler was killed and the end of the war was rapidly approaching.

One morning, forty to fifty girls from our hut, and more girls from other huts, were sent over with water, food, and some blankets to the camp opposite. This camp, for some reason, was called "Mexico." It had no huts, no kitchens, no toilets — no anything. Several thousand girls had been brought there and had been living for a few days under the sky. They were taken away a few days later, to where I do not know. About five or six weeks earlier a large group was brought to Mexico, and a girl came and told me that she had seen my cousin Lea Normand and my aunt. These rumors were rarely true, but several times I dragged across food in iron containers in the hope that I could make contact, but I did not find them.

One morning, Irma Graese walked into our hut. "*Raus* you lazy pigs, to work." Many of us were taken to the empty square in front of the kitchens to carry blocks and shift earth to another spot. It had to be done very fast, of course. When it was done, we had to take it all back, even faster. Then about two dozen of us were taken to carry some very heavy boxes to "Canada." None of us knew where or what that was.

While we were waiting outside the SS offices for the boxes, the windows were open and all of a sudden I saw a girl I thought I knew. She had staring, half-crazy eyes. I moved nearer to see her, and the girl moved as well. Horrified, I understood that I had not recognized my own image in the glass window.

Two had to carry a box which was not only heavy but difficult to get a good grip on. We went up to the gates and the SS guards, with their dogs, presented the written orders. The gates were opened, we turned left and started off toward the open fires again. We were not allowed to say a word and we were afraid we would drop our box. There was one girl who asked in good German if she could put it down for a second. She was kicked, cursed, and above all we saw the dogs baring their teeth and getting ready to jump. We came near the flames and were lucky that we had to concentrate on the box and how we were going in order not to trip. We passed the fire; it seemed an endless journey. We turned left and soon arrived at what was called Canada.

How can I describe what we saw? It was something that only a completely mad mind could think up and produce. Huge piles of hair, heaps of tiny children's shoes, bigger children's shoes, women's shoes, men's shoes, eyeglasses, a large pile of false teeth, and clothes. I was beginning to feel that I was imagining all this. One girl kept saying over and over again, even while she was being beaten, *"Drága Jó Istenem"* ("My dear good God"). We begged her to stop and were afraid for her, but I think something had snapped in her.

On the way back, I tried to whisper to her that she had to pull herself together, but I did not get through to her, and she kept saying, "Those little ones will never walk."

We asked old-timers in Auschwitz why that place was called Canada. The explanation we received was that there were people of so many nations and languages, that the words, *"Keiner da"* ("No one here" — no living person is here, only things) degenerated into "Canada."

Canada can be the pride of the barbaric twentieth century and of the German nation.

The Month of Av

*I*n the month of Av, which starts toward the end of July, we have a period of mourning for nine days, when so many tragedies befell our nation. On the ninth of Av, our holy Temple was twice destroyed, Jerusalem was burnt down, our people were taken off to slavery, and our holy vessels of gold and our seven branched candelabra were taken to Rome. One can see the victory procession on the Arch of Titus, with the slaves in chains and the legioners displaying the candelabra with the vessels, marching through Via Agrippas.

When I visited Rome, I stood near the Arch of Titus with hate and shame burning in me. I, as a freed slave, tried to feel what my brothers and sisters felt being carried into Rome in chains. Then a German group arrived with a guide, taking photographs, and somehow, in my mind, the past and present merged. I was standing there with my husband and I felt tears in my eyes, and I was shamed again by my history of two thousand years and by the barbarism of the present world.

The Germans knew about each and every one of our holidays, and always tried to prepare something special for those days.

Around this time they "liquidated" the Czech camp, which was known as the family camp or Theresienstadt camp. As they were our neighbors — only the double electrified barbed wire fence divided us — we could see, while standing *Appel* to be counted, what went on there. The two-wheeled carts with human horses were busy indeed, either carrying the dead or the very sick, and the *muselmen.*

One evening there was a lot of preparation and running about by the SS guards. We were counted only twice, once by the *Blockalteste* and once by a death's head. We were given our bread and soup and were told that we were under the strictest curfew ever. Anyone stepping outside the hut would be shot at once.

We saw the food arriving at the other camp. They were not in a fit condition to stand for hours to be counted. The poor things had more food than they could eat, as they were so very sick. The rumor was that they had typhus.

As night fell and it became completely dark, we heard the roar of many trucks. At first I thought they were coming for us. My sister became worried and kept asking what was happening. There was a fair amount of noise coming from over the fence, but what we mainly heard were the roars of the SS. No one dared to say a word. I think each of us was listening to her own heartbeat, which was fairly loud.

Dear God, the crematoria and open fire were belching and spitting smoke and flames all night and the following day. There were also no transports arriving, or perhaps just one or two. I made a trip to the buckets, which were of course overflowing. So what? I peeped out through the wall of the utility room and the world seemed to be on fire. When I climbed onto my bunk, I started to recite to myself the prayer which is said at funerals and every year thereafter, on the anniversary of the death of the person: "Merciful God who art in heaven, may You give peace to..."

The following morning we began the day normally, running to the latrines and trying to wash ourselves. At *Appel* we have to be counted; we all look worse than on the previous day. It was raining during the night and there is a small lake between the huts, so we stand in front of our hut. It starts drizzling and then it begins to rain again, even though it is getting lighter and the sun is trying to peep through. I turn round, and above the smoking chimneys and the odd flame escaping, there is a most beautiful rainbow. I feel it is mocking us remaining Jews, but I say the blessing for the rainbow, which thanks the Almighty for remembering His covenant with us and not flooding the world again. I actually felt a flood would be justified. I have a conversation with the Almighty, which I did every now and then, especially when I wanted to ask Him and tell Him that if he killed off all the Jews, He would not get another nation as good as we, who stick with Him, literally through fire and water.

When it is completely light, the rain has stopped and we are all in shock. In the camp next door to us there is not a single soul left. I turn my gaze to the open flames, I can almost see them — the grandmother and the little boy who used to play with his toy, and all those nice civilized looking people, being carried up to heaven. They are all gone. I hope they did not suffer too much. It is a cold morning. Perhaps our blood is frozen. It is the month of July. This morning we get a thin kind of porridge, which tastes so good, just a few gulps and we already feel better. We are all very quiet. Now we have no neighbors. On the other side of our camp is an unpaved road, leading between our camp and the Gypsy camp into Birkenau. To the left of the open flames are two or three crematoria, Canada, and the showers. This was the way we came in from the platform when we arrived in Birkenau on that first night.

The ninth of Av falls on a Shabbat this year, so one does not fast on that day, but on the following day — on Sunday. I do not know if I shall manage to fast because it is a long fast day, starting before sundown on Shabbat and finishing on Sunday evening when it is completely dark. I know that I do not have to fast in these circumstances, but I want to.

The SS allow us to walk about in the camp in the evening so we can go to the latrine again. We meet some girls outside our hut and we are allowed to talk amongst ourselves. As this day is supposed to be sad and quiet, the Germans want to make it the opposite for us. A girl comes to me and whispers in my ear that the *Blockalteste* from hut no. 32 was sitting on the floor with several other girls and reading the Lamentations. I ran to the hut and sat down. She could let only a few girls participate because she should not have had the book of Lamentations at all. The *Blockalteste* was a Slovak Jewish girl; she had been in Auschwitz for several years and most of her teeth were missing. Through her contacts with other old-timers, she must have obtained the book. She starts reading, "How doth the city sit solitary, that was full of people..."

We sit there, a few girls mourning for our holy Temple, for Jerusalem, and for our nation. The *Blockalteste* goes on reading from Jeremiah, about the hunger and all the terrible things that happened in Jerusalem. We feel that we are only continuing our nation's fate — but for how long?

I stayed too long, and now I have to get back to my hut. I have to cross the street, which runs the length of the camp, because my hut is on the opposite side. Everything is burning, today as in the old days. I manage to return without being caught.

The following morning I do not take the warm drink and hope I will be able to last out. After *Appel*, Irma Graese goes into each hut and with a demonic smile says, "Today there is much better food and more food, and you must all eat and can even have second helpings."

When I saw and heard her, I knew at once that if it was the last thing I should ever do, I would fast. I would not help the Germans destroy our souls before killing us. I do not know how many others fasted, but all I know is that no amount of food could have given me the strength I got from proving that I was still my own mistress and there were more important things to me than my hunger.

In the evening, my friend Graete came to me and said she had spoken to one of the *Stubendienst* and managed to put a little food aside for me. I had the food, which was cold, but it must have been good when hot, certainly far better than on any other day.

The diarrhea was plaguing us. Half the camp was barricaded off for disinfection and that meant that we could not get to the nearest latrine, and the others were too far away. I dragged myself there with some other girls, hoping that on the way back we would get no more than a few blows from the *Stubendienst*. By the time we came back, no lesser person was standing there than Irma Graese, with her whip and dog. The road was barricaded, and there was just a narrow space near her to pass by. She started beating us with her whip and kicking us with her boots. I could stand all this, but I was terrified of the dog and did not know how I could stand it if it started mauling my face.

I stood there, turned to stone. She was beating me and I was pouring diarrhea. She laughed at me and said, "This is because you are afraid of me." I said, "No, I am a very sick person," hoping at that moment that she would send me off to the chimney. She laughed again, kicked me, and I fell down. I saw and heard her laughing. Toward the evening, I found myself in the utility room in a heap together with other dead and half-dead girls. Graete came to find me and brought me something to drink, but I could not swallow it — I was vomiting.

The girls and I, in the utility room, could not walk out to be counted on the following morning. Some other girls came to help me go outside so that I should not be taken away. Once the *Blockalteste* knew that neither Mengele nor Graese would be coming that morning, she allowed me to go inside the hut, advising me not to go back to the utility room. A little later, Graete brought me a small piece of charcoal, which was worth gold, and coaxed me to crush it and drink it down with some fluid — this she called black coffee. I gagged on it but slowly swallowed the charcoal, which was meant to treat the dysentery (we had nothing else). I slowly drank a little and nibbled at my bread ration. It was a bad sign that I was not hungry. Toward the end of the day the girls in the utility room were taken away on the two-wheeled cart, some to the sick bay and the others...

It was hot and the flies, like our lice, were multiplying fast. The strange thing was that the entire time I was in Birkenau, I did not see one single bird. Not even by mistake did they come anywhere near the valley of death.

There were still transports coming in from all over Europe, but I think that by the end of July or the beginning of August, all the Hungarian Jews had been delivered. There were also some Polish girls with us, I do not know where they came from, and we learnt many Yiddish songs from them, all of course desperately sad. Compared to them we looked so well fed and so well off that they were not willing to believe that we were Jewish, especially since we could not speak Yiddish, but only German. They could not understand that one's "*Mamelushen*" could be either Hungarian or German.

One day Irma Graese came to select some girls very carefully. They were all good looking, with nice clear skin. I was sure that she was going to take them for the German soldiers. Amongst the girls she took was my friend Graete. After the war we heard that Graese collected girls with clear skin, killed them, and made lamp shades out of their skin.

I never saw Graete again. I tried not to make friends and did not want to have close relationships in case they would be taken away. I found that loosing people all the time was too hard to bear.

Some time in August, a large group arrived, all with freshly shaven heads and desperately hungry eyes. The girls looked as if they were after years of starvation, as indeed they were.

These girls were one of the last transports from the ghetto of Lodz and were crazed with hunger. They were put into separate huts to keep them together and apart from us. These old-timers, poor things, knew the Germans well, and so they tried to mix with us. Yet girls from Lodz could easily be picked out because they looked worse than we did, and their heads were freshly shaven.

When food was brought to the huts, these poor girls would overwhelm, en masse, the girls carrying the bread and soup, although they were not allowed to leave their hut. Unfortunately, they were beaten up time after time by the SS and

Kapos. Some of the bread ration reached the huts, some of it was taken by the girls, fighting like lion cubs, and some of it was confiscated by the SS. The hot soup, which was the main meal of the day, ended up on the ground, and these unfortunates, while still being beaten, tried to scoop up some of it with their hands and eat it.

One morning, one of the Lodz girls came into our hut and offered to sing some Yiddish songs for a dry piece of bread. I realized that we looked so well fed to them that they even thought we had some surplus bread, which we certainly did not. They were also taken separately to the latrines and washrooms, which looked very suspicious. Why were they separated from the rest of the camp?

One evening after about two weeks, when we had been counted and the bread and soup were already distributed, we were told that there was to be a very strict curfew, a *Lager Schperre* — a "blockade." We knew that something terrible was going to happen. There was that deadly quiet which was always felt before an *Aktion*, and it was full of messages of destruction and death. Then came the running about of the SS men and women outside, barking orders. A little later we heard trucks coming from Auschwitz and entering our camp. I think we stopped breathing. No one knew for whom they were intended, but it was obvious that they were meant for a large number of people. We heard the trucks coming nearer and nearer, and so were the SS. All of a sudden we heard the most terrible earsplitting screams from next door, from the hut of those poor girls from Lodz.

They began running and fighting off the attempts to take them away. They were not going to their deaths without putting up a fight. These girls, who had been in the Lodz ghetto for almost five years, since November 1939, under the most terrible conditions, where people died daily of starvation and disease, still wanted to live.

From my bunk I could see, and of course hear, what went on. I was on the top bunk and my wall was near the next hut, about fifteen to twenty meters away. The place was illuminated with reflectors and it looked almost like daylight. Some of the girls managed to get onto the roof, hoping somehow to escape. Some could not get a foothold and fell down, and others were shot down.

I do not know how long this *Aktion* took, but it seemed more than a lifetime. We were simply frozen with horror. *Many times I see these girls in my nightmares. What I see in my nightmares is not fantasy, but I see the screaming girls as I saw them then and how they were dragged off.* The trucks started roaring again, and the screams and shouting died out and away gradually. The poor things had wanted to go on living in this filthy barbaric world.

I wonder what all those death's heads, men and women, who did not belong to the human race, did when they went home. Did they eat, laugh, listen to music, kiss their children, chat with their wives? — because what they did earlier in the evening was only work. It was only "processing Jews." I kept saying to myself, "Merciful God who art in Heaven..." and when I finished, I started again from the beginning, trying to remember the girls I saw screaming and their faces and expressions. After a time I saw the flames coming out of the chimneys, I could not see the open fires from my bunk. I saw the flames and I saw the girls' faces in the flames coming out of the chimneys. I felt I was going out of my mind. Who knows, perhaps I was. If I did not, does this mean that I am normal — if I could live through that and not go mad?

The following morning, running to the latrines, we saw

the hut doors open, but it was dark inside. After we were counted we saw they were gone. We heard that the girls had broken their bunk beds in order to have something to fight off the SS. The starving with sticks against the overstuffed with firearms!

They were all gone after so many years of suffering and starvation, and their ashes were thrown and blown all over Birkenau.

People think that one gets used to hardship, pain, cold, and the smell, but there is just so much one can stand. I found the smell of Birkenau was driving me out of my mind. The nights were cold, and with the rains came the wind. During the day it was not warm enough to dry the mire, so that standing *Appel* to be counted, we sank into it. We tried to clean the mud off our feet with stones and sticks as best as we could.

One morning after several cold and rainy days, we saw a few peasant carts coming into our camp, drawn by male Jewish prisoners. The cargo looked rather strange, dark in color and it was not earth. The carts stopped, and the male prisoners took their shovels and filled the holes that were created by the rain and by so many feet treading on the wet ground. It must have really amused the Germans, the lovers of culture and music, to have the ashes of Jews strewn all over our camp, so that we should have to tread on our own people.

It was a gray, cold day; we were approaching Rosh Hashanah, and the month of September is already cold in Poland. There were more *muselmen*, more selections, and more misery. There were delegations coming from factories, looking for slave labor. I started to think about going on a transport if I could get in, yet I kept pushing it off as I had many sores and most of the time ran a fever. I knew that I could not get through a selection for a transport. When I was able to get a piece of wood with a sharp edge or a piece of glass, I opened my sores myself and reduced the tension. At first my sister did not want to hear of going away, she wanted to stay "near her children"...

The New Year

I remember well the eve of Rosh HaShanah. There was a special atmosphere, and I wonder if this was inside each of us or if it was something created by people who felt alike. We were allowed to walk around a little in the evening to wish each other a happy New Year, a better year than the past one. The girls felt elated to be able to meet friends and to walk about a little in the camp.

I was wondering what special treat the Germans had prepared for us for our New Year. My sister and I were by this time in hut number 12. At one of the countings, one hut would have more or less prisoners and in order to arrange the numbers in an orderly fashion, girls were sent from one hut to another like potatoes. Thus it happened that we were in hut number 12 for Rosh HaShanah. The second in command to the *Blockalteste* was a nice "old lady," probably around thirty-five years old. This "old lady" put out two candles on the funnel running through the hut, lit them making the ritual blessing, and wished us all, "My children, a happy New

Year." We watched her from our bunks. A little later she told us to be very quiet as there was a *Lager Schpere*, a curfew of the strictest kind. The doors of the hut were locked at both ends and there were several *Stubendienst* standing guard with sticks.

The running about and orders shouted were heard, but rather far away, not in or near our camp. Wild screams and the roar of trucks and of shooting came nearer, and we heard the screams of children, young boys, calling *"Tatte, Mame"* in almost all the languages of Europe. These children were fighting for their lives. They had been in Birkenau for some time and knew exactly where they were being taken. They jumped off the moving trucks, were shot down, and the screams were simply heartrending. By now everyone knew what was happening and had lived through several liquidations like this one. Most of us probably remembered the boys we saw on that very first morning, outside the showers. Were these children the same ones? This was the Rosh HaShanah gift of the German nation to us starving unfortunate people, broken in body but not in spirit.

My sister grabbed my arm so hard it hurt me, and said, "What is happening? These are children, the screams of terrified children." The poor thing was afraid for her two little boys. I wonder if she did not know, or refused to know, that the children had been sent straight to the gas chambers.

We did not talk or move, each of us was occupied with her own thoughts. I tried very hard to imagine my home a few years previously, when things were still normal. I tried to see before my eyes the large dining room and the long beautifully laid table with the best china, crystal, and silver, and the family gathering round the table all talking and admiring each other's new clothes. Though however hard I tried, I could not conjure up that past picture — but the nearer past came back to me and I saw the dining room, as I saw it last, when we left the ghetto, with the table pushed to one side of the room, piled high with the belongings of the families who were living in the room, or rather squatting on the floor of the room. This was the dining room I could conjure up before my eyes.

Then I remembered my mother bringing the pink tablecloth out of the house, carrying it carefully so that it should not get creased. This was the tablecloth in which the Torah scroll was wrapped and buried.

Drágá Anyukám (my dear mother), did you take out the tablecloth carefully so as not to crease the others? Oh, and what did you do with the twenty-four napkins which belonged to the set, the matching, starched, and ironed table napkins? Did you throw them on the floor and trample on them?

Drágá Anyukám, I know it is difficult to change a lifetime's correct behavior, but I cannot bear the thought that the people who could hardly wait for us to be taken away, would not even have to iron those lovely tablecloths before using them. Anyukám drágá, now I shall never know because I can never ask you, but I could swear you left it all in apple pie order, and after you took out the tablecloth, you shut the cupboard door, I am sure.

I remember when you took us girls shopping. We went to that lovely shoe shop, where they send home several pairs of shoes for each of us to choose from at leisure. Then you took us to Vadas, the textile shop, to pick the right material for each of us, to be sent to the tailor and dressmaker. These were big worries.

Drágá Anyukám, this is gone forever, but I did go with my daughter, Michal, to choose and buy material for her wedding dress, and that was such a happy day.

Anyukám, you bought and supervised the making of the wedding dresses for four of my sisters, but not for me — but I know you were with me on my wedding day, and all my life.

I cannot remember when we got off to sleep, but at once we were woken up, still in the dark, and we started again the miserable routine of our lives. We hardly had time to run to the latrines and washrooms. My sister and I were sent to the kitchen with another six girls to bring hot black coffee (imitation) which was our breakfast. We had to wait a long time outside the kitchen. It was very cold and in order not to shiver, we rubbed ourselves, or each other, to warm ourselves up a little. We were facing the chimneys and the open fire, and I am sure that all of us were thinking of the children whom we had heard screaming for their mothers and fathers only a few hours previously. My sister said, "Tell me what happened last night? What did they do to those children?" I told her that she knew as much as I did. We carried the coffee in the iron containers back to our hut. There was a long procession of reeling, tottering girls carrying coffee, each group to their own hut.

I did not know the Rosh HaShanah prayers by heart, but remembered a few outstanding things like *Avinu Malkeinu* and *Min Hameitzar Karati* ("I called upon the Lord in distress"). When I came to the words "You have chosen us from all the nations, You have loved us and wanted us," I looked up at the flames consuming the children — I was bewildered and I said it with a question mark at the end. But, I said it again at *minchah* and *maariv*. I thought a lot about what was happening around me, and about the prayers, and decided I did not understand — but the Lord was mine and I was His, and I was a Jew and was desperately trying to cling to my religion. I spoke to the Lord and sometimes asked Him what He was doing, even if He knew what He was doing. He was there for me, and I clung to him with desperation.

Later in the day a girl came in with a *Machzor*. She obtained it from the *Blockalteste* to give to the girls who really wanted to pray, just for a few minutes, so that it could go around the camp. If we had been caught we would have been tortured to find out from where we got the prayer book.

During those two days of Rosh HaShanah, I found myself more and more thinking of home — not the good old days, but how we left the house. All of a sudden I sat up in my bunk, and the girls thought something had bitten me. I told the girls incredulously that we had left all our mezuzot on the doorposts. They whispered unanimously, "So did we." I started counting, and it was clear that we had left behind at least fourteen mezuzot. My dear God, why did we ever do that? My sister said, "Of course we left ours as well. Why should I have taken them off — to give myself more work in putting them up again?" I was stunned. She had not considered the possibility that her family might not return intact to their nice home. My sister started talking about her garden and the fruit trees, which needed tending to, the apples and pears, which should be picked already, otherwise there would be less fruit the coming year. I told her not to fear, there would be plenty of people to pick the fruit.

It made me so miserable to think of the hundreds of thousands of mezuzot being left behind. Then I remembered how we had left all our china and crystals in an orderly fashion, in their places, instead of smashing them to pieces. Of course, we left our clothes hanging nicely. We had offered our clothes to people who did not have enough for the journey, but even then we left behind far too much.

I thought I was crazy. Why should I worry about these things when death was engulfing all the Jews? Nevertheless I could not bear the thought of my enemies taking over with a smile and thinking of us not only as dirty Jews, but as idiots as well.

This was the way we spent our New Year.

The day after Rosh HaShanah a girl came by, completely beside herself. She had given two days' bread ration for a small piece of paper and a tiny piece of pencil, so small that I could hardly hold it. She asked me to write a letter in her name. This was the second letter I had written for her, in German to her Polish so-called boyfriend. This Polish political prisoner came over regularly to our camp with a work gang. She sent the letter via other political prisoners who came to work. Since her first letter he had not taken any notice of her. She begged him to help her with food, gold, or any money he could get. She assured me that she would pay me with bread for writing this letter, once her friend contacted her, and she was sure he would not turn his back on her. I told her not to worry, I was not in the letter writing business and I would not take her bread ration.

I met her a few days later and did not want to ask if she had had a reply, because I was sure that once he knew that she wanted him to help her, he would not come anywhere near her. She told me she had seen him in the camp, and he had simply turned his head away. What happened to her? She was a pretty girl, who was hungry for a piece of bread...

I had a sore on the palm of my left hand and opened it with a piece of glass. I scrounged a little icthiol, a thick smelly ointment, and put it on, but the sore under my armpit was getting worse. It was a cluster of boils, four in all, and I ran a fever. I tried opening them up with a sharp piece of wood, but the area still remained too hard. I managed to find a small geranium leaf and a spider's web, half of which I gave to another girl. I was feeling sick and very weak.

It was cold and raining, and we were approaching Yom Kippur. We were shivering with cold, but were not allowed to show it in the presence of Graese or Mengele.

About this time, perhaps a few weeks earlier, the factory in the town Auschwitz was bombed. We were waiting; I was hoping to be killed by a friendly bomb, rather than by the Germans. The bombing sounded very near, almost as if the next camp to us was being bombed, but the Allied planes ignored the chimneys and open fires.[1]

These were very hard days, and I felt things were getting too hard to stand up against. For one thing, the smell of Birkenau was driving me out of my mind, and I decided that I must either go on a transport — away from the smell — or be taken to the gas chambers, but either way it would be better than staying here.

The day before the eve of Yom Kippur we were taken to Auschwitz by foot for disinfection. We did not take the short route across the railway lines, but went almost to the edge of the Auschwitz township.

We undressed and all our clothes were put into a very large drum with steam. The lice loved it, they simply thrived on it. In the meantime we were let into a washroom to wash

---

1 After the war the Allies were asked why they had not bombed Auschwitz-Birkenau. One of the answers was that they were afraid to kill prisoners. This, of course, does not hold water, since no bomb could kill as many at one time as the gas chambers and the crematoria working twenty-four hours a day. The second answer was that as the air force base was so far away, they could not spare a bomb for the chimneys. The distance by foot from the camps to where the bombs fell on the ammunition factory was only three or four kilometers. The interesting thing was that even in the middle of the raging war, the camps were floodlit. The flames escaping from the chimneys could have endangered the Germans, yet they were not afraid, trusting the rest of the world to give its silent acceptance to their killing us — which indeed they did.

ourselves, without soap, while the disinfection took place. After washing we had to file into another room, one by one, where several Hungarian Jews were standing, each holding a spray. What was in it, I do not know, because this was before the time of DDT. As we came in we had to lift our hands above our heads, and one by one we were sprayed. When this was done, we were handed the crumpled half-wet dresses, and about twenty-five or thirty of us were left without anything to wear on that cold rainy day. I was one of the girls left naked.

We were all marched outside and left standing there for all to see, freezing in body and soul. I tried to convince myself that this was not happening to me, that I was just an onlooker.

Those of us who had no "dresses" were given a piece of blanket in which to wrap ourselves. Being wrapped in blankets made us look far worse than we did wearing clothes, and it was an accepted thing that girls in blankets were taken away in the next selection. Everybody, even our own friends, looked at us pityingly. Somehow we underwent an instant change of personality for wearing the blanket. In a way, perhaps, it was warmer than the thin summer dress we had before, but we had to hold the blanket from inside, so in addition to our starved faces, we had no arms either.

The following day was *erev* Yom Kippur. It was cold and rainy — I was freezing on the outside and inside. I met a non-Jewish lady who used to be our neighbor at home and was married to a Jew. Her son, about my own age, went to a reform Jewish school. I had not seen her since Rosh HaShanah, and those ten days had not done her a lot of good. Somehow, she managed to look like a distinguished lady — even in her filthy rags. She told me she would fast in solidarity with us. I wished her all the best, but did not think she would last much longer. *Recently I asked a friend if the son, father, or mother sur-*

vived, but unfortunately none of them did.

Once again, a very special atmosphere descended on our camp. Every one of our days was a day of judgment, but this was the eve of a most solemn day. I am there now, back in Birkenau, and I am hurrying to the latrines, bundled up in that piece of gray blanket. I pass by a girl from my town, whom I know only by sight. Her name is Perl or Perlman. We nod to each other and I murmur a happy New Year to her. As she passes she recognizes me. She stops me and is shocked that I am wearing a blanket and says that I must not stay with the blanket or, God forbid, they might take me away. She says she has a vest under her dress and wants to give it to me. I say thank you, but I could not take it away from her as it surely keeps her warm. She insists, takes off her dress and then her vest, and gives it to me — *all this from a girl whose first name I do not know to this very day.*

I take the vest from her, gratefully thanking her. It is a hand crocheted vest, without sleeves, old, dirty, and torn. I take it, put it on, and say the blessing I used to say ever since I was a little girl when putting on new clothes, "Blessed art Thou, Lord our God, King of the Universe, who clothes the naked." Although I had said the blessing many times before, it is only now that I really understand it fully, for the first time.

I wondered, *and still do when I think of it,* who crocheted that vest, which country it came from, and what happened to the original owner. It was a short vest, but just long enough to cover my nakedness, so as not to have to wear the blanket. That girl, whose first name I do not know and whose surname I am not absolutely sure of — and whose fate I also do not know — undoubtedly saved my life that day. With the first selection I would have been taken away with the other blanket girls.

On Kol Nidrei night (eve of Yom Kippur) I was fairly respectably dressed, and I still had a piece of blanket, which I spread out as far as it went when lying down. There was a hush over the camp. In our minds all of us were at home, thinking of our loved ones and of our past, present, and future. I saw my mother dressed in white, my father standing next to her, and all of us children coming up to them according to age, each for his blessing: "God make thee as Sarah, Rivkah, Rachel, and Leah..." and for the boys, "God make thee as Ephraim and Menasheh. The Lord bless thee and keep thee. The Lord make His face shine upon thee and be gracious unto thee. The Lord lift up His countenance upon thee and give thee peace." We used to receive these blessings every Friday evening and on the eve of every festival, as well as a very special blessing on the eve of Yom Kippur.

I started praying whatever I could remember. I whispered so that my sister and some of the other girls near me should be able to repeat the prayers after me.

I did not know why, but since Rosh HaShanah I had been thinking more and more of my parents, sisters, brother and the rest of our family. A desperate longing possessed me — I wanted more than anything else in the whole wide world to have my parents' hands on my head and to receive their blessings just once more.

I was afraid that with this intense longing for my family and vivid thoughts of them — going with them to the gas chambers, smelling the gas, stopping to breathe — I was losing my mind and losing control of myself. Then I was back in the boxcar...and I blamed myself that I had never asked my mother or sisters how they managed in the ghetto, what did they have to eat? How did they wash their clothes? How did the children manage? *I had not been at home during the time of the ghetto, but stayed at the hospital, so I do not know about my family's life then. It had not seemed important to ask because I was sure that we would all die together. I was not prepared for going on "living" on my own. After the war, when I was married and my first son, David, was born, I felt that crazy desperate longing to show my baby to my mother. It was almost a physical pain to know that she would never admire my baby.*

The following day, Yom Kippur, the Germans sent a lot of food, of better quality than ever before, to each of the Jewish camps. Irma Graese went round again, from hut to hut, saying that we must eat and could even receive second or third helpings. There were people who ate, but many of us fasted and we gained more strength from fasting than from food. What a wonderful feeling it was that we were still our own masters.

It is interesting that at a time when the Germans were losing the war, when they must have realized that the Reich was collapsing, their great worry was to degrade us — to make us feel subhuman, without principles — before killing us. For this may they be damned forever — for they are the true Amalek.

The chimneys were working day and night, as were the open fires. No birds, no hope, only the terrible routine of running to the latrines, getting something to eat, scratching ourselves, and growing weaker and weaker.

On Yom Kippur, after I had prayed, I decided finally that, should I be able to get into a transport, I should go. As for my fever and sores, I thought either the Germans would pass me or send me to the gas chamber. Sooner or later I was certain that we would all be killed anyway, and I was afraid of losing my mind.

The following day we were told by the *Blockalteste* that there was a transport being organized and it sounded good —

and those of us who thought they could get by should go. They were looking for girls who had been working for at least five years in an electronics factory and were very good with their hands — for delicate work. There was not a single girl I knew who even had any idea where a factory like that was located, but nevertheless hundreds of girls came forward for the interview. Out of the hundreds, they chose eighty-three girls and put us together in a hut, to be called later.

My sister was also among the eighty-three chosen for work, but she was still worried about leaving her children in Birkenau.

The following day and the day after, nothing happened about our transport, and most of the girls thought we had been forgotten. On the third day, which was the eve of Sukkot, after having been counted and recounted, again and again, our *Blockalteste* told us that we were going over to the F.K.L., *Frauen Konzentrazions Lager*, in Auschwitz — which was just across the railway and platform.

I asked around for a piece of glass to open the sores under my armpit. When I had opened two of them, I asked two girls to squeeze hard — one of the sores discharged thick pus and the second would not discharge at all. The third was oozing blood, and the fourth sore was a big hole — so the girls told me. I felt very bad, still running a high fever, but at least I had a flush on my face.

Two SS men and one SS woman came to our hut, we had to stand five in a row, and we went off to Auschwitz. We were taken into a brick hut in the camp of the women prisoners who worked in "Canada" and in the offices — old-timers who had gone through hell on earth. They were mainly Slovak Jewish girls, Polish or German political prisoners, who were the "working" prisoners of Auschwitz, while we were kept solely for annihilation. They all had numbers tattooed on their forearms and were also registered in the Auschwitz records, so that when they died or were sent off to the gas chambers — when it was felt they knew too much, or at the whim of one of the SS — they were crossed off the list.

We were told to strip, were given a piece of soap, which we had to give back afterwards, and taken into a large shower room. The girl prisoners, in striped clothes, turned on the hot water and we started washing ourselves. I washed my sores, trying hard to stop them from oozing. The water was turned off and we stood there for what seemed a long time without clothes. Finally we were herded into a very large room and were told to go in one by one, with our hands above our heads, before the SS officers. There stood Mengele and two women SS — and I knew I was lost.

I walked on perfectly calm, not caring at all what would happen. My sister was just behind me, and in front of me there was a very small girl, who spoke a fluent Yiddish but no German. She was one of the girls who had, after a few months of starvation, a swollen abdomen. As she came before Mengele, he asked her, "*Bist du schwanger?*" ("Are you pregnant?") and she answered, "*Nein ich bin nicht verheiratet*" ("No, I am not married"). They started to roar with laughter, passed her on, and I came next, holding my left arm very high. But as they were roaring with laughter, I was also passed on, with my fever and my horrible sores.

My sister was not passed on, and out of eighty-three girls they chose only thirty-two. Those who were not passed were taken out of the room the way they had come, and we were taken out through another door and given slightly better fitting clothes and shoes. We still did not know if we were really being taken for work or whether, perhaps, together with the other half of our group, we would be taken to the gas chambers.

After some time we were marched out, five in a row, and taken across the rails to stand on the platform in Birkenau, near the central watchtower, under which all trains had to pass on their way into Auschwitz-Birkenau. It was a gray day, and the SS guard who watched over us was one we had known ever since we had arrived in Birkenau — he used to count us, sometimes twice a day, and was not outstandingly cruel. He was a *Volksdeutscher* (a German living outside Germany) from the town of Satmar, in Transylvania. As we stood, waiting for a long time, he said to us in German, "You are lucky that you are leaving the chimneys behind. The further away you get from the chimneys, the healthier it will be for you." He even seemed pleased for our sakes, for thirty-two young girls, who were getting away from the gas and the flames.

Far away, from the direction of the town of Auschwitz, we heard the noise, the puffing of an engine, and soon we saw it coming toward us. The engine arrived with two normal passenger carriages attached to it. We were sure that this could not be meant for us. Six or seven SS guards, all men, alighted. We were then handed over to them, they signed some papers, and we were told to get in. It seemed too good to be true.

We were given no food or water to drink — so I still thought they might take us and kill us. Meanwhile, the engine went on shunting, and when it came back, it was again attached to the two carriages and took us back whence it had come. At the town of Auschwitz, which was only five or six kilometers away, we stopped. There were passengers waiting on the platform, and several more carriages were attached to the engine. The last carriage of the train was ours, with the girls sitting in it. Doors and windows were locked and we were told not to stand up but to sit. In the next carriage were the SS guards, and they also locked their carriage so that no passengers could walk through and see us prisoners.

Here I was leaving behind Birkenau and Auschwitz together with thirty-one girls, amongst whom there was not a single one I knew, and we had no idea of where we were being taken or what was going to happen to us.

We were sitting there quietly, craning our necks to see the wonder of people dressed normally and walking about freely. Ten minutes away by train from Auschwitz and life had not stopped and still seemed to be normal — all because people here were not Jews.

I looked at the girls. There was one group of six sisters, another of three sisters, and another of two. I thought of my sister who has not passed the selection. She still had her high boots and although we had to walk to the selection without shoes, which most of us did not possess anyway, she put her feet halfway into her boots and walked like a cripple. I asked her, begged of her, not to walk with her feet halfway in her boots, but to no avail. As she came up to Mengele, he waved her to one side hardly even looking at her. I did not know what had happened to her, if she had been taken back to the camp or...

Meeting my sister Rici in Birkenau and now not knowing what was going to happen to her was a continuation of being torn away from family and friends. She had looked lost — as if to say, who will look after me now? — although she was sixteen years my senior. I was convinced that sooner or later we should all be killed and I wondered what else would happen before the end. God only knew.

It was only six months after my own liberation that I learned that Rici had survived, having been freed by the Russians at a relatively early date. She had made her way home, recovered her house and furniture shops, and arranged her affairs, waiting for her husband and children to return, which they never did. It was not until January 1951, in Israel, that we met again.

The sisters amongst us spoke to each other, but the majority of us, who had no one they knew, just sat almost without breathing. We came to another station where the train stopped. Many people got on the train, and the platform was full of German soldiers, officers, with wives, girlfriends, children, and babies — the women running around in high-heeled shoes with hats, gloves, fur coats, and handbags, just as it had been in my previous life, when I had been considered a human being with at least minimal rights. It was hard to believe that there were still families with babies, and children going to school, and life going on as if the families next door did not disappear, never to be seen again. Who cared? Those who did were few and far between.

We sat in the train for several hours looking at stations and people as if we had come from a different planet. We were enjoying this new state of sitting up like human beings. It was growing dark and we were still traveling, but there was no question of getting any food.

The train pulled into a station, stopped, people alighted, doors were slammed, hurrying feet were heard, we felt our carriage being disconnected, and after all was quiet outside the doors were unlocked and we were told to get off the train. It was dark outside and there were just a few railway workers walking with lanterns, but I caught a glimpse of the name of the station — Reichenbach. I had never heard of the place. It was cold and dark and we were already so tired and so very, very hungry.

Five in a row, and we started off toward the unknown. We went through the town but we could not see anything; we were in total darkness and just about dropping. After some time, we came to a fenced area, which looked like a large factory. One of the four SS men went in and after a long time came out, shaking his head. He spoke to the other SS guards and two of them went in again. We understood that they did not want us and the Reich would survive without our expert work. The SS men came out, without telling us anything of course, turned us round, and we started marching, shuffling and dragging ourselves into the unknown. We started whispering to each other, wondering if we were going back to Birkenau. We were so down that none of us cared where we were headed. It was evident that we were not going back to the station — this was a different route.

We came to the edge of the town and at a distance we could see trees. To me it was evident that we would be taken into the woods, shot, and just left there.

We entered the woods, and I started to say *Shema Yisrael* and the other prayers said in preparation for dying. We walked on, and I could not understand why we were going so deeply into the woods. The girls were nervous, but did not care too much about what would happen. We were shivering with cold, thirty-two starved girls, guarded by four able-bodied armed men — at a time when Germany was losing the war! As we walked on we came to the edge of the woods and continued. Then far away we saw some buildings, and as we came nearer we were able to see a watchtower and barbed wire and we realized that we were approaching a camp.

When we came to the gates, some argument broke out again and we were not allowed in. We stood outside the gates, longing to have things settled one way or another. Nobody wanted us, even as slaves. It started to rain again, and we were so very cold to start with.

I was so tired that I did not remember that it was the first night of Sukkot. In the morning before we left Birkenau, I told the girls near me that it was the eve of Sukkot. During the journey, I once or twice tried to think of our sukkah at home, but it did not work. The thoughts which crowded in were of the recent tragic things I had lived through and witnessed.

After a long, long time a Jewish prisoner came to the gate, with an SS guard and an SS officer. The gate was opened and we went inside. We were told by the prisoner, in German with a heavy Polish Yiddish accent, to stand in rows of five to be counted, and she then announced that she was the *Lageralteste*. She had dark hair almost down to her shoulders and the shadow of a dark mustache, which looked as if she must have shaved somehow. Later on, I heard from her that she used to live in Auschwitz and that there was a nice Jewish community there before the war. After she had counted us, the SS officer counted us as well and signed some documents saying that she had received thirty-two slaves...or Jewish pigs? Of one thing I am sure — she never signed for thirty-two girls.

The *Lageralteste* told us to follow her and took us into a stone building to the second floor — we climbed stairs for the first time since leaving home. We entered a room with two primitive but normal windows. It was dark except for the light coming in from the searchlights and guard towers. The room was empty; there were no beds or anything else in it. We were shown where the latrines were: outside, some three hundred meters away. We could go there at any time but were not allowed to wander around the grounds.

We settled down on the stone floor next to each other as tightly as we could, because that was the only way to survive the cold of the night. We lay on the floor, without anything to lie upon or to cover ourselves with. We were hungry but I think we were so tired that our hunger was secondary to our exhaustion.

Reichenbach

The following morning, while it was still dark, we were awoken and ran downstairs in rows of five to be counted. The place where we were was called "*Sports Schule*" and it was a work camp, in contrast to Birkenau. We were not given anything to eat or drink, but we appreciated the fact that we could go to the latrines at any time and had water in the taps of the washrooms.

After *Appel*, the girls went off to work and the thirty-two of us were released to go up to our room. We sat on the rough concrete floor and tried to sleep off our exhaustion. Later, when the sun came up, the *Lageralteste* sent for us. We ran downstairs, stood in rows of five, and waited to see what we were required to do. She told us that probably in a day or two we would be going to work at the Telefunken factory. She gave us large paper sacks and showed us where there was straw, and we started filling the sacks with it. We received one of these sacks as a mattress, and it was indeed a luxury to lie on something. We were also given some blankets and were told by the

Lageralteste that we should soon be getting beds. After filling the mattresses, we carried them upstairs, put them on the floor, and admired our unbelievable luxury.

Each mattress and blanket was for two people. I was paired off with Judith Deutsch, from Rákospalota, near Budapest. She was a very pale looking girl with fine features, rather quiet and reserved, the eldest of three sisters present. The younger sister after Judith, a wiry youngster of seventeen with large gray eyes, reminded me of a Siamese cat hunting for food for her sisters and herself. Her name was Zsuzsi. The third girl was a lovely child of barely sixteen years old, with enormous gray-green starving eyes. She seemed to follow Zsuzsi all the time, and they were not only sisters but terrific friends as well. As I said, Zsuzsi seemed to watch over them as a cat would over her kittens. Judith was my age and we became great friends — camp sisters — and we helped each other, sometimes dragging or pushing one another in order to keep going.

There was another group of girls, five sisters, with very strong characters, where the two elder ones kept the others in order. There was yet another girl, Mira, who was not a sister but was separated from her family, so they adopted her and looked after her. The oldest girl was Etu. She was married, but had no children yet. The second was Dori, who was my age, and we became good friends. Then came Duci, Hani, and Lola, a thin overly quiet young child of less than sixteen.

Judith and Dori were my greatest friends, to whom I spoke about home and my past life, which sounded like a fairy tale. They also spoke about home. This was done in whispers during our long marching and shuffling into work. This living in the past helped us to escape from the terrible actuality, at least for a little while.

Later on that first day, we were given a table for our room.

We sat on our mattresses and started introducing ourselves to each other. Toward evening, we were called for *Appel* and each received a small dish, a spoon, and an enamel mug with a handle, to drink from. This was returning to civilization. We were given a fairly thick soup with potatoes and other vegetables and a slice of bread — no comparison in quality and quantity to Birkenau.

The following morning, while it was still dark, there was *Appel*. We were all counted and all the girls except us went to work in various factories. Later on in the morning, a messenger came to our room looking for me. I had to go downstairs where the *Lageralteste* was waiting with an SS woman. I was told that I was being taken to the residence of the SS officers to clean their apartments, do some washing, ironing, and anything else I would be told to do.

The messenger girl also came to show me where the detergents, cleaning materials, iron, and other things were. This girl thought I would be her assistant, as she had been working for the SS for some time.

First I washed underwear, socks, and shirts of the SS men. I hung them out to dry in the sun and wind, and then I moved over to the apartment of the commandant of our camp, a vicious beastly ugly woman, whose name was Grossman. I washed her underwear, shirts, and stockings under the watchful eyes of the SS woman, and every now and then I was given orders by the other prisoner as to how to do things. After some time, the SS woman shouted at the other girl and told her to keep her mouth shut, because I was a better worker than she, and that I was not lazy, as she was.

I felt very sad because it was the first time that I was doing personal work for the SS and washing their filthy underwear and smelly socks, by hand of course. For the first time I felt a real slave.

When I was brought back to the camp in the evening by the SS woman, the *Lageralteste* said how lucky I was to be able to go on working as a personal maid to the SS and not have to walk several kilometers to and from the factory in the rain and snow. That night, after Appel, seventeen of the thirty-two girls were counted and sent off for night shift. I was not included. I noted that two sisters had been split up, one to work the night shift and one to work by day — they would have met only on Sunday. I quickly asked the sister on the night shift if she wanted to change with me. She was terribly grateful and I stepped into line instead of her, hoping, because of the dark night, that I should not be discovered.

Once we were outside the gates and nearing the woods I was almost happy to be going to work in the cold, cold night. It seemed to take us a long time to walk through the woods and we found the walking hard going, but we were stimulated by the things we saw. We went through the outskirts of the town and finally came to the factory. There must have been a mistake about the gate where they took us in, or perhaps it took them too long to accept us, because it was the only time that we met the men prisoners coming out. From a few meters away they started shouting out names in the hope of finding wives, sisters, family members, or girls from their town. These were Jewish prisoners from Hungary, and although they were beaten by the SS to keep quiet, they went on shouting names and asking where we were from. One of the men shouted out, "Girls, do you know tonight is Simchat Torah?" I knew it, but I was happy to hear and have it confirmed that up to that evening I had managed to keep a correct count of the calendar.

The men were chased out, and we waited outside for a long time until it was decided where to place us in the various departments where they needed workers. Then, as soon as a list was prepared, we were herded into a large hall and then taken into an office; a German civilian was sitting behind a desk and a middle-aged woman prisoner with fairly decent clothes and hair was standing near him. I cannot remember her name, but she was an engineer from Holland from the Philips factory. She was Jewish, and it was said that she collaborated with the Germans and therefore could stay alive and receive better treatment. *I heard that after the war she was tried in Holland and sent to jail for collaboration and giving away secrets of the Philips factory, where she had been working before the war.*

When they needed interpreting for the girls, I was called upon. Then SS women took us into separate departments and handed us over to prisoners who had been working for some time at the Telefunken and Philips factories. These girls all came from Holland and had been in Reichenbach for some time now. When the Philips factory was evacuated from Holland, the workers were taken to Auschwitz-Birkenau, had numbers tattooed on their forearms, and the same day were taken on to Reichenbach to work in Telefunken. They had better clothes than we did: they had either received better clothes or were left with their own clothes from the ghetto. All of them looked much better than we did.

Together with these Jewish prisoners were twenty-two non-Jewish girls, students who had demonstrated against Germany, been arrested, taken to Auschwitz, and sent straight off to work. Since they were non-Jews, these girls had much better treatment. They were also allowed to keep their hair and the clothes they originally wore. They sometimes received Red Cross parcels — after the removal of cigarettes, chocolate, and some other items the Germans were particularly interested in. We, the Hungarian girls, called them *"Hajasok"* — the hairy ones — so they should not understand that we were talking about them.

In the department where I was put to work I think there was no one else from my group. We received a metal desk with a lamp fitted on it, a magnifying glass, which we had to learn to fit onto our eye and work with, and a soldering machine, which worked with the touch of one's foot. In this department there must have been more than a hundred girls at work. Most of them were from Holland, some were Polish Jewish girls, and some of them were Russian or Polish non-Jewish civilian workers. We were not allowed to talk to the civilians. There were German civilians as well, but they worked mainly in the storeroom of each department, handing out work or controlling finished work. The head of the section of the large hall was an ugly disgusting looking little German called Kindler. Every now and then, he would walk through the many rows of desks and working girls. Sometimes he stopped near me and I could feel his gaze piercing through my head. My hands would start to shake and of course I could not work, since the work was very delicate and accurate.

We were soldering filaments onto a base, which when finished was a small bulb. Each of these pieces went through several departments until they were finally filled with gas. Later on, in winter, when our hands were swollen and full of sores, it was terribly difficult to work at these delicate tasks.

After about two weeks, there was a German woman who came round with a stopwatch and sat behind me to see how much I could produce in an hour. I did too well, but others deliberately worked more slowly so that the demands on their productivity would be less. The German did not say a single word, but watched every move of my hands.

As soon as I could, I went out to the toilets. This had to be approved by the SS in charge of the hall, and after that one had to obtain permission from the SS outside the toilets. There

I met some Dutch girls, who saw that I had tried to work fast while being stopwatched, and told me that I had made trouble for myself.

At about one o'clock in the morning we were given warm food. During the winter we had soup, and sometimes even a few small green boiled potatoes. We were also working in more human conditions, sitting on a chair, drinking from a tin cup, and eating off a tin plate in a warm hall. The toilets for the prisoners were separate but reasonable. Our great trouble was when the weather started to freeze. We were given extra clothes, underwear, some sort of a cardigan, and a thin coat. All these pieces of clothing were marked with red oil paint. A large red cross on the back of our garment ensured that we could not run away.

Even with these extra clothes, in the freezing winter — dragging ourselves to work in the dark, through the woods in the rain, hail, and snow, and arriving to work with frozen hands and fingers — it was terribly difficult to start our delicate work straightaway. When we warmed up, things went better, but working for twelve hours, whether by day or night, was very hard indeed. There was a time when we came in for a night shift in the pouring rain with the wind howling, and by the time we arrived at the factory, we were not only soaked but completely frozen.

We used to hang our coats in the corridor of our toilets. Mostly they did not dry out in twelve hours because there were several layers of coats, one on top of another, hanging limply and making puddles underneath.

As it grew colder and my hands and fingers grew swollen, I started falling behind the amount of bulb bases I should have produced. The harder I tried to hurry, the less I succeeded and the more filaments I spoiled. In the morning we were given our quota of raw material that had to be completed and not spoiled. Sometimes the Russian civilian girl who was in charge of our raw material could help us by giving us a few extra things to replace what we'd ruined. Some of the girls were caught not producing enough or spoiling the raw material. They were punished either by having their heads shaved again, which made one suffer terribly from the cold, or being shot, or threatened with being sent back to the chimneys of Auschwitz.

At the farthest corner of this large hall was a room separated by glass walls, where the manager, a tall German, sat. He could see all the workers, and when he appeared in his white coat and started walking about, we were all shaking. I mentioned Kindler before, but he was a subordinate of this other German civilian, whose name I cannot even remember. The Dutch Jewish engineer also worked in that room, as well as a tall blond Dutch girl.

One day when I was on the day shift, this tall blond girl prisoner came out of the cubicle heading straight for me and told me to come with her. All eyes were on me. She called to the others in Dutch that if they did not want to be in trouble as well, they should not waste their time, but work! I was taken into the cubicle, where the German looked at me and told me I was lazy and not working hard enough, that every day I was producing less and less, and did I want to go back to the chimneys of Auschwitz? Unless I mended my ways I should finish up as smoke coming out of a chimney. Meanwhile my punishment would be washing the floor and keeping the hall and toilets clean. "And work fast," he told me.

I started to wash the floor of the hall with a bucket of cold water. My hands became numb and turned purple. After some time, one of the Dutch girls managed to switch my bucket for another, but this time with warm water. God bless her! It was very hard to wash the floor for twelve hours under the watchful eyes of the SS, who saw to it that I should do it on the double.

One of the things that made life hard was that when we were given underwear, I received, instead of pants, a very large corset, to the great amusement of the SS. At first I did not know what to do with it, but as the weather grew colder I wrapped it around me and tied it with its laces, and this kept me nice and warm. There were several metal strips in it, instead of whalebone, and that made it difficult to bend. I decided that as soon as I returned to the camp, I should somehow have to take out these stiffeners. We had no scissors or real knives, but we had the use of a sort of knife to cut the bread. When we returned to the camp I took off my corset, and with the help of my friends I managed to make a hole in the material and started pulling one stiffener and then the other. It was difficult to dislodge them as they had been sewn in several times. I pulled out the first one and it was wrapped in Polish money, twenty and fifty zlotys, if I remember correctly. When we finished pulling out all the stiffeners, there was quite a lot of money, and we decided to get rid of it by throwing it down the latrines and hoping that by morning it would be covered with excrement.

Most of the night I was wondering about the poor woman who had worked hard to hide the money in order to save her and probably her family from starvation, and then, on arrival to the camp, she was either killed or was now starving and struggling to stay alive somewhere. As we were fairly near Gross Rosen, which had a crematorium and gas chamber, it was probable that our clothes came from there, rather than from Birkenau.

My shoes simply went to pieces — we were given a wooden sole and on it a ten centimeter piece of material, which was supposed to keep our feet in place. As soon as we started walking in the snow, it was pure agony. The strip of cloth got torn and we had to try to tie the wood onto our feet. The piece of wood did not bend, so we could walk only by lifting our foot and putting it forward rather than walking in the normal way. This way of getting about was terribly tiring and if, on top of this tortured walking, we had to go straight out into the howling wind, sleet, or rain, we could only triumph over the elements by joining forces with each other. All five of us in a row linked arms and leaned forward into the wind. We were afraid to stand or walk about alone in that wind because it seemed impossible to stand up against it. We went to the factory and back to the camp, after twelve hours of work, shuffling and dragging each other and ourselves, not knowing how much longer we should be able to withstand these hardships.

When we were on the day shift we suffered from the tantalizing smell of freshly baked bread. We left the camp in darkness and arrived at the factory while it was still dark. On the outskirts of town we used to pass a bakery. Sometimes we saw the bakers working inside the warm bakery. I wonder if they ever felt sorry for us, did they ever feel they would like to give us a piece of bread? I was sure that I should never in my life be able to eat my fill of fresh, warm bread.

Sometimes when we were going back to the camp after our day's work, we had stones thrown at us by youngsters. *These same youngsters, when they were in their thirties or forties, were able to look into people's eyes and say, "We had nothing to do with anything. We did not know and we did not see." I personally have not met anyone after the war who knew, heard, saw, or was responsible for bringing Hitler to power or having had anything to do with the camps.*

Meanwhile, the girls asked me if I would apportion the food, and I accepted this responsibility. *Today I wonder why I did it. There was no advantage in it for me and it meant more work. While the girls could gratefully fall onto the floor to rest, I would be dishing out food.* There were two very young girls of under sixteen, Lola Friedman and Hedi Deutsch, and we all agreed that they should each receive an extra spoonful; on the very rare occasions when there was a bone in the soup, one received it one time and the other the next time. On the rare occasions when the soup did have a little meat in it, I am sure that it was either horse meat — or worse.

Amongst us thirty-two girls there were so many different types. Some of the girls came from religious backgrounds and others from completely assimilated homes. There was a very tall sad looking girl from Budapest, and there was another girl whose name I think was Ilus, who always looked on the verge of crying. Nevertheless no one ever cried; we were beyond crying. Ilus was an only child of elderly parents. One day she told me of her terrible sorrow. Her parents, who were a loving couple, started quarreling about her once the deportations had started. Her father wanted her to run away and hide, while her mother was against it. Her mother was afraid she would not be able to manage on her own and wanted her to stay with them. Her father tried to push her out through the door, her mother stood in their way, her father pushed his wife aside and struck her hard. Poor Ilus could not bear the idea that because of her, after thirty happy years of marriage, they started bitter quarrels and then did not speak to each other at all. This is the way they came into Birkenau.

Poor Ilus didn't survive. She was growing weaker and weaker and many times we had to push and drag her to work. We were taken away from Reichenbach through the hills in deep snow. At one of the camps we passed through, she was taken to the sick bay, and when we were sent on to another camp, she and some other *muselman* girls were wrapped in blankets and put into a peasant's cart, dragged by several girls, and taken away. I saw her when we left and told her to keep warm and that we should be seeing her at the next camp. I do not know whether she believed me or not, but I never saw her again, or the human horses who took those poor sick girls away.

There was another girl, also an only child, whose name was Oli. She was a quiet youngster, eighteen years old. I think her father had died, and she and her mother lived in Budapest. Oli went round the corner to buy a few necessities and was picked up outside her house. Without being able to say good-bye to her mother, she was taken to Birkenau. She kept saying, "My mother does not know what happened to me." The poor child wanted to live so much and to go home. She did all the right things with determination, but exactly two weeks before our liberation, we buried her, the only person we were allowed to bury. Oli became sick, but she wanted to keep going to work. Within a day the doctor diagnosed typhus, not that it mattered what the diagnosis was, since there was no medication or any sort of treatment. She soon lost consciousness and died a few days later.

There was a very good looking girl from Yugoslavia with her friend, Panni, and another rather tall girl called Jancsi, who once saw a loaf of bread fall off a truck, and also a few potatoes. She threw herself on the rolling food, but an SS guard saw it and started beating her. The bread was taken away from her, but she tried to hide the three raw potatoes. She was beaten until she gave it all back. We picked her up, brought her back to our barracks, and laid her down on her bed. She reached into her so-called dress and pulled out a small raw potato, which she had managed to save.

There was a slightly older girl of about twenty-nine, who was an authoress and very cultured, but early on something snapped in her. Sometimes she would tell me about the books she would write in which the characters present could be the central personalities. She became stranger by the day. When we were taken away from Reichenbach, with the Russians only a few kilometers away, she asked me to join her in running away. I told her not to do it. We had no hair, no money, no proper clothing, and only a thin coat which had a very large cross painted on it. I told her she would have no chance of surviving. She assured me that the plot was all worked out, and she was disappointed in me for not taking the right opportunity to step out to freedom. On the second day of walking over the hills in deep snow, and far away from any town or village, she came to me again and asked me to come with her. When I refused and begged her not to go now, because I considered this escape plan as having no chance of success, she said she was leaving anyway. Later on in the day I looked for her and asked around, but she was gone. I remembered having heard a shot earlier on.

I hope she survived, but it seems most unlikely. I cannot remember her name. It is interesting and I am sure that I could recognize any of those girls should I meet them, and I could also recognize their voices as well, yet I cannot remember the names of many of them.

There was a strange looking lady, probably no more than thirty-five years old, whose name was Juliska. As she was the most senior of us all, we called her Juliska Néni. *Néni* is aunt in Hungarian. She was a very strange character and looked rather a dissolute person. She told me she tried to go into hiding, was caught, beaten, and put into jail. She survived until the liberation but I do not know what happened to her after that.

There were the other fifteen girls from our group of thirty-two, who worked on another shift. Although we lived together in the same room, we only met them on Sundays, because on that day no one went to work.

Another girl who was in our shift, who came from somewhere in Hungary, was a pretty young thing who, at home, must have been lovely. She hardly spoke, except about everyday necessary things. I have no idea if she had parents, siblings, with whom she came to Birkenau, or what was her background. Her name was Ida and some of us had a lot of trouble with her, to say the least... When we were given our beds, Ida was sharing a bed on the top bunk with another girl. For the first few nights all went well but when the really cold weather started, she began wetting herself. In the middle of the night, her bed partner began complaining that she was wet; the other girls wanted to sleep and told them to stop quarreling. Later on that night we heard water dripping, and the girls who slept below them started shouting and so did the rest of the room. We were in darkness, since the small amount of electricity we had was turned off in the evening. Some of us tried to make peace and to sleep on, but the girls on whom she had urinated would not go back to sleep, and so the remainder of what was left of our rest was lost. After this incident, no one was willing to sleep with her and she had to sleep on the floor. We managed to get her an old mattress made of paper.

In the middle of the next night we again heard water dripping onto the concrete floor. The girls woke up and again there were arguments going on for the rest of the night. When we came back that evening, the room stank terribly. The girls wanted to throw Ida's mattress out but her blankets were soaking as well. It was decided to put her on the floor next to the bed of Judith and myself, which was the first one in the room. We took upon ourselves to wake her up several times during the night so that she should go out to the latrine. We woke her, but she would not get up, and only after I told her that if she would not get up she would have to take her mattress and sleep somewhere else, did I manage to send her out. She came back too fast, but swore that she had been to the latrines.

The stench was getting worse. The Dutch girls at the factory began complaining about her smell. She was very cold, sleeping on the floor in wet things, so she would not take off her coat either, but slept in it. She was a complete pariah, and we had to keep a constant watch on her. When I started going out with her to the latrines, she began urinating on her mattress, blankets, and clothes the moment we woke her, so as not to have to go out. The poor girl became even more withdrawn. The others called her some very unpleasant names and no one would have anything to do with her.

As winter wore on, the walking to work and back became more and more difficult and full of suffering. I used to say my prayers on the way to work or coming back after the night shift. Judith and some of the other girls used to ask me to say my prayers aloud because they drew strength from them. They did not repeat them after me, or pray on their own, but it was comforting for them to hear me reciting my prayers. Although we were supposed to walk in complete silence, nevertheless, with the noise of the howling wind and the breaking of branches as we went through the woods, the guards could not hear my prayers anyway.

I was afraid of coming face to face with a pack of wolves because as a child I heard of many cases of farmers being eaten by them. In Birkenau, as well, I was more afraid of the dogs than of being beaten or killed by the SS. Once when Irma Graese beat me up and kicked me, I was watching her dog sitting next to her and baring his teeth. I knew that on an order from her, the dog would be tearing me to pieces.

On Sundays we had *Appel*, and most of the time we could rest in our room but we had to be quiet. I suggested to some of the girls that we take a little straw from each of our sacks and give it to Ida so that she could throw away her old straw and put in fresh, even if she would have less straw than before. She was not even interested — she was in a deep depression.

On Sunday morning when we had *Appel*, the men's camp also had *Appel*. They were right next to us, separated only by electrified barbed wire. We sometimes saw them from far away, but this time we saw them standing only twenty to thirty meters away. I think the men looked worse than we girls; they seemed somehow more deteriorated. One of the Dutch girls amongst us discovered her husband. She had had no idea that he was there or even that he was still alive. Of course she became terribly excited and tried to make signs to attract the attention of the men. One of them saw her waving and pointed toward her husband. Unfortunately, the SS woman commandant, Grossman, was watching her and wanted to see who it was she was so interested in. This continued, on and off, for some time until the husband got the message that someone was waving to him from the women's camp. When he recognized her, he must have forgotten where he was and started waving back to her.

The SS woman Grossman and an SS officer in the men's camp pounced on each of them, cursing and beating them as well. We were counted and so were the men and then released to go indoors, except for the couple, husband and wife, who had to stay behind. They were questioned about their relationship and whipped, each of them having to watch through the barbed wire fence while the other was being beaten. Then the real punishment started. The SS officer had a bicycle brought to him and the poor husband had to start running in front of it, faster and faster. The poor man could not run for long and he fell. The officer ran over him, whipped him, kicked him, and he had to start running again. His wife had to watch all of this through the fence. Every now and then she was also whipped. Later they brought a dish of hot soup to the husband and he was told to eat it while running but without spilling any of it. This, of course, was impossible so he was beaten once again, his hands tied behind his back, and he had to run in front of the bicycle again.

Psychologists say that prisoners start identifying themselves with and even developing a crush on their jailers. We had a tall beastly SS woman sergeant who used to count us and take us to work with several other SS men and women. When we two looked at each other there were sparks of real hatred between us, which I was not very successful in hiding. She was everywhere and seemed to have eyes even in the back of her head. The most incredible thing I found was that the girls started calling her Mutti, "Mummy." They used to say aloud so that she should hear, "Look, Mutti is here." She looked at them with disdain and said, "So I am your Mutti, you cows." I was very careful not to come into contact with her.

One Sunday morning, this was the one and only time she announced at *Appel* that we should bring our underpants to the storeroom and we should get clean ones instead. We went and stood outside the storeroom for a long time. The SS women were ready to exchange our underwear, but she sent a messenger to them to say they must wait for her. We were holding our pants in our hands, but I did not have pants as I had been given instead a dreadful looking corset.

When she arrived she singled out several girls, myself included, to come in at once. She changed the pants of the other girls and turned to me demanding where my pants were and from where had I got a corset. I told her, in clear good German, that I had never had pants in the first place but only a corset, which I must have been given by mistake. She started screaming at me and called me "a liar" and continued to say, "and now Mutti will show you what happens to *Schweinhünde* like you." She picked a thick wide piece of wood and with both hands started hitting me straight onto my face and head — for how long I do not know, because I woke up on my bed only when it was growing dark and the girls were shaking me to get up and go down to *Appel*. My nose and face were terribly swollen and there were bumps on my head. I was sure my nose was broken and I could see with only one eye. I was lucky that I was not then on the night shift because I could not have gone to work or done anything at the factory anyway, not in the condition I was in.

After a few hours of rest I went off to the factory along with the day shift. I was helped by my friends to get there.

As we were approaching Chanukah, the Feast of Lights, I told the girls we would have to plan on lighting candles on at least one out of the eight nights. We started planning to have the bare necessities ready for the first night of Chanukah. We discussed the dangers of lighting, as we would have to steal every item except the wick, which we could make from our clothes. I told the girls that lighting the Chanukah candles represented our freedom of spirit and the eternity of the Jewish people.

There were a few girls among us who had never celebrated Chanukah but were nevertheless keen to take part in the preparations. One of the girls managed to steal a raw potato. We looked at it several times a day, and it was a miracle that no one ate it up before Chanukah. Our biggest problem was to get hold of a small container, so that one of the girls who worked on a machine using a small amount of oil could take a few drops a day for our purpose. One of the girls got hold of a tiny container without a lid, but even so, the amount of oil we needed was collected. We still needed matches. This was organized by a girl from another room who also wanted to take part in the celebrations. When she went to the kitchen to bring food for her building, she managed to lift an almost empty box of matches.

The girls were becoming excited, as far as they were able. The potato, which would have made such a lovely meal, even though uncooked, was still waiting, hidden by one of us and carried to work and back. On the evening of the first night of Chanukah, when we had come back to the camp and had finished eating our warm soup, we started preparing for the great event. We took the potato and with a spoon scooped out enough of it to make a little depression in which to put the small amount of oil. We took threads from our clothes and made a wick. The next thing that had to be solved was how to arrange that the light should be put near enough to the window so that it could be seen outside. According to religious law, we should light up in a place where the light could be seen from far away so as to advertise the miracle.

When everything was ready, we turned off the dim light in our room and I started lighting the one and only light for the first night of Chanukah. I said the blessings: "Blessed art Thou, O Lord our God, King of the universe, Who has sanctified us with His commandments and commanded us to light the light of Chanukah. Blessed art Thou, O Lord our God, King of the universe, Who performed miracles for our forefathers in those days at this time." The third blessing thanked God for keeping us alive, sustaining us, and letting us reach this time. We stood there, all of us, neither moving nor breathing, admiring the wonderful sight of that tiny light. Then we burst into the song which is sung after lighting the Chanukah light, "*Maoz Tzur Yeshuati...*" We sang as loudly as we could, not caring whether we shattered the silence of the camp.

We waited. I was sure that very soon the SS would burst into our room, beat us up, and start questioning us. No one came, which we found to be a miracle. We turned on the light again and prepared for bed, because we knew that soon the electricity would be turned off.

The little light was still flickering. I looked at it and it was telling me so many things. It was telling me to lift my head up higher, for I belong to a nation who, through centuries, time and time again, had to be Maccabees, had to fight in order to keep the eternal light of the Jewish people going.

I shared a bed with my friend Judith, and as none of us could sleep because of the excitement, we started talking quietly. We told each other about how we celebrated Chanukah at home.

After Judith dropped off to sleep, I tried to conjure up Chanukah at my grandparents' house. After my grandfather kindled the oil lamp in his lovely, antique silver candelabra, each male member of the family lit the Chanukah lights, each in a different candelabra. Then came the singing and after that we went into the large dining room, with the crystal chande-

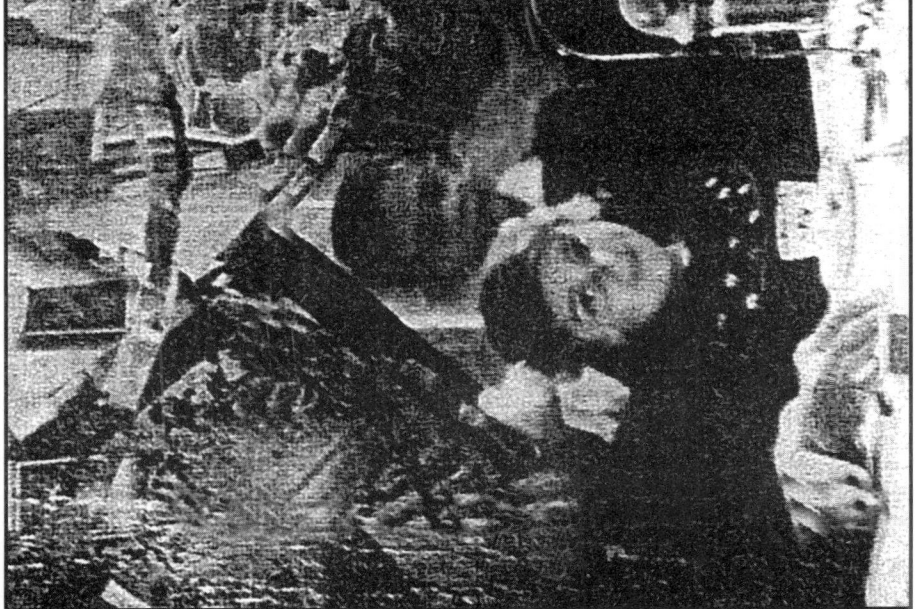

Two pictures of my family in the sukkah. I'm the young girl with pigtails.

The big synagogue in my town with 1200 seats.

The inside of the synagogue with the original decor.

The big synagogue after the war in 1994 with the original decor. The woman in the bottom left is my daughter.

PARANCS.

A „Ghettó" felett a parancsnokságot átvettem.

Parancsaimat csendőrök hajtják végre. Feg... használat a csendőrségre érvényes szabályok sz... Minden kilengést, a szabályoktól minden el... megtorolok. A táborrend betűszerinti végreha... megkövetelem.

Felszólítok minden zsidót, h...

1. azokat az értéktárgyakat (készpénzt, ékszert, arany-, ezüst nemi... értékpapírt) amelyek még birtokában vannak, a leány gimnázium földszinti h... működő átvevő bizottságnak ma 16—20 óra között szolgáltassa be,

2. aki kereszténynek bármilyen vagyontárgyat, bármilyen címen f... 22. után átadott ma 16—20 óra között ugyanannál a bizottságnál írásban... Részletesen fel kell sorolni, hogy milyen tárgyakat, milyen értékben, kinek... foglalkozás, község, utca és házszám) mikor és milyen címen adott át... aláírása alatt tüntesse fel foglalkozását és bejelentett lakását. A bejele... előllemezze. Ugyanez a kötelezettség terheli azokat, akik ilyen esetekről tu...

3. akinek saját, vagy családja 14 napot meghaladó szükségletén felül... élelmiszer van, a felesleget ma 16—20 óra között szolgáltassa be az ugyanott n... bizottságnak.

Holnaptól kezdve a Ghettót csendőrökkel átkut... aki a fenti parancsaimat nem tartotta be, büntető tábo...

Ezt a parancsot a ghettóban minden házban a kapu alatt, emelete... kívül minden emeleten is ki kell függeszteni.

Nagyvárad, 1944. május hó 10.

The Order proclaiming rules in the first ghetto in Hungary. Found after the war in the Jewish Museum in Budapest.

Gateway to Birkenau — its control tower.

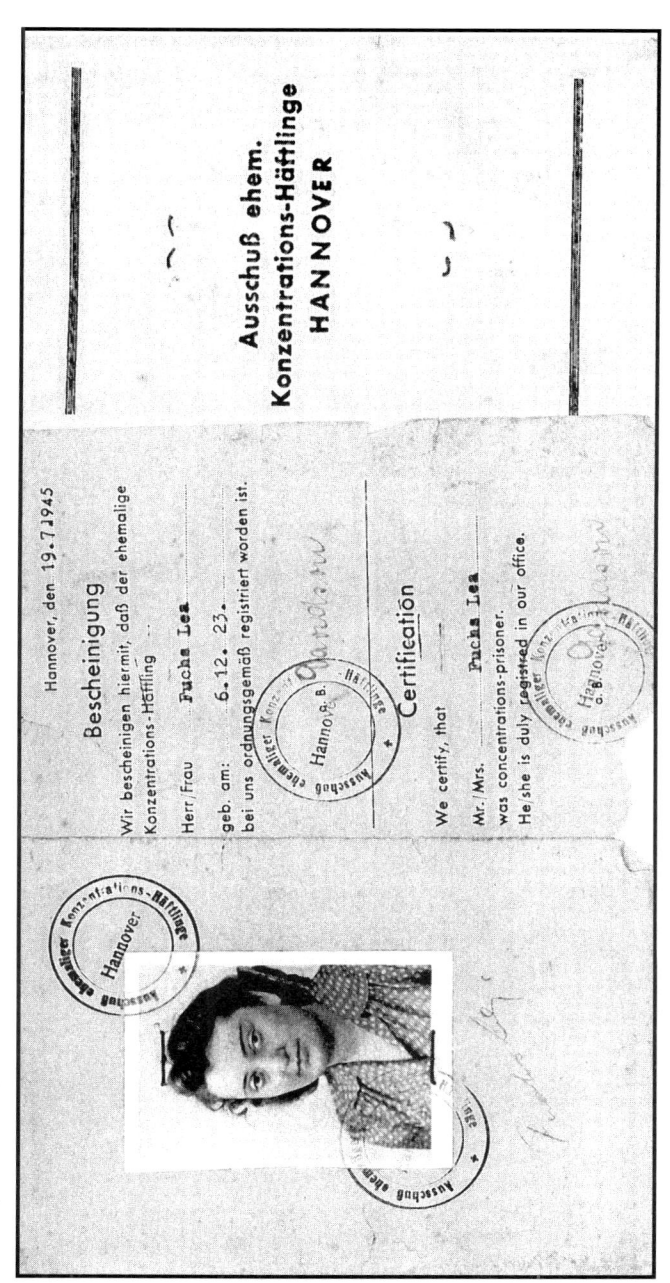

Ausschuß ehem.
Konzentrations-Häftlinge
HANNOVER

Hannover, den 19.7.1945

Bescheinigung

Wir bescheinigen hiermit, daß der ehemalige
Konzentrations-Häftling

Herr/Frau   Fuchs Lea

geb. am: 6.12. 23.

bei uns ordnungsgemäß registriert worden ist.

Ausschuß ehemaliger Konz.
Hannov. B. Häftlinge

Certification

We certify, that

Mr./Mrs.   Fuchs Lea

was concentrations-prisoner.

He/she is duly registered in our office.

Ausschuß ehemaliger Konz. Hannover Häftlinge

Ausschuß ehemaliger Konzentrations-Häftlinge
Hannover

Ausschuß ehem.

Identification as an ex-concentration camp prisoner.

THE CONCENTRATION CAMPS

Between 1939 and 1945, six million unarmed and innocent Jewish civilians - men, women, children and babies - were murdered in Nazi-controlled Europe, as part of a deliberate policy to destroy all traces of Jewish life and culture. As many as two million of these were killed in their own towns and villages, some confined in ghettoes where death by slow starvation was a deliberate Nazi policy, others taken to be shot at mass-murder sites near where they lived. The remaining four million Jews were forced from their homes and taken by train to distant concentration camps, where they were murdered by being worked to death, starved to death, beaten to death, shot, or gassed.

Among the hundreds of thousands of non-Jews sent by the Nazis to concentration camps were anti-Nazis, Jehovah's Witnesses, homosexuals, the mentally ill, and the chronically sick. In addition, more than 250,000 Gypsies were murdered, in a Nazi attempt to eliminate Gypsies as well as Jews from the map of Europe.

In many of the camps shown here so-called "medical" experiments were carried out, without anaesthetics, solely to satisfy the curiosity and sadism of the doctors. Hundreds of otherwise healthy "patients" were tortured and murdered during these experiments.

Auschwitz concentration camp in which more than 2 *million* people were murdered between 1941 and 1944, including Jews, Gypsies, and Soviet prisoners-of-war.

Camps set up solely for the murder of Jews.

Other camps in which Jews and non-Jews were put to forced labour, starved, tortured, and murdered in conditions of the worst imaginable cruelty. Most of these camps had "satellite" labour camps nearby.

0   100 miles
0   100 km

© Martin Gilbert 1978

North Sea
Baltic Sea
Klooga ESTONIA   Vaivara
LATVIA
LITHUANIA
U S S R
Stutthof
Neuengamme   Ravensbrück   Treblinka
Bergen-Belsen   Sachsenhausen   Chelmno
Mittelbau Dora   P O L A N D   Sobibor
Gross Rosen   Auschwitz   Majdanek
Buchenwald   Belzec
G E R M A N Y
Flossenberg   Plaszow
Natzweiler   C Z E C H O S L O V A K I A
F R A N C E   Dachau
Mauthausen
A U S T R I A   H U N G A R Y
RUMANIA
Gospic   Jasenovac
Y U G O S L A V I A   Sajmiste
Adriatic Sea

The concentration camps

lier looking like hundreds of stars. The table was laid, and we usually had goose liver, smoked goose with potato pancakes, and the most delicious thing was toast rubbed with garlic and dipped into hot goose fat.

With my brother Moishi we used to plan our parties and how we would play and be partners in our winnings. Somehow I was always pushed aside even when I was promised and assured that this year I was already old enough to come into the partnership with my brother and Lea and Ari Normand, who were our cousins. Lea Normand was two years my senior and Ari was six weeks older that I. But it was made clear to me at every occasion that I was the youngest.

In those days, it could be cold or snowing outside but the maid kept on stoking the fires with wood.

How incredible it seemed that only a short while ago there was a family, home, food, natural relationships, and now all this was gone forever. I knew that most of my family, if not all, were killed right away on arrival in Birkenau. What had been would never be again.

We were very cold, or perhaps, thinking of home, of the warm family atmosphere, of the cheerful elegant house, of the food, all this made us feel our bitter hopeless situation even more keenly.

Having thought of my family at home, I finished off by thinking of them going into the gas chambers. My mother, my sisters, my sisters' children, my grandfather and father. I did not know what happened to my brother Moishi, nor did I know anything about my youngest sister Chanah's husband — did they stay alive or not? Thinking of them, and wondering how long it took them to die, and wondering if they suffered very much. At the end I always found myself smelling gas, holding my breath, and almost choking.

My friend Judith noticed my breathing difficulties. She found it impossible to go back to sleep — bothered by her memories as well — so we talked in whispers most of the night.

The following day, we were all more depressed and rather quiet; there was nothing to look forward to. It was a sort of let down.

The fifth night of Chanukah was my twenty-first birthday. I received many precious presents from the girls, my new and only family, none of whom I knew from home. I was given a small wooden comb about two-inches long. I had no hair to comb; nevertheless, it was something very precious. From Judith's youngest sister Hédi, that young child with enormous starving gray green eyes, I was given a red checkered handkerchief. What an unbelievable luxury to have something to wipe one's nose on. Goodness only knows where she got it from. To be in possession of any object which we did not receive from the SS was dangerous and a serious offense. I also received, like everyone in our room on her birthday, an extra spoonful of soup from the bottom of the container, as the last spoonful of soup was thicker.

The girls wished me a very happy birthday, and again I was transferred back home, remembering and remembering.

A few days later at the factory, we were witnesses to a drama. One of the Dutch girls was accused of sabotage and sentenced to death by the tall red-faced director, who a few weeks previously asked me if I wanted to go back to the chimneys of Auschwitz.

I remember her coming out of the glass cubicle after sentencing, white and shaking, but behaving with enormous dignity. She was taken by one of the Dutch girls to a chair in the corner of the hall, where our food was distributed, and she was given a glass of water to revive her. After a few minutes, the SS woman on duty chased them both back to work.

We thought the poor thing would be taken to Gross Rosen, which was both near Reichenbach and had gas chambers and a crematorium. A few days after the sentence had been passed, she was picked up in the middle of the night by two SS guards and taken off.

The following morning I heard from the Dutch girls at work that the guards came back fairly soon after they took the girl away. The SS left her bloodied clothes, with a hole on the upper left side of the dress, outside the storeroom. It is interesting that the murder of one single girl could depress us, when we had seen and lived for several months near the chimneys of Birkenau where several thousand people were murdered every day. Auschwitz-Birkenau was a well and smoothly run factory for death.

After a few days the girls stopped talking about her. I suppose this is called self-preservation.

It is so very difficult to explain what made us go on, why we bothered to put one foot in front of the other. Some time ago, I was giving a lecture on the Holocaust. An American girl who had made a special study of the camps and of people's sufferings, and had been to Poland several times, said, "If I could not have had a shower for a whole month, I would have just sat down and told them to shoot me." Even this girl could not understand that she would not have been shot, but she would have been beaten and tortured, put through hell on earth, until she herself would have gone on, just like all of us, dragging ourselves and going through the motions of living.

However, much as one tries to tell, explain, to recreate the atmosphere of the camps, one fails because no normal human mind can understand the abnormal beastliness of the German nation.

The very fact that they found plenty of volunteers besides the SS, so-called normal respected people who could do these atrocities, proved that there was — there is — something terribly wrong with them.

These are the people who did not know, did not see, did not hear about the camps, about their neighbors the Jews disappearing, and their homes, belongings, and businesses taken over by the Germans. They also found willing helpers from other nations, but the organization, the beastly thoroughness, was all theirs. This was the success of the great educators Hitler, Himler, Goebbels, and others.

If you would find a group of children who put to death twenty cockroaches in different slow and beastly ways, and felt so proud of their achievements that they would take films in order to document their efforts, I am sure that they would be taken for treatment to psychologists and would be considered both disgusting and abnormal. Not so if a whole nation does it, against millions of Jews.

The German civilians and the SS were preparing for Xmas, but their preparations were very subdued. They did not seem to have anything special for their holiday. We were looking forward to not having to go to work on Xmas day and resting from the hard long walk to work and back in the wooden clogs.

The snow would get stuck to the clogs, and as we went along the layer would get thicker and thicker. The trouble was that the layers did not build up on each of the clogs equally, so sometimes if we could not stop for a few seconds to scrape off the snow, we would walk like cripples, one leg sometimes as much as five inches longer than the other one. From this torturous walking, our backs and our feet would hurt, and even worse, when the walking really became difficult, the one and only strap of the clog would tear off its base and one would be left with not even a piece of wood between one's foot and the snow. The mud sometimes could be the worst of all, because one would sink into it deeply, and if one was not careful how she pulled her foot out, she could loose the clogs altogether.

The amount of energy and thought required just to put one foot in front of the other was enormous, and I found that reciting my prayers or a particularly beautiful psalm helped me overcome some of the misery.

On Xmas eve we heard loud singing coming from the SS quarters. "*Schtile Nacht Heilige Nacht*" — love and goodwill on earth, love of mankind, and so on.

We were in bed, bundled up together against the cold trying to sleep, when all of a sudden SS guards burst into the buildings shouting, cursing, and chasing us out for *Appel*. The lights were not switched on and in the pitch dark we could not find our clogs and our coats in order to wrap up our feet and ourselves. We were chased downstairs, falling over each other. I managed to find only one of my clogs, and there we had to stand to attention and hear the ravings and curses of the Commandant Grossman, who charged about with her knotted leather whip, slashing out left and right, ranting and raving. We thought they were all drunk, since it was Xmas.

We could not stand still, however much they beat us, because of the bitter cold. Then they started counting us again and there was one girl missing. More beatings and punishments — the guards were completely bloodthirsty because we had spoiled their Xmas eve celebrations. They had to search the buildings and around them for the missing girl. No one was found. More curses and promises of what would happen in the morning and we were released to go to our rooms.

From standing in the freezing cold weather, all of us had to run to the latrines. The snow was frozen and very slippery.

There was a long line of girls waiting impatiently for their turn. We were looking for Ida, the girl with the bed-wetting problem, to make her come with us to the latrines, but unfortunately we could not find her. Judith discovered her bundled up under the table, far enough away from our beds so that we couldn't wake her and send her to the latrines. Judith, who had been treated for the last couple of years for her kidneys, amazingly was managing as well or as badly as any of us. According to her sisters, at home she was considered a delicate girl who needed a lot of rest.

Afterwards, we rubbed our feet, and each other's as well, to get a little warmer so that we could drop off to sleep.

The following morning, when daylight broke, one of the girls while going to the latrines discovered the missing girl inside the cesspit. What a way to die! She must have run there either before or during *Appel*, slipped on the frozen surface, and fell in. It was made of wood, both the floor and seats — some of it cracked and broken. A little later on, we had *Appel* again and were told that because of us *Schweinhünde*, on Xmas morning they had to get up early in order to count us. Later on we heard from the *Lageralteste* that the reason for the ravings of Grossman, the head SS officer, was a telegram which she had received from the army with the news of her husband's death.

Of course, we Jews, the communists, were responsible for his death, and for the German army's defeat on the Russian front.

There was less raw material at the factory now, and every now and then we saw a few German refugees.

In January the Allies started bombing Reichenbach. There were some Italian prisoners of war whose job was repairing and cleaning the machinery. While they worked they used to sing the news to us under their breath. When they could not talk, they would make the sound of a pig and grind their shoes into the ground, then smile. This meant the German pigs are going to be beaten and killed. These Italians were free to come and go without guards. There was no danger of their running away and going back to Italy to fight. They were happy where they were to wait until the end of the war.

One evening, several girls were sent to take food to a building where some new girls were staying. We thought they would be working at one of the factories in Reichenbach. Just before lights out, two girls came looking for me. They had taken food over to the newcomers and found out that they were on their way to Gross Rosen. Amongst them was a girl from my town, in fact, from my class at school. The girls told me her name and said she was behaving in a rather strange way.

Her family used to live not far from us. She was an only child — light curly hair, a ready smile, nicely brought up. Already in the ghetto she had been treated for depression. At first I did not know if I should go and see her. What could I tell her? Should I tell her not to be afraid, and as an old friend give her a last hug and kiss? The last one ever! Or would she prefer to be left alone and forgo the companionship of a childhood friend.

Her name was Ági. Often we met on our way to school and we used to kick a piece of rag in a game which had well-defined rules: the rag had to be on the move all the time, and above all we had to be careful not to be caught by parents, teachers, siblings, aunts and uncles, because we knew this was not the way well brought-up girls behaved.

My dilemma was solved because the lights were turned off.

The following day we left the camp still in darkness. I kept thinking of my friend Ági and could hardly wait to see her — without saying anything to her, just taking her in my arms. I wondered if she knew and minded why she was taken to Gross Rosen. Was she afraid of dying? Would she want to see me?

At the same time I was troubled with a very bad toothache that was getting worse. This had been going on for almost two weeks, but I knew I could not do anything about it, so I tried to keep my face warm, which at least did not aggravate the pain and even relieved it a little. In the evening when we arrived at the camp, after distributing the soup and bread, I finished eating fast and set out to see my friend. I told Judith where I was heading, but she urged me to go first and see the doctor. By then my face was swollen and very, very painful.

I arrived at the block where the girls were supposed to be. I went into several rooms to ask about them, but the information was the same: they had been taken away by trucks, and the sick girls from our camp were sent off with them. So, after all, Ági went off to Gross Rosen without a hug, without knowing that someone cared for her. She was also only twenty-one years old, like myself.

I did not go to the doctor, I seemed to have forgotten about my toothache. I dragged myself back to my room and told the girls that I missed Ági. Nobody said a single word. Judith came to me and started rubbing my arms vigorously. With the rubbing she expressed her feeling of sympathy.

My tooth would not let me sleep. The following day was Saturday, and it was too difficult to keep up the steady work that was demanded of me. In the evening I went to the doctor — to her room and not to the sick bay. It was not good to be seen at the sick bay. She had nothing to give me against the pain. She had a look at my tooth, suggested we have it extracted — as she put it, "Who needs a thing like that in one's mouth?" — and reassured me it would be all right. The doctor suggested that on Sunday morning, after *Appel*, I come to her room, where she had some sort of a dentist's chair, probably one hundred and fifty years old.

The following morning, after a second sleepless night, I went to her room. She had boiled an ancient looking tongs and pliers and a small hammer — laid them all out on a sort of small table — and invited me to sit down. She tried to look very calm, which she was not. I felt sorry for her. She had an assistant, her niece, a nice girl, who handed me a sort of a cushion, or rather a whole lot of rags bundled together. She said, "Squeeze it, or tear it to pieces. It does help, you know." They were so nice to me.

I sat down, very tense. The doctor kept up a light conversation, saying, "Before we even realize, it will be over." She also said, apologetically, that we should try and do it as quietly as possible. I understood.

She put in the pliers and started pulling. I arched my back and thought she was pulling out my heart and brain. Another few yanks, and I realized her niece was telling me it's over — which it was not. She stopped so I could wash out my mouth, because I was gagging on my blood. I saw her wiping perspiration off her forehead, then off mine as well. One more second, it is almost out, but I was not sure that I would survive to see my tooth drawn. It took her another few pulls and yanks, and at last the tooth was out.

I tried to say thank you, but did not have the strength even for that. I washed out my mouth with cold water. The socket was bleeding freely, and the doctor suggested she put in a plug to stop the bleeding. The only bandage she had available was a diminishing roll of toilet paper. She rolled up a piece and told me to bite on it. It never occurred to me that I might get septicemia. I could die from so many other things that a little blood poisoning was nothing to worry about. She wiped my face with cold water and said, "It was nice seeing you, and we'll forget about the whole thing." They cleaned up, put away everything, and left the room, but not together with me.

It was so good that I could recover in comfort: it was Sunday and we were on the day shift, so I was off duty till Monday morning. Toward evening before *Appel*, the doctor's niece came to ask me how I was and if the socket was still bleeding. It was agony during *Appel* standing in the cold wind and not being able to cover my face.

A few days later, the doctor's niece had a stomachache with vomiting and fever. The doctor told Commandant Grossman about it, and she said she would take her to a hospital. We were all certain that she would be taken to Gross Rosen. Ten days later she was brought back by an SS woman, looking much better than before. She had been operated on for her appendix, stayed in an ordinary ward, had the same food as the other patients, and when she started eating she was even given white bread. She had a proper bed with sheets, just like a human being.

At *Appel* she was shown to all of us, and Grossman, the SS officer, said, "Now that you see what wonderful treatment we give you in Germany, when you are sick or unwell or you are weak and it is difficult for you to work, come forward — you will be treated and then returned." Thank God nobody fell for her cunning.

The following night at 10:45 the sirens started screaming. I knew the time because there was a large clock opposite my work bench. The SS were shouting and rounding us up in order to herd us to the open fields. We were told to lie down on the frozen snow, while the civilians and the SS jumped into slit trenches. It was rather nice to see the tracers and then having flares coming down, which lit us up. The bombing started. The tough Germans were terrified; not so the so-called cowardly Jews. We were waiting to welcome a friendly bomb.

After some time it was impossible to lie on the frozen ground, so we all sat up. The SS and their dogs were watching us nervously. They started shouting that we should lie down or they would shoot us. We did not take any notice of them, because it was better to be shot than to freeze to death. Later, when the all clear sounded and we went back to work, the SS and all the civilians were served hot drinks. It seems we did not need it because we were not considered human beings.

The bombing cheered us up because it showed that things were not going so well for the Germans. Soon there was bombing every night, and in order to prove to the German population that the Allies had air supremacy, they came over every night at exactly the same time. Often they came back, wave after wave, but they always started at the same time.

After a few days, the German population received the message that exactly at a certain time, the bombing would start. I loved watching the Germans ten minutes before the sirens would sound, getting ready, putting on their coats, so the moment the sirens sounded they were out of the building. The factory had glass ceilings and they were afraid to be injured by flying glass. Twenty minutes before the time of the sirens, there were people walking up and down the different departments of the factory to see to it that no one would get ready before the sound of the sirens.

It seemed that things were going better for the Allies, and

they started coming over and bombing also in broad daylight. The same thing happened during the day — at exactly 12:00 noon the planes appeared and swooped down to drop their cargo and cause as much destruction as possible.

The SS let us sit on the ground or even stand without moving. We were watched by their dogs, and with one word from their masters they would have torn us to pieces.

We, the so-called hysterical cowardly Jews, stood there relaxed, rather enjoying the fact that the brave Germans were frightened out of their minds. We enjoyed it enormously, but tried not to show it. The bombardment went on day and night, almost unchallenged. I do not know how much damage was done in town to property, but the damage to the morale of the population was great.

We had no idea which of the Allies did the bombings, but as we were nearest to the Russian front, we thought it was their planes coming over all the time. *After the war we heard that most of the bombing was done either by the U.S. or British air force.*

I was getting good at my work, which entailed making very small bulbs for use in German aircraft. Some of the girls were sabotaging the bulbs, but as each one passed through a number of phases, it was impossible to discover this until it was completed. Then each bulb came to the control desk, where two German civilian girls worked, checking each bulb carefully with a microscope.

The manager of my section, the ugly little German, Kindler, called me to his desk. I thought now I shall really be sent back to the chimneys. I decided that I am not afraid of anyone or anything, and I went to him. Kindler looked up at me. "Fräulein Fuchs, are you clever?" I replied, "I do not know." He said, "I want you to come and sit here with my other two

assistants and work in the control department of this section."
I could hardly believe my ears, just imagine for once I was
called Miss Fuchs — and not some degrading name.

This was a tricky position, because if I did not discover
the spoiled bulbs, I could be shot, and if I did I would get our
girls into trouble, including myself.

Thank God each day there was less raw material available.
Our factory, the Telefunken, had not been damaged yet, but
there were ammunition and heavy industrial factories which
were hit and not functioning anymore.

Toward the end of January, a single girl prisoner was
brought to our camp by a policeman. She was a Greek
non-Jewish political prisoner who was in the death march
from Auschwitz. She told us that many of the prisoners died
on the march or could not go on. At a place where they were
being put into boxcars, she went to relieve herself and was left
behind. The train started moving and gathering speed, and
she begged the station master to signal the train to stop but it
was too late. This was in the middle of the night. Instead of
running away — she had fairly normal clothes, shoes, hair —
she went to the police station and there she was told to come
back in the morning. Finally she was brought to our camp.

I asked her why she had not run away, hidden, worked,
whatever, just to stay free. No, she said, that would have been
too difficult, and she preferred the companionship of the prisoners in the camp.

From her we heard that the Russians were advancing.
Auschwitz had been liberated a few hours after they left. She
also told us about the *Sonderkommando* blowing up one of the
gas chambers and crematoria. She herself was working in Canada, sorting out clothes and other things which came off the
trains. She had a number tattooed on her forearm. The gas

chamber and crematorium which they blew up were the ones next to Canada where she worked. The Greek girl told us how they shouted some prayer, like all the Jews shouted before going into the gas chambers, and also sang their national anthem.

The Sonderkommando, *Jewish prisoners who worked at the gas chambers taking out gold teeth of the poor victims and going through their bodies to find diamonds and gold, managed to save a lot of gold for themselves. They knew that about every three months, the boys were changed by killing the ones who worked there and getting new prisoners for another three months to work. The reason for changing them every few months was not to let them accumulate too much gold or knowledge of the running of Auschwitz and Birkenau. The Germans were afraid of prisoners running away and telling the world about the mass killings.*

The boys, knowing that their time was up, wanted to do something for their own people, the Jewish people. By destroying a gas chamber and crematorium, they slowed down the daily killings in Birkenau by 2,500 people. These brave people said Shema Yisrael and Hatikvah and were murdered, but they also did something that no one else has ever done in Auschwitz before or after them. Hashem yikom damam, *may the Almighty avenge their blood.*

The Greek girl was put to work at the local kitchen where there were other political prisoners working.

On the way to work, or coming back from the factory, we met German refugees — hordes of them — pushing piled-up baby carriages or bicycles loaded up with their belongings. They were running away from the Russian army by the thousands. I thanked the Almighty that I lived to see the suffering of the Germans, who were the personification of evil.

The bombings became more frequent, and the tough German population were not looking so well under the strain.

During the night shifts we hardly worked; there was lack of raw material and in any case the sirens were going on and off all night long. Coming in from the freezing cold and not having any work to do made it difficult to keep awake. Several times after air attacks we had to clean broken glass and other debris from the factory floors.

We started hearing hollow thuds from far away and thought it might only be wishful thinking that those were the guns of the Russian army. Slowly, after several hours, the sounds were coming nearer to us. After our night shift, going back to our camp, we saw people coming from all over Germany with babies, chickens, pulling along children, going on foot.

In the middle of the day we were woken up by a lot of noise: the wooden clogs and excited talk of the girls who were on the day shift at the factory, but had come back to the camp. The girls told us how there were waves of non-stop bombings; no sooner would the all clear sound, than the warning sirens would start again. The Telefunken factory was hit, buildings were burning, and people were wounded. The prisoners were told to get ready to go back to the camp, but when the sirens sounded again, our girls were abandoned because the Germans ran for shelter. The girls saw how many people were wounded and did not want to stand near the factory, so they made their way through the burning town back to the camp on their own. *It might seem difficult to understand, reading this, why they did not run away or hide. One has to understand that without money, food, proper shoes, or clothes, without hair in the middle of winter, they could not have survived.* In the evening we were not taken to work, and I never saw the factory again.

The fighting was definitely coming nearer, and we were hoping to be captured by the Russian army. There were a lot of preparations and running around at the SS lodgings and we heard, and it was obvious, they were getting ready for something.

All day we did nothing except speculate if we still had a future, or if this was the end.

In the dark of the night we were chased out for *Appel*. By that time we heard constant thudding and pounding of guns. The Commandant Grossman was even more vicious than usual and was cursing the daylight out of everybody. We were told we were leaving. We ran back to our room and tried to improve our shoes. We tore our mattresses, which were made out of thick paper, hoping the SS would not look in the rooms before we left. We wanted to wrap our feet in the paper and tie the clogs to our feet with rope made out of the paper.

Screaming for *Appel* could be heard again all over the camp and we went downstairs. The tension amongst the SS was great and Grossman was raving as we had never seen her before.

The men from the camp near us must have left earlier because there was no sign of life from there. There seemed to be some trouble with one of the *Blockaltestes*, a good looking tall girl from Transylvania, who also had a younger sister with her. She was liked and trusted by Grossman, but she stood alone to one side and looked in great trouble. All the girls who worked at the Telefunken factory were set aside from the girls who worked at the ammunition factory.

We were given a small loaf of bread, which was for three girls, and we started moving out of the camp. The *Lageralteste* and *Blockalteste* who was in trouble stayed behind. I never saw Grossman again. I do not know how many SS guards we had, some men, some women, and their dogs.

Odyssey of Death

The SS loaded their belongings and their food onto bicycles and made the girls push them. We all had to take turns in pushing and dragging their belongings. Soon we came to the bottom of a hill, and we started climbing uphill in the snow. It was impossible to push the bicycles. Two girls had to carry a bicycle, and the belongings were dragged by other girls separately. We had to take turns in carrying those things, because it was difficult enough even to drag ourselves.

The heartwarming music of the guns was with us all the time. The sun came out, the hills looked beautiful, everything was covered in snow. That must have been a lovely ski run. We found by the side of the path log huts for resting and sheltering against rain, snow, and wind. The SS made good use of these huts, while we stood outside waiting for them. At one of these log huts the guards went to have a rest. We turned round and looked down toward Reichenbach; our hearts gave a big lurch because we could see a column of tanks advancing toward the town.

The oldest of the Friedman girls, Etu, saw three cows standing nearby, and being a tough practical girl, walked up to one of them and started milking it. They drank a little milk, but as soon as it was discovered by the guards, it was stopped. At least we were not cold, with all the effort of climbing and carrying things. I do not know how many kilometers we covered, but it was amazing that we managed to walk at all. Later on, with the sun shining, we tried to make a more cheerful atmosphere, and Judith, Zsuzsi, Hédi, and I started singing Zionist songs, and others joined in. There was one song in Hungarian describing alien countryside, in which we were now walking although we wanted to go to Eretz Yisrael — to the land of Israel. The refrain was *Am Yisrael chai* — the Jewish nation lives. Looking at the girls, we did not look very much alive.

We still had not eaten. We did not want to touch our bread because we did not know when we would be getting more food. Toward the evening when the sun started to set, we still could not see where we would put down our weary limbs, and a completely hopeless feeling settled on us.

From behind us came thirty to forty prisoners of war; they seemed to be officers with large funny hats. As they came alongside us with their guards, they asked us in English who we were and where were we going. We told them we were Jewish girls and our destination and future were unknown to us. They were shocked by what we looked like and started taking off scarves, throwing them to us with any food they had on them.

Their guards started pushing them. Our guards took away everything they threw to us and started beating us. These men were Australian and New Zealand prisoners of war. It must have been the first time they saw concentration camp prisoners, judging by their reaction. They were shocked and started arguing with our SS guards and with their own as well. The more they argued, the more we were ill-treated. The prisoners of war were pushed on ahead of us.

The light was beginning to fail, and by the next turn we saw a most picturesque village between the white hills. This put a little strength into us. We came to the main street, and our guards did not know where to go. Two of them went off to find a place for us for the night but came back, it seemed, empty-handed. More guards went off in search of a place, and we overheard the SS women saying to each other that people did not want us here.

Further down the street we saw the Australians and New Zealanders on the front porch of a peasant's house, arguing. Their guards were trying to push them into the house. We were too far away and too exhausted to listen to what their argument was about. Standing still, not walking, we felt the biting cold, but we knew that none of us could walk any further.

In 1947, when I was already married and living in England, my husband, who was working at the Southend-On-Sea General Hospital, asked me if we could host a young surgeon from New Zealand who was rather lonely. We invited him for dinner one evening. He told us he had been a prisoner of war in Germany, and we started talking about Germany and the Germans. I told him I had also been a prisoner, but under a lot worse conditions. He said he could not imagine anyone surviving the treatment of the SS which he witnessed once. He told us how he had met a long column of Jewish prisoners, girls or old women he could not say, because they hardly looked alive. Then came his description how the prisoners of war, he amongst them, were taken by foot over mountain paths away from the Russian guns without much to eat. Compared to those women, he said, they had been very well-off. In fact, he said, they took off scarves and pullovers and such food as they had with them and threw them to the women. All the things were confiscated and the women were beaten up by the guards, he said.

His group had been pushed on and later the group of women came into the village as well. They tried to refuse to enter the house until they made sure that the women would have something to eat and a place to sleep during the night.

Here I took over the story, by describing the main street of the village and the house with the front porch in which they were billeted for the night. He said that they left before daylight, but they saw SS guards standing further up the street, so they understood the girls must be resting there. He was amazed that any of the girls survived that march.

I told him we stayed the night in a rat infested barn.

Our main worry was to hide our bread from the rats, because that was our only food. For drinking we had snow. I slept near the entrance, and there the rats walked around freely. I sat up sometimes to chase them away, but finally nothing could keep me awake.

I cannot say that in the morning any of us felt refreshed from sleeping on the floor of the barn with just a little straw as a mattress. As soon as we were allowed to go outside to the fields to attend to our biological functions, at least we could wash and refresh ourselves with the frozen snow.

We started walking again, going into the unknown. I no longer saw the girl who tried to talk me into escaping with her. I asked the girls if anyone knew where she was, but they could not remember seeing her. On the way, several times we heard shootings. I think those must have been the girls who went crazy and tried to run away, or those who simply would not or could not carry on walking. I do not know how many girls were missing because no one counted us anymore.

We needed all our energy just to keep going and help

those nearest to us. There might have been girls left behind on the way without us realizing it.

It was another lovely sunny day. Where we were treading there must have been many refugees who had walked before us. Dori, Etu, and her other sisters, Judith, Zsuzsi, and Hédi, and Mira and I walked together or near each other.

I am mentioning this rather often, but this was a very important factor with whom you walked to work and back, and of course on long marches, both for physical and moral support, we relied on each other.

Oli, the girl from Budapest, was walking near us, so was Panni with her friend, and another few girls with whom we tried to keep together. I cannot remember when and where I saw Ida the last time. How did we loose her, poor thing? We tried desperately to keep up our morale; the going was a little easier, not so much climbing. We were telling each other about our families, about home, and I found myself thinking again how my family lived through their last hour and minutes packed tightly in the gas chambers. I smelled gas again and found I had difficulty breathing.

This happens even now, after fifty years, when I am with my family in thought in Birkenau.

The second day we were going much more slowly, and the SS had to chase us all the time. There were many stragglers, and every now and then we heard a shot. The SS women also found it difficult walking and complained to each other about not having good enough shoes. They also complained to each other about their food and about the fact that people with higher ranks did not have to walk. At intervals we tried jollying along the stragglers helping them keep up with the others.

It was almost evening when we arrived at a ghost town. It seemed as if the whole population had died out. As far as I remember, the place was called Fallersleben. Near an abandoned factory there was also a sign: *Stadt Des K.D.F.*, whatever that meant. We went inside the abandoned factory, and in one wing there were dormitories with beds. I think these dorms were put up for foreign civilian workers. We laid down gratefully on the beds, and a few minutes later I heard a commotion and happy squeals of the girls. I rose to see what was happening.

Some girls were shouting hysterically, "Mutti is here, Mutti is here!" It was the SS sergeant from Reichenbach whom a few crazy girls called Mutti (mother). She hated me, and I hated her at least as much again. She arrived by transport, not by foot. She was jeering at the girls saying, "So I am your Mutti?" From far away she saw me and shouted at me, "Hey you, you never call me Mutti? Why not?" I stood there, and I knew I should never let those words pass my lips.

All of us passed out on our beds, after we had a little piece of our bread which we had brought with us from Reichenbach. We had nothing to drink, there was no water and no snow outside either. Luckily there was electricity so we did not bump into each other in the darkness.

We were awoken, or rather forced to regain consciousness, by shouting and cursing.

I think the cursing did not matter anymore; we almost did not hear it. Those of us who suffered from being called the lowest things were gone a long time ago. The only way to keep sane was to shut one's mind to it all. *The important thing was not to let one's spirit be broken, and even to feel superior to the Germans and think of them as pagan savages without any law, except the law of the jungle which they made up to suit themselves.* Again we were not counted. We got organized with our friends near us, five in a row, and we started off into a gloomy morning.

The sun and snow had disappeared, and it was a gloomy dark day to go on our wanderings. The only thing which gave me a little strength was that the SS looked down and out, and some of them were hobbling on their blistered bandaged feet. Our feet were full of sores from frostbite and the straps from the clogs, which rubbed off the skin and cut into the flesh — *I honestly do not know how we put up with so much pain* — but we went on.

That day there was no singing. I hardly had the strength to say my prayers. At the end of our morning prayers we say the Thirteen Articles of Faith expounded by Maimonides. The one before last expresses the belief in the arrival of Mashiach. "Although he tarries, nevertheless I shall await him." This I said, and said again, not believing that the Mashiach would come to me, but to some Jews in faraway places — so that our nation should not be annihilated. This time it seemed the absolute end of the journey, for after today I could not imagine anyone being able to walk anymore.

In the afternoon we came miraculously to a factory which looked abandoned but was not. The gates of it were locked, and I was desperate because no one opened it for a long time. Two of our guards went inside and after some time came out with someone with keys, which looked like the keys to the kingdom of heaven.

We went into this large empty weaving factory, with all the looms standing still. We were taken to the part of the factory where there was a dormitory. By now the sun peeped through the clouds and a few welcome rays of it shone in through the windows. We lay down; we had no more bread left, but we were not hungry as hunger is felt under normal circumstances. We were lightheaded and I, at least, felt that I was floating. I seemed to have stepped out of my body and was looking on the girls and myself from far away.

A few girls came into our dorms, speaking Polish and Yiddish. They wanted to know who we were, and we told them we were Jewish prisoners being dragged about Germany away from the Russian army. We also told them about Birkenau. They would not believe we were Jewish because we did not speak Yiddish, and they would not believe us about Birkenau.

These girls had been brought to the factory from the Lodz ghetto; there were about twenty of them still with their own, very old clothes. Their heads had not been shaved and the conditions there were much better than any we had seen up till now. The girls had a room with a few things in it which they brought from the ghetto — they even had a cupboard next to their bed. They were fed regularly with better food and more than they had in the ghetto, where hunger, disease, and conditions in general were dreadful. They had to work hard, but were glad to do so.

They were given printed postcards to send back to the ghetto, to family and friends, saying that they were well treated, working under good conditions, and receiving enough food not to be hungry. They urged their families to volunteer for transports going away from the ghetto because their conditions at work would be better. They never received answers to their correspondence because letters could not be sent out from the ghetto. We told them that we saw the last girls from the Lodz ghetto come into Birkenau. The sad thing was that these girls were treated at the factory better than at the ghetto, and were willing to believe the Germans rather than us.

There were two wonderful things which put a bit of life into us that evening. The first one was hot soup — the first hot or cooked food in three days. All we had eaten the last three days was a third of a small loaf of bread. I started sipping the soup slowly; my stomach had to get used to food again. After a few sips I started getting stomach cramps. It seemed a long time since I had had cooked food.

The second good thing was a hot shower with plenty of hot water. The last time we had a shower was before our selection for going to work in Reichenbach, which was five months previously. We were not given any soap, but just to feel hot running water on our filthy frozen bodies was wonderful. We washed our sores, our infected wounds on our feet, and thought we would have a lovely night's sleep. There were girls who started a panic, saying that "this was not a shower room, but a gas chamber." After a few girls showered, it was clarified that it was a shower room.

I laid down next to Judith, but I could not drop off to sleep because of cramps in my stomach and pain all over my body. I should imagine every one of the girls felt more or less the same.

The following day and night we stayed on at the same place. During the day I had many opportunities to talk to the girls from Lodz. Finally they believed us that we were Jewish and told me that they were worried because they had not been working for several days. The civilian workers left and the factory was going to be closed. They had not been told what would happen to them. They were hoping to be evacuated together with us.

On the second day we were again given hot soup. Early the following morning we were given a small loaf of bread, either for three or five girls, I'm not certain.

We were told to stand five in a row. Without being counted we started moving. The girls from Lodz were looking at us enviously, but they stayed behind on their own with a

few SS guards and the civilian with a key to the large iron gate
of the factory. *I hope the girls survived the remaining two months
until we were liberated, for this was already the middle of February,
1945.*

The open boxcars were waiting for us not far from the factory. The rails came beyond the gate, specially built to bring or
take away from the factory whatever was needed.

It was a crisp, cold, sunny day. We managed to climb into
the boxcars and were so tightly packed that it was almost impossible for all of us to sit down. I cannot remember how
many boxcars there were or how many girls were in each car.

As soon as the train started moving, we realized that it
was a blessing to be so tightly packed because of the cold and
wind. We were sitting there next to and on top of each other,
not moving, talking, or even thinking. We were behaving like
people awaiting their deaths after having been sentenced.

I remember Juliska, an "old lady" of thirty-six, the most
senior amongst us, who found it very hard to sit on the bare
floor of the boxcar.

We did not want to break into the bread, which was our
only food, because we did not know when we were likely to
get more nourishment.

As we were climbing into the boxcars, I said the blessing
which is one of the first said in the morning: "Blessed art
Thou, Lord our God, King of the universe, Who giveth the
weary strength," hoping that we would be allocated some extra strength in order to be able to carry on.

The train started the "puff, puff, puff" and the "chu, chu,
chu," the mysterious language of the train which millions of
Jews understood as "death, death, death."

We all thought back to when we started off from the

ghetto with our families, with the same "puff, puff, puff" and "death, death, death" trains. We were completely apathetic, not caring what would happen or where it would happen. We were all without even the energy to talk, but Juliska Néni started to hold forth about what a lovely platinum blonde she had been. She sounded completely crazy, poor thing, and we just let her talk without interrupting. We hardly listened to her because all we were interested in at that moment was not to be too cold and to be bundled near friends who, though I had known them for only a few months, were family as well, since I had no one else left.

After some traveling we came to the outskirts of a town which was being bombed, and the rails had been destroyed. We stood there for a long time and then the train started chugging backwards and took a different direction. The train was traveling very slowly; we came to signals which were red and we could not continue. From the distance we again heard bombing. We were in the midst of the bombing of the railway lines time and time again. This was our only comfort. I remembered the prayer of Samson in the Book of Judges: "And Samson said, 'Let me die together with the Philistines.' " I felt I should be happy to die, but would like to see the Germans and Germany go down with me.

The following morning the sun disappeared and we were so frozen that our biological functions were non-existent. We could hardly move, and worse still we were not interested in moving or speaking to each other because of lack of energy. At night we arrived at the outskirts of a large town which was being bombed by wave after wave of bombers. It was a beautiful sight. The planes came in, many of them dropped their bombs, turned, another formation came along to drop its bombs, and so on: an unending and almost undisturbed destruction of a German town. We did not know what town it was and we had no idea who did the bombing. Toward morning, when the bombing stopped, they took us on one of the railway lines furthest from the city. I was amazed to see that the place was none other than Dresden. *After the war, I learned the British air force bombed the town and that Bomber Harris was the brilliant man behind it. God bless him, and may he rest in peace!*

I tried not to think of the tragedy and misery of the individual Germans or of the children in that town. I was full of our own tragedy and I saw before my eyes the terrified looks of our Jewish children: getting out of the boxcars in the middle of the night after three and a half days of traveling, cooped up without water to drink or wash with, being chased out of the boxcars, being screamed at and forced to leave behind their last and only comfort, the one toy they had been allowed to bring with them from the ghetto. Those children, instead of clutching their teddy bears, dolls, little cars, or books, stood on the ramp in the middle of the night seeing hundreds of shiny SS boots and dogs. Those children witnessed the breaking up of families; they left their mothers or fathers and witnessed the end of their world. Why should I think or feel sorry about the German children? I was happy to see the collapse and downfall of evil people and of an evil nation.

It was a cold gray morning and all that we saw wherever we looked was destruction. The train went on, coughing and wheezing, and we girls no longer minded what would happen to us, but wanted it to happen as fast as possible.

The train stopped outside the siding of a station and some of us stood up to look about. It was no small effort to pull ourselves upright. Outside the siding two young women stood looking at us. After a long time, they looked right and left, and then shouted at us, "Who are you?" We answered, "Jewish girls from Hungary." We felt that this was perhaps our only chance to let people know what was happening to us. They started to cry. They asked, "What is your destination?" I drew my finger across my throat, meaning, "They are going to kill us." The two women stood there for a long time, sobbing their hearts out. I do not know who they were. They might have been Jewish women in hiding, or perhaps just two German women who somehow stayed human beings.

The train started its "chu, chu" and "death, death" again, but it was so slow that I think we could have walked faster. Slowly, slowly we passed a station, and it was Riesa. I am not sure if we still had a little of our bread ration or not. We were lightheaded and no longer hungry; on the contrary, I was afraid to eat in case eating a little bread would wake my bitter hunger.

More bombing, stopping. The SS ran to the nearest safe place, sometimes woods, sometimes trenches, but they always left their dogs near each boxcar. Many a time some of the SS guards were wounded. The strangest of all things was that I did not hear of or see any of us getting even a scratch from these friendly bombs.

We started moving again and traveled fairly smoothly for a long time, or so it seemed. Most of the time we were sleeping, or perhaps we were only half conscious because of our weakness, hunger, and cold. It started snowing again, and we were covered with a lovely white blanket of snow. We could eat the snow instead of coffee, tea, soup, or water — at least we would not become terribly dehydrated. We had been sitting like zombies in the same spot for over forty-eight hours without needing to perform our basic bodily functions. The sun peeped through and far away we could see villages and small towns. I pulled myself together and realized that I had been rather slack during the last two days in telling the girls the day of the week and the Jewish date. As it happened, the next day was Purim. I told the girls it was Purim and that hopefully, in another few years' time, surrounded by our families and in our own homes, it would be difficult to believe what we were going through today — not of course believing what I was saying.

Juliska Néni looked up and said, "Who is Purim?" I said, "It is *Farsang*," which is the Hungarian name for it. She said, "Every one of you is crazy if you have nothing else to think of." She looked all in. She turned to me and said, "Tell me, after the war, will you please come to visit me in my elegant apartment in Budapest? I shall receive you in my most elegant clothes, and by that time I should have long platinum blond hair." I certainly cannot remember her near or after the liberation.

So it was Purim, the jolliest holiday, when friends send each other the most delicious cakes and chocolates. People wear costumes and eat big family dinners. It seemed to me impossible to eat so much and such heavy food. Even if we should survive, I thought I could never eat a normal dinner again. All I wanted was bread and a warm soup. Juliska Néni asked in a crazy voice, "Are we all going to die here together? Please, girls, who knows? Do tell Juliska Néni."

We were completely covered with snow and I thought, "What a nice way to be buried, under fresh white snow." The rest of the morning I cannot remember anything special. We were quiet because we did not have even enough strength to talk. There was no bombing so we could sleep.

Later on in the afternoon, the train stopped suddenly. We had run into what looked like a monument made of rails: the rails were piled several meters high. Without any warning of sirens, the planes began coming one after another, but this time their main cargo was propaganda leaflets. Some of the planes flew so low that we could see the faces of the pilots. Our long train of open boxcars was abandoned by the SS and they ran into the nearest woods for safety. They left a dog near each boxcar, to watch it.

We stood up, at least those of us who still had enough strength, and started waving at the planes. They flew over us time and time again as low as possible and dipped their wings in greeting, dropping loads of leaflets. We stood there, waving and cheering, no longer caring who saw or heard us. The planes turned round and when they came back, they machine gunned the SS in the woods. They flew over us again, dipping their wings.

We started reading the leaflets, which were written in German: "People of Leipzig, we have nothing against you. Do not let your leaders destroy you, your town, and your homes. Lay down your arms, you have lost the war, and save whatever you can." After a long time — I think that the all clear did not even sound — the SS began hobbling and helping each other back to the trains. Some of them were bandaged but I do not know if there were any dead or badly wounded amongst them. Having read the leaflets, we knew that we were in Leipzig, or rather outside it.

We were wondering where the SS were trying to take us. I could not imagine that we were still intended for work, as most of us looked more dead than alive. The train started shunting; we turned round since there was no possibility of going straight ahead. We were traveling again, gathering speed. I was sure they were taking us to a convenient place to kill us. One thing was sure, we were not in a fit condition to dig our own mass graves. To kill us and leave us to rot was dangerous for the German population because it would cause disease. We had no more food, had had nothing to eat and no bodily functions for the last three days, but at least we had snow to lick.

During the night I stood up, just to change my position, and looked at my friends, who had become my family as well. I thought, "Thank God my mother did not have to go through all this suffering — just the suffering of the gas chamber."

The train was slowing down and it was twisting and turning. The trees were covered with snow and everything was white and clean. Suddenly I had a terrific urge to jump out of the train. I knew I could not survive, but to die as a free person and not as a slave rather appealed to me. I kept telling myself, "Jump, jump and just for a second before you die, be a free person." I was longing to die on that lovely white surface amongst the beautiful trees and with no one present except the Almighty.

I was bitterly disappointed at my failure to jump out of the train and did not look on it as a suicide attempt. This in itself is evidence of my muddled thinking, or rather lack of thinking.

I tried to jump — but I would have to pull myself up to the edge of the boxcar and then throw myself out. I tried several times but did not have the physical strength to do it. I stood there rather broken on that night of Purim and realized that whatever the Germans wanted to do with us, that was what was going to happen.

I tried to sit down, but there was no longer any room where I had previously been sitting. I stood there until I dropped off to sleep, or rather became semi-conscious, slid down, and sat on one or perhaps two girls. They moved and I was sitting again as before, in some manner, between them.

Our train's stopping and starting, or shunting and going back whence we came, seemed to be the most natural thing. In the middle of the night we arrived somewhere, though we had no idea where. There was a train standing on the rails parallel to ours. People were getting into it and we heard Hungarian being spoken. Some of the girls shouted across to them, asking who they were. They said they were a small group from Hungary and were on their way to Palestine. They also said that the Rabbi of Satmar was with them. The following day I checked with the girls to see if they remembered seeing the train during the night. They all said the same thing, just as I remembered it. It was difficult to believe, because in the morning the train was no longer there.

On the other side of us, on the parallel rails, a train stopped. It was a hospital train with red crosses on the carriages. The wounded were obviously from the regular army and they looked at us with a little more humanity than the SS. We overheard the guards telling some of the wounded that here they were going to get rid of us.

A regular train came in a little later and people started alighting under SS guard, some of them in rags, not looking much better then we did. We asked them where they were from and they answered, although it was forbidden for any of us to communicate. They were from Drancy and some of them were still in their own clothes, having been picked up in the street in France or Belgium. We envied these people because they were going into a camp and could stop their odyssey. *Little did we know that those people getting off the train would die of typhus or starvation. The place where we were was none other than Bergen-Belsen.*

We had no idea where we were and why we could not get

off. We started shouting in German, appealing to the wounded soldiers to kill us now rather than leaving us to freeze to death or die of hunger. Some of the SS officers came back from wherever they had been and told the guards that the cargo would not be accepted at the camp. They flatly refused. They said they had enough of their own, in fact, more than they could deal with. As far as I could see and hear, their main disappointment was that they could not get any food for themselves.

The guards were given orders and opened each boxcar. They chased, or rather tried to chase, us out of the cars but we could hardly move. They told us in the coarsest possible way to go into the fields and perform our bodily functions. Some of the girls suggested that we should lie down in the fields and let them shoot us. They might have beaten us up, but would not have shot us because, as it turned out, they had to deliver us to another factory for work.

We dragged ourselves and each other back to the boxcars, and with the greatest difficulty we pulled ourselves up and settled down again, to be taken, we were sure, for execution. We were not cold or hungry — I do not think we felt anything anymore. The train started its usual death song with the puff, puff, puff and chu, chu, chu, and with all the energy it could muster it slowly crawled along.

A guard appeared, not one we knew or who had been with us for any length of time. He was no ordinary SS, but had a death's head and cross bones on his hat. He produced a whole loaf of bread and said, "Girls, do not give up now. You must not. If you have lived up till now, you should try and make it — you have just been saved from certain death. Take this loaf of bread and give it to the weakest and the youngest. It is only a matter of another few weeks." We took the bread, thanked him, gave a tiny piece to Juliska, who was reluctant to open her mouth to eat it, and gave the rest to the youngest and weakest girls.

The train was speeding along with no bombing this time. I think we must have slept most of the time. Then the train stopped, not as usual, outside the station, but within a small station in which was written in large letters "Porta." The guards opened the boxcars and again we had to get off as best we could, which was with the greatest of difficulty. We said to each other that we simply could not walk anywhere. Our legs were stiff and our feet and hands painful from frostbite, and on top of everything, we were terribly weak. The SS guard who had given us the loaf of bread told us quietly, "Hang on, girls, it is only another few weeks, you must not succumb now."

Five in a row and the unbelievable happened: we started walking. We did not look round but concentrated on putting one foot in front of the other. We walked, who could tell how far or how long it took us? It seemed days or weeks but was probably only a few hours.

We lifted our eyes and were happy to see a camp with watchtowers, a place which was to be "home" for us. It was a small camp. As soon as we arrived, the commandant of the camp received us, counted us, and immediately gave orders to release us and place us in huts. He was not an SS man, but a pilot who was recuperating from his wounds and was given the responsibility for the camp until becoming fit enough to rejoin his unit. This was our greatest stroke of luck, because if it were not for this convalescing pilot, I do not think many, if any, of us would have stayed alive.

We gratefully went into our huts and chose our beds near our friends. Each hut had about two to three hundred beds. There were some blankets with which to cover ourselves and we all drifted into a so-called sleep. Just before evening, we were called for *Appel*. As soon as we stood in rows of five, the commandant came down the few stairs from his office, counted us, and we were given a piece of bread and a soup, which was thin but nevertheless warm and put some life into us. We went back to our hut but were too tired to look around to see what sort of camp it was or what they were going to do to us.

The guards who had brought us and had been with us since Reichenbach were released, and others, locals, took us over. I remember an SS woman, tall, dark hair and blue eyes, with skull and crossbones, who wore a long black cape for warmth and protection against rain. I thought she could be very pretty if only she could have looked human.

The following morning, I think fairly late, we were called to *Appel*. The women guards started harassing and barking at us. The commandant was looking out of his window, and instead of letting them count us several times while we stood to attention, and letting them beat and curse us, he came out of his room, down the stairs, counted us once, and gave orders to release us.

We had warm tea — at least that is what it was called — and went to investigate the washrooms, where there was water trickling which we could use any time, as long as the water came through. I decided that however cold and weak I felt, I should wash myself. It was very problematic because there was nothing to dry ourselves on and it was freezing cold. I went to the furthest corner, where it was less windy. I started taking off my clothes, folding them, and putting them on the floor. I washed myself in a split second, because I was shaking and my teeth were chattering with cold.

I bent down to pick up my clothes to put them on, and

my eyes caught a small piece of green cube. It shook me because it looked like the piece of soap we were given in Reichenbach. I bent down and did not want to touch it, but wanted to make sure that it was a piece of soap. While I was looking at it, a girl came in and asked me if I had found a small piece of soap. She picked it up and left.

Two or three months previously, in Reichenbach, each of us had been given a piece of soap. It was light green. I watched the Germans handing it out, which they never did unless there was some special point in it. As I took the soap from the SS, I held it like a delicate baby and started shaking. We were told to use it, that it was good soap. This was the finest German sense of humor, to use soap made of our parents, sisters, cousins, or just fellow Jews. Later I went downstairs, buried my piece of soap in the snow, and said the prayers for the dead which is customary at funerals. I had never seen soap like that before. Hooray for the civilized German nation!

I went back to my hut and lay down. I was cold but the little water I had splashed on myself made me feel fresher, or perhaps mentally tougher, which was even more important. Toward evening there was once again *Appel*. The commandant was watching us from his window, and the moment we stood there he strode out of his room, counted us, and dismissed us. This was a wonderful piece of humanitarianism. If we had had to stand for hours at *Appel* being beaten and tortured, none of us would have survived.

Two or three days later, after the morning *Appel*, we were given a piece of bread and marched out of the camp to work. For the first time we saw that there was a small village in the valley, and on the way to work there was lovely mother nature to admire. How far we had to walk to the factory, I have no idea, but we had to help many of the girls to get there and I was sure that in a day or two there would be far fewer girls coming to work. Some of the girls looked as if they were living their last few hours. They could have stayed behind at the sick bay, but that would have meant a death sentence. Of course I only saw the other girls and how terrible they looked, but I did not see myself.

We started slowing down as we approached the side of a hill. We entered the hill and descended on iron stairs, although there was also a lift. On the second floor we came across some girl prisoners who had been living and working inside that hill. They had a horrible white complexion, which is understandable since they never saw the sky or daylight. There were male prisoners as well, but they were deeper down in the bowels of the hill.

We were taken further down and came across familiar machinery. In fact we were going to do the same work as we did in Reichenbach. The Dutch girls squealed when they found their names scratched on machinery from the time they had been working for Philips in Holland. The Germans had simply dismantled all machinery from the Philips factories, taken it to Germany, and integrated it into the Telefunken factories.

We were each given a place at which to do the same work as we had done in Reichenbach. The place was very cold. There was no natural daylight but only electricity, and one was constantly aware that one was in the bowels of the hill.

Before we started working we had to go to the raw material storeroom to get our quota for the day. We lined up but were given only half of what we needed, and were told to come back later when we had finished this. By lunchtime we went back for more raw material and the people in charge seemed annoyed with us for bothering them again.

While we were inside the hill and the factory, we could not hear bombing or fighting, but on the way to and from the factory we could hear every now and then the thuds of the guns from far away.

Porta Westfalica is near Minden, in Northwest Germany; we therefore hoped that the US and British armies were closing in on us. We seemed to be going to the factory and coming from it in almost broad daylight. Sometimes there was no water supply, but luckily enough there was still some snow in which we could wash ourselves. The quality of the food was getting worse: the pieces of bread were getting thinner and the soup more watery. As far as I remember, the girls who had been working and living in the factory were transferred to the camp after we came, but the men stayed on at the factory, underground. We were not particularly beaten, except every now and then. It may just be that we were used to the beatings and took them in our stride; or perhaps it was the commandant, who was more humane to us than anyone we had seen before; or perhaps it was the fact that the US and British armies were encircling our area.

Once, coming back from the factory, we saw the signs of spring: the bushes growing wild near the path already had buds and some of them even had tiny leaves coming out. As I passed by, forgetting for a moment where I was and rejoicing at the sight of renewal of life, I reached out and broke off a twig. The response came instantly. One of the SS guards saw me performing this great crime, came up behind me, and with all his might hit me on the head with the butt of his gun, calling me all sorts of names. I cannot remember how I got back to camp.

Some days we went to work and worked for only two or three hours, and the rest of the day we had to sit at our workplaces without talking or dropping off to sleep, however weak or tired we were. We even reached a stage where we came to work and most of us did nothing.

As all the machinery at the factory was stolen and brought out of Holland, the Dutch girls every day discovered on the machinery names of people who were long dead.

On the eve of Pesach, which was on a Wednesday, we went to work but did not do anything at all. As it was *erev* Pesach, when we were given soup and a slice of bread at lunchtime, I did not take it because I was trying to avoid eating leavened bread. The soup itself had some oats in it, which is not allowed on Pesach. It was certainly not easy to refrain from eating the slice of bread or the soup, but I wanted to try to hold out as long as I could and not eat anything leavened. By then we were all suffering from malnutrition. Amongst other things, we had gingivitis, which was very painful, and our teeth were so loose that we were afraid they would fall out. During the last few weeks we had had a lot less food and of worse quality, and even the water supply in our camp was very erratic. It might be that the main pipes had been bombed. On rare occasions we had a soup with four or five very small green boiled potatoes. I was hoping that by a miracle we should be given boiled potatoes and I could eat them. The little green potatoes were meant for cattle fodder, and even when we had them cooked in the soup, we used to get stomach cramps and our abdomens were terribly distended. Lately we had not had such great luxuries.

After the girls had their lunch, I started wilting and found it difficult to keep awake. One of the girls appeared with an enamel cup with warm water. She managed to heat it on her machine, and another girl got hold of a little salt, Lord only knows from where. My friend Judith told the girls that I was not eating anything and organized the wonderful warm water. I started sipping it slowly and it put strength and even some energy into me. The girls were happy to be able at least to help someone keep Pesach.

We felt that the civilian workers and even the SS were restless. The food was distributed to the girls earlier than usual and the atmosphere was rather panicky. After the girls had finished eating, the order was given to hurry up and pack up our work desks, which we had not opened as there was no raw material to work with. We were told to stand five in a row immediately and they marched us upstairs, out of the hill and into the open air. During the morning, the ventilation had been switched off twice and the light had been dimmer than usual. Without the ventilation it was most unpleasant, some of the girls began fainting. I also thought of the possibility of the Germans leaving us without electricity or ventilation: it would be worse and take us much longer to die than in the gas chamber.

When we went upstairs we were glad to see the sky and daylight. We started off toward our camp amidst the thud, thud and boom, boom. It was evident that the Germans would either finish us off or take us away again. Where to? was the big question, and also, were we still able to start wandering?

One of the girls said to me that she would take out my bread ration and keep it for me until the time when I would start eating bread again. After about three days, the girls said, "Look at her. See how much better she looks." Her face had filled out a little, but no one suspected anything.

Our friend Oli, a youngster of eighteen from Budapest, was lying unconscious in the sick bay, and when I went to see her the doctor said she might die at any time now. In the evening Judith and I went to see her again and she was sinking fast. The doctor told us that if we wanted to stay with her a little while we could do so, because the commandant had given permission for some of her friends to stay with her in case she regained consciousness before dying. There was yet another girl with us, I think it was Dori, and we sat around Oli's bed.

I told the doctor that it was Pesach and Seder night. I suggested to the girls that as we were sitting there, we should hold a Seder and tell the story of the Exodus as best as we could remember it by heart. I started reciting the traditional wording and it was amazing how much one does remember by heart. We had, of course, no unleavened bread, nor did we have bitter herbs to remind us of the bitter life we had lead in Egypt, but I think our own lives were bitter enough to understand what it was all about.

I started reciting, "We were slaves of Pharaoh in the land of Egypt," and went on to say how we were led out to freedom by the Almighty. There we were reciting about the bread of affliction which our forefathers ate, but we did not even have that. We each sang our families' traditional songs and after several hours, the doctor said we should go back to our huts because poor Oli seemed to be dragging on and on.

I was very hungry. Lunchtime I had a cup of warm water with salt in it, and after that nothing to eat or drink. I crawled on my elbows and knees to the SS dust bins, hoping I would not be discovered, and found a lot of potato peelings. There was no water in which to wash them, but I had a small piece of rag and started to wipe each piece and eat it. I made a good meal out of the peelings and was living in the hope that at least for the first two days of Pesach I could manage without eating the soup or bread. I crawled back to our hut and thought I should be very tired going to work in the morning.

During the night we could hear the thud, thud, but it was not near enough for my liking.

The following morning we were called to *Appel* and did not get anything to drink, not even something warm which they called tea. They released us and we went back to our hut; it seemed that we were not going in to work. In fact *erev* Pesach was the last time we saw the factory.

The food was becoming less and worse, and many of us walked or crawled to the SS dust bins to pick up nourishing potato peels. The water supply to our camp stopped. It was obvious that Germany and the Germans were in trouble. We realized that the Germans could not leave us alive to tell the world what they had been doing to us.

Not working but just sitting or lying on one's bed and being hungry was very demoralizing. I realized that we were in the process of dying slowly, unless the Germans killed us at once. This slow dying frightened me because one became a *muselman* and a zombie.

The following day there was again *Appel* in the morning. And again there was no food. I saw that a number of our guards were Ukrainian. I would not insult the animal kingdom by calling those SS animals, I prefer to call them subhuman. Their appearance was disgusting and frightening. The decency of the commandant certainly saved us, for the Ukrainian SS were restrained by their officer, the recuperating pilot.

By Saturday morning we saw that the SS were packing things up, and I was sure that we should either be killed or dragged somewhere else. I thought that the circle must be getting rather small and that our area was probably surrounded.

In the early afternoon on Saturday, Oli passed away. I could not bear this constant losing and losing, first my family and then my friends. A peasant's cart was produced by two

Ukrainian SS guards, who took a crudely made coffin into the
sick bay and came out laughing and joking. They flung the
coffin with the remains of Oli into the cart; we were not sure
but supposed that Oli was in the coffin. We were given orders
for ten to twelve girls to come to the burial. One of the girls
was Zsuzsi, Judith's younger sister, and myself, but I cannot remember who were the other girls. There were no horses so we
started pulling the cart, with the SS barbarians leading the way
downhill into the valley. This was a new landscape for us because on the way to work we did not see the village with the
red roofed houses and the church spire. It looked very pretty
and it was difficult to imagine that villages like this produced
murderous monsters and were not even ashamed of it.

This was the first time that we buried or heard of burials,
except for mass graves where people were shot at the edge of
the grave and fell into it as they were shot. They were covered
with earth before most of them were even dead. Small children as a rule did not even merit a bullet, but were thrown
into the bottom of the grave and then the adults fell on top of
them and suffocated them.

It was a long way down to the village and we were all
hanging on and holding back the cart to prevent it from running down the hill. The further down we went toward the village, the more clearly we heard the guns.

We came to what seemed to be the main street running
through the village. The street was flanked by peaceful looking houses on both sides of the road. We came to a cemetery.
The gates were open and we had to maneuver the cart through
them. We took off the coffin and carried it by hand to the end
of the cemetery, where there was a small chapel. On its right
hand side there was already a grave dug and the commandant,
the pilot, was waiting for us. At the edge of the grave we put

down the coffin. The two Ukranian SS opened it and amidst laughter, tipped Oli's remains, wrapped in a dirty, filthy blanket, into the grave which was too small for the body.

We girls took the shovels standing there and started filling up the grave, sobbing our hearts out. This was the first time I had cried since the train journey before our arrival in Birkenau. This normal act of burying a friend brought out the normal reaction to the death of a sweet eighteen-year-old girl, who had not even started living and yet we were covering her with earth. During our time in Birkenau, where we daily saw two to three-and-a-half thousand people being murdered and burned, we did not cry. We were too stunned.

The pilot stood there all the time, watching the burial, and said to some of the girls and later repeated to me, "You will not be able to say I was not decent." Was he already looking for an alibi, or perhaps he did not want to be remembered together with the SS scum?

We finished burying Oli, and I looked at the girls and remembered that today was the Shabbat of Pesach. On this day, the portion of the Prophets read in the synagogue was from Yechezkel, "And He said unto me, 'Son of man, can these bones live?' and I answered, 'O Lord God, Thou knowest.' Then He said unto me, 'Son of man, these bones are the whole house of Israel.' " I stood there gaping at the girls, at the dry bones of the house of Israel, and I was sure that even if by some miracle we stayed alive, none of these girls could lead normal lives. I could not see myself, and for that I was rather grateful.

We started going back to the camp, pushing the cart uphill, which was no easy thing to do. Neither on our way to the cemetery nor on our way back did we see a single person in the street or in the gardens. I should think they were told to stay inside their homes.

We were pushing the cart with all our strength so that it should not roll back onto us. I thought if Oli would have passed away a week later it would be unlikely that we would be strong enough to push the cart. We were growing weaker by the day, and I was worried that the spirit of the girls would break. I felt so terribly weak that I decided to start eating the bread, which I had not eaten since early Wednesday morning.

When we arrived at the camp we received a terribly watery soup and no bread. I went to my friend to ask her for my three-day ration of bread, which she had taken and looked after for me. "Unfortunately," she said, "someone has stolen it." I had to accept the fact that perhaps I was meant not to eat bread on Pesach for yet another day. I crawled out again to the dustbins but there were so many girls scavenging that there was hardly anything left of the potato peelings.

To the sound of distant gunfire, I crawled back to my hut, lay down on the bed, and thought about the funeral and of poor Oli, lying in a Christian cemetery in an unmarked grave near the chapel. I drifted into sleep and it seemed very soon that we had to get up for *Appel*. That morning we were divided up. A few hundred girls, myself amongst them, were told to stand to one side and the others stood some distance from us, whispering that they were going to a better place. Some of the girls tried to convince me to go across to them but I simply left everything to fate.

The weather was a little warmer, the snow had melted, and even the sun started to come through the clouds — and there we stood, hungry and weak, on the second day of Chol HaMoed Pesach, almost a month since our arrival, preparing to start our wanderings once again. I was almost envious of Oli, but I kept thinking what a shame it was that we could not have buried her according to Jewish rites and in a Jewish cemetery.

We, the prisoners, were not apprehensive about our future. The SS women were coming and going and saying goodbye to each other. The tall SS woman with the black cape, black hair, and blue eyes did not stay still for a single second and from her restlessness I drew strength, at least enough to start walking or standing. Above all I saw she was giving the SS bad news and they all became agitated.

As we stood and waited to see what would happen to us, the inevitable cart with the human horses appeared, packed tightly with *muselmen*. Amongst them was Ilus, a girl from our group, just sitting with her eyes open. I do not know if she saw us or knew what was happening. Two days previously, I had gone to see her in the sick bay, when she could still remember and understand a little. I sang her favorite song, "Life is only one day, life is only one kiss." She smiled then, perhaps she remembered something pleasant. I held her hand, gave her a hug, put her hand down gently, and left. I turned round for a last look at her — she was no longer smiling but just looking and perhaps not seeing anything at all.

We started dragging ourselves, five in a row, but at least I was together with my camp sisters, the only family I had. We boarded the train at Minden. It was a very long train, all cattle trucks. We crawled onto one of them and sat on the bare floor. By now we did not look for water, food, toilets, or any other luxury meant for superior beings. We had plenty of room for sitting but were so far gone that we did not even appreciate it. The train stood still for a long time but we heard orders being barked and then the big heavy doors of the cattle trucks being rolled shut.

We started feeling cold without the sunshine and we could on no account figure out where they were taking us. I said my prayers and told the girls the Jewish date and the day of the week. Although I wanted to talk to them about Pesach, I did not have the energy, and I should imagine the girls would not have wanted to listen to me either.

The amazing thing was that we could travel uninterrupted by fighting or bombing. The Germans were probably running round in a small circle, which was getting smaller every day. We did not hear any gunfire, or at least I cannot remember it.

After traveling for some time the train stopped, and through the cracks of the cattle truck we could see open fields with no station and not even farmhouses. In the distance we saw trees. A lot of orders were barked together with curses, and then we saw male prisoners — or rather starved half-dead figures — being driven into the fields toward the trees. We were jealous of them because they had reached their final destination. *Little did we know at the time how very final the destination was and how soon they were lying in a mass grave.*

The train started moving again but I have no idea how long our journey took. I was still counting the days but the weaker we grew, the less we spoke to each other. Amongst us there were several girls who were very ill with high fever, and it was obvious that they were suffering from tuberculosis. Almost all of us had infected sores on our feet, legs, hands, and everywhere on our bodies. In addition we had scabies and, of course, the rags we wore and called clothes were full of lice. We had no lice in our hair, which was still very short, less than an inch long. The amount of energy we had to spend in scratching ourselves was terrible, and I felt the dirtiest girl on earth. I could not visualize the time when I had had baths, clean clothes, and could choose what to wear, yet I was the same person and it was most important to me to know that I had not changed in myself. The change I had suffered was only physical, I told myself.

The train stopped, not at the station but probably just outside, and we were given orders to alight. I do not remember how we managed to put one foot in front of the other or how far we had to go, but all I know is that, miraculously, we arrived at a camp where we were put into a square room in a hut with a door and a window. There was a heap of filthy blankets on the floor; we each took one to cover ourselves with or to lie on and then from hunger and exhaustion, fell off to sleep.

As far as I can remember, the Germans did not particularly ill treat us in this camp, but neither did anyone take any notice of us either. No one was interested in counting us, and we were given virtually nothing to eat. We just lay there growing weaker from day to day. The most amazing thing is how the sick people among us lasted so long.

I do not think we had much, if any, contact with the old-timers in the camp, except to ask around for family and friends, which none of us found. We moved when we had to. The weather was growing warmer, so that we did not suffer badly from the cold. Of course, we were already veteran sufferers, and suffering which a year previously would have been hard to bear was taken in our stride. March turned to April, 1945. We were not excited about our future, I, for one, being convinced that we should be killed. The other girls, those who could still think, partly thought they would go home and await the arrival of parents, grandparents, little brothers and sisters, in fact the whole family. Having been in Birkenau and seeing the chimneys of the crematoria puffing smoke did not make them think that it might be their family or friends who were burning. They knew that people were killed day and night, tens of thousands of them, but refused to think who the people might be. Perhaps this was the only way they could go on existing.

By the 11th or 12th of April, discipline and order were almost gone. There was no food given out at all, at least to our group, and there were rumors that some of the SS had deserted. It was either on the 12th or 13th of April that some prisoners broke into the kitchen and food store because they were sure that the SS had abandoned it. When the Germans saw the fighting for food, mainly raw material, they half-heartedly stopped the rioting. They did not shoot any of the prisoners but beat up a few of them. When one can hardly stand up from weakness, hunger, and sickness, one hardly feels the beatings and certainly does not hear the curses.

Some of the girls came back to our hut with a few rotten onions, some small green potatoes, and half-rotted parsnips. All these were fit, even when fresh, for fodder for cows and other animals. I remember sucking and chewing a small onion. It gave one pretty bad indigestion and a stomachache.

The end was approaching fast, that was obvious to us. We heard the fighting getting nearer and the Germans were in disorder, yet we just sat or lay on the floor of our hut and did nothing. I think we were almost beyond caring what happened to us.

In the late afternoon on Friday, on my way to the latrines, I saw in the distance some soldiers in uniform, but not the bluish gray of the German army. Some of the girls said that they were Russian soldiers. Another theory was that the Germans had dressed up in Russian uniforms in order to escape. I personally thought that the Germans had indeed dressed in uniforms other than their own and were surrounding the camp in order to pour petrol around the huts, put a match to it, and then run away.

Somehow, that Friday night we went on with our existence, very quietly through lack of strength. I remember saying the welcoming Shabbat prayers lying in a fetal position on the filthy floor, dropping off to sleep or semiconsciousness and not knowing how far I had reached with my prayers.

I woke up in the dark to a very strong smell of gas. I sat up and saw my mother, two sisters, and my sister Miriam's two little boys. I touched the girl next to me, my friend Judith, and asked if she could smell the gas and said that we were going to die now. She sat up, not even excited, and said she was not sure if she could smell it or not. I asked if she had seen my mother and sisters. She only said, "I never met them." I realized it was a most convincing dream — that I had been in the gas chamber with my family, inhaling the gas, and we were very calm.

I knew then that this was the beginning of my becoming a *muselman*. Luckily enough, I was sure, we were going to be killed soon and this was our last night ever.

I desperately tried, with all the concentration I could muster, to remember a Friday night in my parents' home. I wanted to conjure up my mother lighting candles, but all I could see before my eyes was my mother being kicked down the road by the Hungarian gendarme and rolling down the road on our way from the ghetto to the cattle trucks to be transported to Auschwitz. I so much wanted to see in the eyes of memory the large table surrounded by family and sometimes with guests as well, all of us singing and welcoming the Shabbat. The master of the household would sing in honor of the lady of the household, "A woman of worth, who can find?" from Mishlei 31. We, the children, would then line up according to age to receive the traditional blessings. For the boys: "God make thee as Ephraim and Menasheh," and for the girls, "God make thee as Sarah, Rivkah, Rachel, and Leah. The Lord bless thee and keep thee..." After this my father would lift the heavy crystal decanter full of red sweet wine, fill his large silver cup, and everyone would fall silent as he started the blessing.

However much I tried to remember, all I saw was the table pushed to one side of the room with several people sleeping on the floor and their belongings piled high on the dining room table. This was our dining room in the ghetto — and I thought that even as a farewell from life I could not have the luxury of seeing again how we once lived. I must have dropped off to sleep and when I awoke, the sun was up and Judith said, "Was it a nice dream you had? You were shaking your head and kept twitching." Then she said, "Dear God, we have to start another day." She was a very sick girl, having had trouble with her kidneys. Her complection was something between yellow and gray and there was an expression of constant suffering on her face.

We both stood up and shuffled out to the latrine and in search of a little water to drink and, if superlatively lucky, to wash our hands and faces. There was no water. The noise of fighting was growing nearer but by then we were used to it, and believing that in any case it would not bring our salvation any nearer, we were blasé.

It was still early, judging by the position of the sun, but there was a lot of activity and nervous running about by the SS. The two of us wandered to the barbed wire fence, where there were already several girls standing. One of the girls told us that the soldiers in the fields were Russian because she had seen with her own eyes the hammer and sickle. The soldiers kept coming nearer to the camp, and we could see that they were armed but could not make out what army they belonged to. Very far away there were several tanks; they were not coming toward us yet we could hear and see the firing of their guns. A girl came and told us that none of the German sentries were at their posts. There were no SS to be seen, and the girls were coming out of their huts. There was one girl who advised us that if the Germans set fire to us we should run onto the electrified fence. "Less suffering," she said wisely. But the electricity had already been cut off.

The tanks in the fields now started to move toward the camp and the soldiers were also closing in on us, when we heard the drone of aircraft — and suddenly the heavens were filled with hundreds of white mushrooms against the clear blue sky. The mushrooms grew bigger and bigger until we could see the paratroopers with their parachutes and then they must have landed somewhere near us.

Liberation

We stood there dazed, those of us who could still stand, not believing our eyes, when one single tank drew up to the gate of the camp, an officer jumped down, opened the gates, and told us simply, "You are free."

We were stunned. It was the US army who liberated us on April 14, 1945, in the town of Salzwedel. The SS officer in charge of the camp walked down the stairs from his office with his hands raised above his head, and after him came the others, their badges of rank torn off, without their pistols and without the hateful look on their faces of *"Deutschland uber alles"* (Germany above all).

The soldiers who had surrounded us for the last thirty-six hours came in from the fields as well, and they were overjoyed that the Germans had not killed us. These soldiers were Jewish French officers, prisoners of war, who had been separated from the non-Jewish prisoners by the Germans. According to the Geneva convention, they were not supposed to differentiate between Jewish and non-Jewish prisoners of war. These Jewish officers, some of them high ranking, were working in a sugar factory for the Germans. This was also forbidden by the convention.

As the fighting had grown nearer, these twenty-odd officers had made preparations to save the girls in the work camp. They knew of the girls and had also seen them going to work, and when the fighting came near to the town they had made a deal with their guards, who were from the *Wehrmacht*, the ordinary army. Their deal was to get arms and ammunition from their guards, as well as the keys to the storerooms where the Germans kept their food supplies. In return for this, if the guards were caught by the Allies, the French officers would vouch for their decent behavior and that they had put down their arms before the town had surrendered.

We stood there gaping, not wanting to wake up from this fantastic dream. I went to tell the sick girls in the hut what had happened but found I could not speak — not Hungarian, German, or English — not a sound would leave my mouth.

I went outside again and we found some of the women SS who had cut their hair and put on some sort of a dress so as to look like one of the prisoners. Needless to say, they looked quite different from us starving, weak, and ill-treated girls. They were rounded up together with the other SS.

I went outside the gate to touch the tank and at least to smile at the US soldiers, if I could not welcome them in any other way. As I stood there, I saw the SS man who was in charge of the kitchen and supplies running like mad in the ditch surrounding the camp. I tried to shout but could not — I was making some sort of noise and desperately pointing at the running figure. From the top of the tank, one of the soldiers shot him dead.

We still could not understand that we were liberated, even as we watched the SS being marched off by one single American soldier.

The French officers urged us to come out through the gates with them, but not to wander off alone. These wonderful people had prepared bread for us together with meat conserves, but this unfortunately was the tragedy of many girls who ate and became very ill from the food, many even dying. We had to get used to eating again — slowly. I ate a little bread and tasted the meat but, luckily, could not eat it.

The streets were deserted and it looked as if the population of the town were made up of Jewish concentration camp prisoners, and a few French officers dressed in old crumpled uniforms and US soldiers who were sitting on top of their tanks gaping at us. In every single window there was a white sheet hanging, in lieu of a white flag. I wondered what the American soldiers thought about us. I realized that none of us looked like civilized young girls. I passed near one of the tanks, and on top of it stood a young lieutenant waving a prayer shawl as a sign of solidarity with us. We stood gazing at each other, the lieutenant moved beyond words and we hardly realizing that it was not a dream.

We started shuffling toward the center of town. There stood a door of a house, wide open, and some of us went in. How strange it was to see a normal household again! We walked into the kitchen. The table was laid for breakfast. The news of the US tanks arriving must have reached them halfway through their meal. There was a baby's high chair with an egg only half eaten, an overturned chair, and something spilled on the table, dripping onto the floor. Here, before my eyes, were the signs of the mortal fear of a family with children.

We walked into the other rooms, full of heavy elegant furniture and with carpets on the floor. We came into a doctor's clinic with X-ray machines and a white coat hanging on a hanger. The girls opened wardrobes in the bedrooms, and I asked them not to take anything, as in the Bible it is written in many places, "They did not take part in the plunder." I was certainly not sorry for these Germans, but I did not want to see any more misery because it reminded me of my murdered family.

We came to what seemed to be the main street with shops. All the shop windows were smashed, with most of the goods on the floor, and dozens of Polish collaborators with the Germans were looting. We went into a large textile shop; there was hardly anything left on the shelves. I moved to the back of the shop where I saw bales of material. An elderly couple came out from behind a crate and said in artificially sweet voices, "Please do not damage our shop, we shall give you anything you ask for." I became angry and, infuriated as I could be, told them they were German swine, that I was not a beggar so they could not give me anything, and that I was going to take what I needed because it was my right to do so. "I shall not pilfer, not because of you Nazi swine but because of my own self-respect." I took hold of the first material I saw. It was a navy blue silk-like material, and I took a few yards of it. I also took some yards of a heavier beige suiting with darker stripes

We dragged ourselves back to the camp, completely exhausted. On the way back to our "home" I realized that I had started talking again and that there was no permanent damage to my speech.

As we approached the camp, we saw with delight who our new and trusted guards were. They were two French officers, armed, guarding us against the odd Nazi who might want to come in and finish their murderous job. The French officers, with the help and advice of the US army, organized bread and a warm drink for us and were working on mending the water supply. Meanwhile they took charge of our camp and were told by the occupying army that within two to three days we would be transferred to a better and cleaner place to await the end of the war. We were also advised not to wander around outside the camp for security reasons. The army knew that some of the SS had escaped and were probably hiding in the vicinity. Several girls who went for a walk in a nearby park were murdered. Every day escaping SS were caught by the American army.

I am often asked, "What did you feel when you heard the words, 'You are free'?" To be honest, I felt nothing. We were stunned, weak, ill, and not in a condition to be overjoyed or even feel any happiness as we should have done. The first day or so I was dazed, and what we all wanted most was hot showers and clothes without lice. Even the cold water dripping from the taps was something to be appreciated.

On the third day after our liberation, it was announced that trucks would come for us to take us away, but before that we would be given clean dresses and we were to leave our lice infested ones in a heap in the courtyard. The only other things we had were dirty blankets which were full of lice, but we were told that there would be as many clean blankets as we wanted available at our new dwelling.

The trucks came for us and started taking groups of girls after they had put on clean dresses. The girls were helped onto the trucks, and the soldiers and the French officers stood by to assure that nothing infected was taken. After the camp was cleared, the army burned it down so that it would not spread disease.

We did not travel very far and arrived at a place which looked like heaven. There were two-storied buildings built in a rectangle. In front of the buildings was a nicely kept garden with no flowers but a shrubbery and trees. The place was spotlessly clean, and as the trucks drew up in front of each house we saw prisoners of war from the German air force waiting for our arrival with a US soldier. We went into the houses and were allowed to choose our rooms together with the girls with whom we wanted to share, four in a room. It was a nice room with two double-decker beds on opposite walls. The beds were all made up, like in a hotel, with clean white sheets, pillows, and plenty of warm blankets. On the wall opposite the door, there were two long windows looking out onto the greenery, and between the windows was a long mirror. Next to the door was a wardrobe and in the middle of the room was a table with four chairs. On the table was an ordinary glass jar with some leaves and green twigs in it. The place was spotlessly clean, scrubbed until everything shone.

I was asked by the American soldier, "Is it all right, miss? Would you like anything else in your room?" I asked if we could please have two small tables and where should we go to fetch them? He answered, "You do not fetch anything. These are here to do it for you," nodding his head toward the German prisoners, who were air force cadets. They went off to find two small tables, and meanwhile we tried to push the beds closer to the windows to make more space near the door. When the US soldier came back with the prisoners, he was angry with us for doing the shifting of the beds on our own. "You must not do that," he said, and told the Germans, "Get on with it." He said to us, "But I don't speak their language — you tell them what to do so that they don't get lazy."

It was hard to believe that these were the arrogant Germans, trampling down the whole of Europe and trying to do so to the rest of the world as well. Their looks of superiority had disappeared and I think the most shocking thing that had happened to them was having to serve and clean and scrub for Jewesses, who, in their eyes, were subhumans. Not only were they prisoners but they themselves had to vacate their air force schools and see us settling in and taking them over.

The touching treatment by the American force occupying the area was incredible, particularly as there was still a war on. What wonderful human beings those soldiers must have been to realize that we were young girls, who had been tortured mentally and physically and were starved and sick, and to put in so much effort and thought into our rehabilitation. God bless them for it, they restored my faith in the human race.

A sergeant went from room to room, knocking on the door, to hand out a bar of soap and towels for each of us. He also told us that there would be hot water in the showers twenty-four hours a day and should we need anything please ask for it. The metamorphosis from being less than dirt and subhuman to being treated in an accepted, polite, and civilized fashion was so sudden that it dazed us.

We were told to be at the dining rooms at seven o'clock for supper. The very first thing we did was to take a hot shower with soap. We had as yet no change of clothes so we put on the same clothes again and went outside to see where were the buildings with the kitchens and dining rooms.

I wandered about for a while, alone with my thoughts. "What now? Where do I start?" I knew I had no parents, no grandparents, and out of four sisters and one brother, there was possibly one sister left alive: my eldest sister from whom I had been separated in Birkenau when I had been taken with the group of thirty-two girls to work at the Telefunken factory.

Of my four brothers-in-law I had no idea who might be alive. I heard only that one of them never went into the camp but was taken to the gas chambers together with my grandfather, father, and brother.

I knew that I did not want to go back to the place I had once called home in order to claim back worldly goods. I hated the people I would find occupying our house and using our things. I would hate walking in the streets of that lovely town, where thirty-five to thirty-seven thousand people had been taken away and so very few would have survived. I could imagine the disappointment of the Hungarian families in the Jewish homes and businesses when a survivor would return. I wanted no part of that; on no account did I want to go back. I knew with all my heart and soul that I had to move heaven and earth to go to Palestine, or as we called it even before the State was established, "Eretz Yisrael," the Land of Israel. I was sure that would be the only place where I could rehabilitate myself and where it would be worthwhile to make the effort to go on living. My plan was to go into a religious kibbutz, to work with all my soul and strength and try to make the kibbutz my family. The big question was how to get there.

In the open air, under a tree, I said my afternoon prayers all on my own, which was also a new luxury. When I came to, "And let our eyes behold Thy return in mercy to Zion," I was longing for Zion and to be part of it. There was a bench nearby. I sat there, thinking of my family. As soon as I started thinking about them, I smelled gas — and I was in the gas chamber, naked, together with them, and I was holding the hand of my sister's little boy and was watching them choking and falling down, not quite dead, one by one. I tried to stop thinking about the gas chambers, but can one reverse the flow of a river? I had lost my family and had not shed one single tear for them nor had I mourned for them in the accepted way. The grief was with me, in me, not only for my family but for my nation, which I had learned to love and for whom I ached.

I went back to my room. The girls were not there. I took my wet towel and bar of soap and went to have one more shower before supper. All the showers were full, with the girls scrubbing themselves raw as if all physical and mental hurt could be scrubbed away. I had my second shower in three hours, and then we waited for the gong to go for supper, as none of us had watches.

We lay on our beds, still dazed, and then the sound of the gong was heard. One of the girls said, "Probably we shall get a plate and cup in which to receive our food." The double doors to the dining hall were open and at the entrance stood a US officer. We came into a large dining hall with the tables laid with knives, forks, spoons, salt cellars, and glasses, and we sat down at a table again, like human beings, to eat on a normal plate with a knife and fork. There was a jug of water on the table together with bread and salt. I cannot remember what we ate because the most important thing was the salt. We ate bread with a lot of salt and could not get enough of it. We could not eat much because we had to become used to eating again and holding down the food. After supper when I said the blessing after food, it did not sound ridiculous because for the first time in over a year I had eaten my fill. ("And thou shalt eat and be satisfied and thou shalt bless the Lord.") It was an amazing feeling to be sitting at a table. There were even paper napkins.

We were asked not to leave the building after dark as there might be German fugitives around. There was no longer any blackout, since even though the war had not yet ended and the fighting was still going on, there was nothing to be afraid of from the German air force.

We went back to our rooms, picked up our towels and soap, and had our third shower in eight hours. This became an absolute mania. We went to sleep in our clothes, exhausted and hardly believing that in the morning we should wake up in our own beds, with sheets and pillows and warm blankets. One to each bed, dear God, what luxury!

As I write I wonder why we were not afraid of the Germans coming back to kill us or to recapture the place. We had such complete faith in the US army and they were so wonderful to us that it never crossed our minds to be afraid. The other thing which I am proud and glad about is our behavior toward the German prisoners of war. Those air force cadets, who were cleaning the place and making things comfortable for us, were simply ignored rather than being subjected to nasty remarks or ill treatment. Perhaps it was because they did not belong to the SS.

The following morning we woke to sunshine, and after showering we waited for the gong. We did not feel well, most of us had stomachaches, indigestion, sores, scabies, and several other things.

For breakfast we had a thin porridge, which was just right, and some bread as well, but we could not eat a great deal. We put salt onto spoons and licked it. Many of us took bread and salt back to our rooms, not being able to trust or imagine that there would be food available whenever we wanted it.

We decided to go to the hospital, which used to be used by the airmen and was not far off, in the compound. The staff were all Germans but there were US soldiers and doctors as well. I was hoping to see anyone rather than a German doctor. After waiting outside the clinic, I was called in by a US orderly who did not speak German. I came in and found a German doctor, and he started talking to me as if I was someone off the street. "What's the matter?" he shouted at me. I tried to keep my temper and answered, "I have a terrible stomachache, weakness, and indigestion." "Aha," he said, "you guzzle too much, you smoke too many of those American cigarettes." I answered, "You German swine, you forget that today it is *'Deutschland unter alles'* and *unter* us as well. You are a prisoner and I am free." I told the US orderly to keep a close eye on him. "Yes," he said, "some of them Krauts, never heard of discipline." The doctor was red in the face and said in English, "You must not say things like that." I left and decided it was far better to suffer or even die than be treated by a German swine. I waited for the other girls and one of them told me that there were several girls lying in the hospital but there were American orderlies watching that the German doctors didn't bother them. I did not feel very happy about this.

On the way back we met several girls dragging what seemed to be a white tent. They said, "Run quickly, there is an airfield at the back of the buildings and there are a whole lot of parachutes, which can be used to make underwear and blouses." We went to the airfield and four of us tried to drag a parachute; more girls came and somehow we managed to drag several of them back to our rooms. We were glad to have found the white parachutes made of pure silk. I had no idea how to sew but there were several girls who were experts, at least that is what they said. Some of the girls had cotton thread for sewing, we got hold of some needles, and we asked one of the US officers if we could possibly be given two or three pairs of scissors because we wanted to make ourselves clothes from their parachutes. He found it a very unusual idea and was happy to help us.

One of the girls, whose name was Edith, and my friend Dori started to organize the cutting and sewing. We were firstly in urgent need of underwear, two sets each, so that we could wash out one set. There were no sewing machines so everything was sewn by hand, with a back stitch.

We were called for lunch but I was not sure if I could eat anything because of my distended stomach and constant cramps. We looked pregnant, with swollen puffed-out abdomens and swollen legs and hands, but we were beginning to look cleaner. It was a joy to go into the dining room each time and see the tables laid and be received by a lovely whiff of cooked food. I remember having soup and mashed potato and eating it very slowly. We were told that after lunch there would be a distribution of clothes, so that if any of us still had lice in our clothes we could throw them out and they would be burnt.

After lunch we went back to our rooms and in the central hall there were large crates of clothes, mainly jackets. There were army boots from different European armies but not from the German army. I took a pair of Italian army boots, several sizes too large for me. It did not matter much because my feet were swollen and full of sores so I needed to wrap them in bandages and rags. The boots were a light tan, and I will not say that they were chic or easy to walk in, but they were more comfortable than the German football boots I had been given by a girl who had taken three pairs from a shop. I took a jacket, which was from the Yugoslav partisans, as I was later assured when the Serb and other prisoners of war arrived at our camp. There were Belgian, Yugoslav, Polish, and many, many Italian ex-prisoners of war.

As soon as the Italian prisoners of war arrived, the whole place looked and sounded different. First of all, every one of them seemed to have been an opera singer. Even if this were not strictly true, they certainly could sing and they did. There were certain favorites like "*Mama son tanto felice,*" "*O sole mio,*" "*La donna e Mobile,*" and many others.

We had not seen our French officers since we settled in at our new location, but when we inquired about them we were told they had been repatriated. Poor people, a lot of heartache awaited them. They had been in the army since the beginning of the war and had no idea whom they would find at home, if anybody was still alive.

The showering went on unabated, and we had a new craze besides that: sewing feverishly by hand underwear, skirts, and blouses, the underwear and blouses being made from the parachutes. We did not particularly worry if the fit was good, the main thing being to have two of each so that we could wash them every day. That had also become a mania. We had no possibility of ironing so we simply stopped worrying about it. Our main activities of the day were showering, changing our clothes, and washing them.

We were still crazy about licking salt and kept taking the salt cellars back to our rooms. After lunch a non-commissioned officer stood at the doors, holding out his hand and asking, with a smile, for the return of the salt cellars. After supper we were asked to stay in our rooms because a doctor was going to go from room to room in order to examine us. It was not a comprehensive examination but at least he dealt with the people who were sick and needed urgent attention. To most of us he would smile and say that with plenty of good food we should be fine.

We had been liberated on Saturday, April 14. On the Tuesday or Wednesday of April 17 or 18, we heard through the grapevine — the only way available for passing on news —

that a camp called Bergen-Belsen had been liberated the day after us. This was the first time we heard the name Bergen-Belsen and of the terrible conditions the Allies found there. We heard there were many people from Hungary and that survivors kept dying of typhus. The hope arose that perhaps some of our families might be alive. I went to the clinics of the local hospital to try and find out who was in charge of medical services. The sergeant wanted to know why I wanted to know, and when he heard that there were several girls, including myself, who wanted to volunteer to go to Bergen-Belsen to nurse the sick or do anything else necessary, he smiled and said, "Look miss, you can hardly stand up or walk yourself. You would only be one more person to be looked after over there."

We started making up lists of girls who had survived, listing them alphabetically according to towns. We were told that the International Red Cross would come, take our lists, and bring other lists from other places. This was the only way we could find out who might still be alive. A US soldier gave us pencils and paper to prepare the lists and for the first time in well over a year, we started writing. How lucky that we had not forgotten how! There were those, however, who had forgotten. They had survived physically, but mentally and emotionally they were dead. I was in that lucky age group who had had no children, nor had I been married or engaged. I wanted to write a letter to the address of my past home, hoping that perhaps one of my brothers-in-law might be alive and receive it. I also wanted to write a letter to my eldest sister, from whom I had been separated in Birkenau, hoping she might still be alive — but I could not remember our address nor my sister's married name nor her address.

I sat down to write my first letter, hoping I would remember their names and addresses later. How could I start a letter to someone who I did not know was alive? How could I not tell him that, to the best of my knowledge, with the exception of myself and possibly my eldest sister, every member of my family had been murdered, wives and children, and that their ashes were somewhere in Birkenau?

I decided to ask how to send letters. Perhaps the Red Cross would take them. I was told that post did not exist in Europe except for to and from army personnel. So, after all, I did not write my letters, but slowly started remembering names of people and places.

We started preparing the list of names in a very orderly fashion, but soon people came along and added their names without bothering about alphabetical order or towns. That is how it was everywhere, and for a whole year the main obsession was reading through thousands of names so that we should not miss anyone from the family or friends. My eldest sister, who survived physically and went home to wait for her two little boys, husband, parents, and family, never put her name on a list. A few months later, I heard she was alive and living in her house.

There was still a war on, but the US airlift came in and landed on the airfield undisturbed. Our source of information was the US soldiers. There was no radio station, even if we had had a radio.

On Friday night, almost a week after our liberation, the US army organized Shabbat prayers for us in one of the auditoriums. An army chaplain arrived and handed out a few prayer books, which he collected after the prayers with an apology. At the end of the prayers it is customary for the male mourners to say Kaddish, and because there were no male mourners present, the chaplain asked all of us to say Kaddish with him for our parents and loved ones. The girls refused to say the mourner's prayer because they would not believe that their parents and families had been killed. The poor chaplain was rather bewildered by the girls' reaction. Only a few of us admitted to themselves and had known all along that our families had been murdered. To many people this ignorance was a way of escaping reality and was probably the only way they could go on living.

We went back to our rooms, most depressed on this, our first Friday night after liberation. Each of us was thinking back about what had been home and would never be again, although only a few of us were brave enough to admit it.

A few days later we were told that the area of Saltzwedel, where we were, would be handed over to the British reconnaissance forces. We were duly taken over by the British forces, but it did not make much difference to us except that by that time we started to be fairly crowded with people from almost every country in Europe except Russia. There were many collaborators from Latvia, Lithuania, Estonia, Poland, and Hungary. There were even people from Holland, who had come to help the Germans, but not many.

As we gained a little strength, we were burning with the wish to start normal lives, but where to start and how none of us knew. The girls almost all wanted to go home and I wanted to go to Palestine. Both alternatives were impossible because the war was not yet finished and we realized that traffic and life in general would be chaotic in Europe.

I had a navy skirt with white pure silk blouses — two sets of them, together with underwear. The mania for showering and washing continued. The sick girls were taken away in army ambulances and we knew nothing of what happened to them. On May 3 we heard that Berlin had fallen to the Russians.

The British forces had to try and normalize life for the indigenous population and for the tens of thousands of displaced persons. The Red Cross kept bringing new lists of names. One day, an ambulance driver, a woman from the Canadian army, came and introduced herself. She told us she was Jewish and wanted to know if there were any girls from Poland because her mother came from there. She asked many questions, and cried, and promised to send off letters to the USA or Canada for girls who had relatives there. She told us we should not go to the USA or Canada because anti-Semitism was terrible there, but that we should go to Palestine. I agreed with her wholeheartedly but asked her, if life was so terrible in Canada, why did not she and her family go to Palestine as well? She could not give me a convincing answer.

The British were looking for interpreters. They could not pay them but I wanted to work and was eager just to get a room away from the crowds. I thought that perhaps through work, I might find out how to start on my plan to go to Palestine. That Shabbat morning, there were boys and girls coming to each building and asking people to join them in settling in a place near Hamburg in preparation for going to Palestine. As it was Shabbat, when one is forbidden to travel, I did not go with them. Had I done so, I should have missed meeting my future husband and would probably never have known what true happiness is.

The Struggle to Live Again

The healthy girls among us, and I include myself, tried hard to make plans for the future. The difficulty was that none of us had the slightest idea of where to start or to whom to turn for advice. Of course we were rather weak and swollen, but we began to look like, if not young, at any rate girls again. We were still showering several times a day, washing our clothes, sewing, and constantly talking and planning our future.

One of the shattering things I heard from some of the girls was that now the whole world would be open to us and that we could go anywhere we wanted to because the world would be delighted that somehow we had managed to stay alive. I could hardly believe what I was hearing and argued that we would be a nuisance and an embarrassment to the world. While I was sure that the Jews of the world would open their hearts and purses, I doubted if they would open their homes as well in an equally free fashion. I told the girls that my grandfather had had a younger brother in New York, living, as far as I remembered, in Long Island — but I would not make any effort to find him and his family until I was settled in Palestine. I could not bear their thinking that I wanted them to support me.

It was a very interesting feeling, not having anything or anyone to answer to; I felt that whatever I did and however I behaved it was purely my own choice, without family or social pressure behind it. Yet each day, when I found it so very difficult to go on with life, physically, emotionally, and mentally, I remembered my mother saying, "I do not know what will happen to us but of one thing I am sure, and that is that you will be all right." This she said in the cattle truck just before we left the borders of Hungary on our way to Slovakia, Poland, and finally Auschwitz. My mother said these words in the presence of my two sisters, one brother-in-law, and my brother. I often wonder why she singled me out and entrusted and burdened me with the words, "I am sure that you will be all right." This was meant as her will and testament to me to carry on our family's traditions. I wonder if, for a split second, she saw our future clearly and knew that I, the youngest, would be the only one to survive and build a family again. This call of conscience gave me the push to go on and fulfill my duty, for I knew that if I had stayed alive, I would have to go on living and fulfilling my mission however difficult it might be.

In the long mirror in our room, I looked at the girl reflected opposite me and started to recognize her; she reminded me a little of the young girl I once was. My sisters thought that, being the youngest, I had been spoiled and allowed to do things never permitted to them. One thing I was sure of: no one would ever spoil me again.

One morning we heard from two of the girls that they

were going to work for a Captain Butcher, who was the doctor in charge of the local army. As far as I know, he had been a general practitioner. The army took over a large, very pleasant, private home for the surgical and medical administration, and the British soldiers came there on sick parade all day long. There were several orderlies and ambulances standing outside the house. The two girls told me they were going to keep the place clean. I asked them if they would ask the doctor if he needed an interpreter for his dealings with the local population, and I would help with the cleaning as well. The answer was yes. The three of us were picked up by an army ambulance, and I remember the driver asking us where our luggage was and thinking that I did not know what he meant by luggage. He started a whole pantomime of carrying a suitcase and was amazed that we did not have anything at all to take with us.

The army commandeered a nice large room for us with an elderly family. I do not know if the authorities paid them or not. We did not receive any payment for our work but we had food and the room for the three of us, away from the crowds, and for the little work we had to do it seemed fair payment. We had no money at all and I cannot say that any of us, certainly not I, wanted any. Without money or anything of value, each of us managed to get by.

As the war was drawing to its close, the army had to make certain arrangements for the local population. Captain Butcher needed me for his contacts with the Germans, but most of the time I was helping the girls with the cleaning. I must say that the British soldiers', sergeants', and officers' behavior toward us was impeccable.

On May 7, 1945, the invincible German army surrendered to the Allies. On May 8, everybody from all over Europe, except the Germans and their collaborators, celebrated and were almost crazy with happiness.

I went out for a short walk in the town, just to get the general atmosphere. I found it unbelievable how the "Ruling Race" had collapsed. I found soldiers and officers without any dignity lying tired, hungry, and thirsty in the streets of the town. They were waiting and hoping to be taken prisoner and to get a hot meal. *I try to remember what I felt, besides disgust. Revenge? I knew that nothing would bring back my family, my people, or my youth. I could not understand how a so-called tough, strutting, barking, murdering, and inhuman army could collapse as they did. They were a huge balloon, which kept blowing itself up until the Allies put a pin in it and the air rushed out together with their self-esteem and respect.*

These were the regular army, the *Wehrmacht*. The SS collapsed even faster — they were not fighters but just a gang of murderers from the Middle Ages. As I walked around and saw the Germans as low down as any nation could sink, with German children running after British soldiers calling "*Onkel Tommy*" and begging for sweets, chocolate, and even food, I wanted to get away and not to see them, not even humiliated as they were. I remembered a psalm, "They have said, 'Come and let us cut them off from being a nation, that the name of Israel may be remembered no more.' " This certainly spurred me on to rehabilitate myself and go to my country, Eretz Yisrael/Palestine, and help rebuild it. I did not think about marriage at all, although I was already twenty-one years old in years, but much older in looks, seriousness, and experience of life.

On the evening of May 8, when the war in Europe was officially over, two of the sergeants took the three of us back to our camp to see the celebrations there. The British officers and other ranks who were running the place were celebrating wholeheartedly and making plans about going home to their wives, families, studies, and so on. They kept asking us, "Aren't you girls happy?" They said, "Look at the Italian, Belgian, and Serb prisoners of war and how happy they are. Why can't you celebrate with us?"

We tried to explain how grateful we were to them for winning the war and how happy we were for them that they could stop fighting and pick up their lives and continue living, but that we had nowhere to return to. I had registered myself as stateless. I was not going back to a place where my family had lived for several generations, where there was a street named after my grandfather, where we had many roots and yet were thrown out like people who were contaminating the world. They asked what were our plans and each of us had a different one, but none of us knew as yet when and how we could start implementing it.

Every few days we asked the ambulance drivers or one of the boys to take us back to the camp in order to look through the new lists of names, if there were any. I was looking for my eldest sister and for my cousin, Lea, who was two years my senior and with whom I had been very close. Lea, her brother, Aron — who was six weeks older than I and would never let me forget it — and I, had been brought up together. Aron had been in the Hungarian forced labor service, in Hungary, so I was hoping he had survived together with Lea, who was a strong good-looking girl, and that I should see their names on one of the lists. During the summer of 1939 Lea had been sent to England to improve her English accent. She was fluent in English and was hoping to become an English teacher.

In 1932, I had had a governess called Bertl, who taught my brother and myself German literature, Jewish history, English, and general good behavior. I remember how we children went out for walks in white cotton gloves, so as not to pick up any infection. Then my aunt became sick, and as Lea and Aron's governess had just gone back to Austria, Bertl went over to Kolozsvar to look after them. The town they lived in was a university town, where my uncle worked as a general practitioner with specialization in diabetes. As we were not very far away, only 160 km, we used to travel there by express train, though as a child I loved the slow trains because I could enjoy the beautiful scenery of the Transylvanian mountains, with their waterfalls and villages.

Bertl had been born in Fulda, in Germany, where she lived with her parents and family. When Hitler came to power, she started to be worried about developments. In late 1934, as far as I remember, she went back home to see what was happening. She saw how bad things were and that they were growing rapidly worse, so when she heard there was a chance of going to England as household help, she applied and was one of the lucky ones to be accepted. I do not know what year it was when Bertl arrived in England but when my cousin Lea arrived in London in the summer of 1939, Bertl was friendly enough with the family where she worked to invite my cousin to come and see her. There Lea met a young medical student who was the brother of the head of the household's son-in-law, and they started to go out together.

Then, on the first of September, the war broke out in Europe, and when England entered the war two days later my grandmother became desperate and insisted that Lea be brought home. My aunt was a very sensible woman and at first was in favor of leaving her in England, but later gave way, and Lea was told to come home. She traveled by train across Europe and arrived home either at the end of October or beginning of November. She was given a reception worthy of someone who had escaped certain death. Lea told me about her trip and of the medical student — tall, dark-haired, and a most impressive personality. She hoped that the war would soon finish and they would meet again.

The medical student, whose name was Mark, finished all his examinations but before joining the British army had to do six months as house surgeon, which he did at the London Jewish Hospital. There he was wounded when the East End of London was bombed. Before joining the army he talked things over with his family and decided to send Lea a telegram asking her to marry him. In his telegram he quoted from Psalms, "This was the Lord's doing, it is marvelous in our eyes." She was very happy and straightaway sent a telegram of acceptance. My aunt then wrote Mark a long letter, which he received.

I wondered how he had fared during the war, hoping that she was alive and well and that he would soon be reunited with my cousin. Yet her name did not appear on any list, neither did her brother's or my sisters'. I once thought of finding the address of the London family, and perhaps through them I could find out where Lea was, but I was afraid to contact them in case they or Bertl might think that I wanted financial help from them.

One day I heard from some girls — who had heard from some other girls coming through our camp with Red Cross lists — that many girls from our town, including my cousin Lea Normand, had been in a camp in Studhof. They heard that they had been put on a boat which either was deliberately blown up by the Germans or hit a mine. I did not want to believe this because when one hears things which have been passed on several times, they are not reliable. I continued looking through lists and putting my own name on them, and kept on hoping.

I asked Captain Butcher, the doctor for whom we worked, for the second or third time if he could please make inquiries about how I could set about going to Palestine — as I was a stateless person who had nowhere else to go and who did not want to go anywhere else either. He was very polite but told me each time that Palestine would be the most difficult country to get to, and advised me to try the USA or a South American country where life would be easier than in Palestine.

We three girls worked all day and toward evening went back to our nicely appointed room, where we had a double bed in which the three of us slept together. I slept on the edge, and it often happened that I fell out of bed or was thrown out because of the nightmares which one or all of us had. We shouted and screamed, sobbing in our sleep. In the concentration camp we had not had nightmares. Life itself was a nightmare, and besides we never slept long enough without being woken by one of the girls, who wanted to turn onto her other side.

There were many German books in our room and one night I took out a novel just to start reading again, but I could not concentrate even for five minutes. I read and reread a page but could hardly remember what it was about. I felt bitter and angry. I got out of bed, dressed — I had no dressing gown or nightdress — knocked at the door of the living room of the German family, and with a perfectly straight face asked the woman, very politely, if she had a copy of the poems of the great German writer Heinrich Heine, because I should please like to read it. There was silence and then her husband rose and very politely said he could offer me other *"Dichter"* (poets). I assured him I was interested in Heine. I also told the woman that all our things including our families had stayed in Auschwitz, and I needed a good pair of scissors with which to cut my nails after fourteen months. She immediately brought me a pair of scissors and I took them from her and tried very hard not to say thank you. I still have that pair of scissors.

I thought it was silly of me to ask for Heine, a secular Jewish poet whose books had been burnt by the Germans in the big book burnings on May 1, 1933, despite the fact that he had left Judaism. These people knew of course why I wanted to read only Heine but the result was that they went off to sleep and I could not drop off for a long time. When I did, I woke up choking and smelling gas. I was back in the gas chambers, all of us naked and choking to death and my sisters, mother, and two children falling down in a heap, not yet dead, while I was standing, inhaling the gas and watching them. I got out of bed and wanted to wake up the Germans and ask them if they could also smell the gas and if not, why not. I wanted to torture them by at least describing my nightmares but decided against it. I was angry with my poor parents for having brought me up to behave in a civilized fashion even with uncivilized people.

I sat down in a small armchair and watched the girls thrashing about, having their nightmares. The girl who slept in the middle was the youngest amongst us. She was a true platinum blonde, not pretty, small, with a very coarse voice and an uneducated accent. Poor thing, she kept saying in her sleep "Mame, Mame" very slowly as if each syllable belonged to a different person.

The girls woke up and we had no idea what time it was, but after talking a little while, we decided to get dressed and go to the park for a walk. It is true that we were not supposed to

walk about in the dark; there was a curfew and there were SS
and other German fugitives lurking around and killing girls
who wandered about. All three of us were in a murderous
mood and we said that if we caught a German, God help him!
We were, I think, totally mad.

We went out, making sure that we banged each door so
that the Germans in the house would wake up, and started not
walking but almost running, going nowhere in the dark, and
then we came to a bench under a tree where the three of us sat
down exhausted and dropped off to sleep. We woke up because we felt cold and because at dawn the birds started twit-
tering. All this brought our thoughts back to Birkenau, where
we never saw or heard a bird.

It was nice and peaceful, too peaceful for us. We went
back to our room, very depressed and tired. I was hoping that
someone from the household would ask us what had happened during the night. They did not do so, and I went on behaving like a civilized person and hating myself for it.

It is interesting that I can barely remember what
Salzwedel looked like. I was not interested in it and when I
went anywhere I hated the people and was sorry about every
house that had not been bombed. There was little damage in
the town itself, which was probably not important enough
strategically to be bombed.

We were told by the sergeants and by Captain Butcher as
well that the British forces would have to withdraw and that
the area would be occupied by the Russian army. This was the
beginning: when the Russian zone started and stayed as such
until the Berlin Wall fell and East and West Germany were reunited.

I asked Captain Butcher if there was any way to get transport to the British zone. Under no circumstances did I want to

be locked up behind what came to be known as the Iron Curtain. He promised to do whatever was possible. Two days later, he told me that a large army truck would be available and packed tightly it could take thirty to forty girls. I went back to the camp and told the girls to come with us, but most of them wanted to stay, trusting that the Russians would take them back to Hungary. In fact, some of the girls said, "We are staying here until we can go home."

The following morning, a large army truck came for us and twenty to thirty girls piled in at the back. We said good-bye to our friends and off we went on a bumpy and very breezy journey. We passed through what had once been a town, with streets upon streets of ruins, and so we traveled on and on.

We arrived at a DP camp outside Hannover, full of people of all sorts of nationalities but amongst them there were no Jews at all. We did not like being together with Poles, Rumanians, Hungarians, and, in fact, people from all over Europe. We were given two rooms but we asked for one large room, since however crowded we might be we wanted to stay together and keep an eye on each other.

We could either eat in the dining room for company or take the food back to our room. We most certainly did not want the company of those people, so we took the food and hurried back to our room. The food was plentiful and prepared probably by Polish cooks; the Poles were the largest contingent in the camp. I do not know what the place was before all the nationalities descended on it but it had probably been some sort of army camp, with trees and rather pleasant surroundings.

We decided not to run around a great deal. It was obvious that we were rather popular with the Poles and Rumanians.

Even the worst anti-Semite loves Jewish girls.

The next day we went to register. This was the first time we received a DP card, a displaced person's card. We asked if there were any other DP camps in Hannover and how we could get into town. Hannover had been a large town before the war. During the war it had been bombed until almost the whole of the town was in ruins. It was the headquarters of the military government of the British, American, French, and Russian forces.

At this time there were already buses running into and within the town. While we were waiting for the bus, four or five of us, one of the girls said, "We cannot go in by bus because we have no money." I asked her if she was completely crazy. We entered the bus and sat down.

"Hey, tickets," the conductor said.

"Will you address us not as 'hey' but as 'miss.' We have no money, no home, no parents, no family, no nothing, and you should know better than anyone else what you did with all our families."

"Please, please..." he said and went off.

I waited until he came near me again and this time said to him, "Do you want to know why all the other people have money and decent clothes and only we Jewish girls have nothing?" He lifted his hands and said, "Please, miss, please."

We went to the military government building, which was in perfect condition. The area in which it stood was far less damaged than the rest of the town. We decided to go to the French military government offices on the assumption that people who had personally suffered from the Germans would be more sympathetic and helpful to us.

We went in, and everybody there looked like a most important general. Then a tall, thin, bespectacled officer came in, resplendent with a sword, and said to us, "*Shalom aleichem*," which in Hebrew means "Peace be upon you." So we felt we had arrived home. He told us there were other places in and around Hannover where there were decent people and not collaborators with the Germans like the people in the camp where we were. He did not like the idea of our being there and promised to arrange transport within a day or two.

When we went to get our evening meal, a huge Pole with a white apron and a cook's hat walked up to me and tried to explain something in Polish. Finally he brought someone to interpret for him. In Polish German, I was told that the gentleman was the chief cook, and a very good cook, and that this food was not good enough for me. He was going to be my friend and would bring me good food. As soon as he went into the kitchen, I took my ration and together with the girls, hurried back to my room.

In less than hour, he was brought to our room by the girl who worked in the office. He came in with a huge smile, holding all his pots and pans. The man was huge, with blond hair and a pig's face. He invited the other girls as well to take part in the feast. We had just eaten and none of us could or wanted to eat. He tried showing us that my face was "*dobje*" or a similar word and he invited me to dance with him.

I showed him that my head was hurting and that my feet were hurting. The idiot sat there looking at me adoringly. I kept saying in Hungarian, "What have I done to deserve this?" Some of the girls started giggling and finally he stood up and left. We had a good laugh but we locked the door and did not leave the room.

The following morning three of us went into Hannover to our French officer — I had no idea of his rank — and told him my "success story." He did not like it either and told me not to go back at all, but that the other two girls should return on the truck with two French soldiers and tell the remaining girls to gather up our few things and come back with them as quietly and quickly as possible. Then we would be taken to another more decent place where there were Jewish girls and Jewish boys, as well as a few Rumanians who were probably collaborators.

Toward evening we were settled into our new place. It was a large school and the rooms had been filled with bunk beds. In the middle of our room there was a large table with chairs. The food was minimal but who cared? I was so relieved to get away from my adoring Pole.

We started being more normal and decided to arrange Friday evening and Shabbat day meals with the boys and girls, who wanted to remember Shabbat meals at home with their families. We sat round the table in our room and those who came later, when the five or six chairs had been taken, simply sat on the beds. We tried to make the table look a little more ornamental in honor of the Shabbat, even decorating it with leaves and small twigs from a tree. Most of us saved up the two slices of bread and spoonful of jam which constituted our supper. The oldest and most serious of the boys, an old man of about thirty-five, said the blessings before the meal. I begged the kitchen staff to lend us a jug and we even had a cold tasteless ersatz coffee, made of hops and chicory I think. It certainly never approached anything that looked or tasted like coffee. Coffee, cocoa, and cigarettes were the hard currency at that time in Germany.

We sat round the table. Luckily the light in the room was very dim, so at least at the beginning we did not see the tears in everybody's eyes. We all tried our best but one after another of us started crying. The first one who started, almost shouting and choking on her words, was a tall woman of about thirty-five with a large nose, who began looking round with her eyes bulging. "What am I doing here, without my children?" she cried and stood up and ran out of the room. I wanted to run after her, but one of the boys said, "Let me go, she told me about her children." We sat in silence, then someone sitting on a bed started sobbing. This was terrible for morale.

The "old man" who had said the blessing suggested that we sing the Shabbat songs which were customary at meals. He looked at me and said, "You start. What did you sing at home?" My mind went completely blank. Even if my life had depended on it, I could not remember a single thing.

I wanted to leave the table, to get away and go outside, but I could not budge. I was giddy and wanted to vomit, and with shaking legs I got up and together with another girl, holding onto each other, we left the room. We went to the bathroom to wash our faces in cold water and in a corner sat the tall lady with the big nose.

"Tell me," she said to me, "was it your idea to interfere with people's lives? Hasn't God given you any brains?" She was right, I thought. I should not have arranged a Shabbat meal, just to get everybody worked up. The three of us had a good cry and arm in arm returned to the room. There was nothing on the table and no one sitting around it.

I went downstairs to walk around in the schoolyard. It was a nice clear night with the stars shining. I could not bear the thought that there might be Germans enjoying this lovely evening and that I was sharing this beautiful sky with them.

I wanted to have a conversation with Heaven, which I had not done for some time. Before I could start, a well-fed Rumanian, a collaborator with the Germans, attached himself to me. He introduced himself, but I shook my head, meaning that I did not understand. Then he said, "You are from Transylvania and people do speak Rumanian as well." I shook my head and started to go back to my room. He climbed the stairs with me and told me that he liked me, that he had noticed me from the first day and kept an eye on me all the time. I said goodnight, went in, and locked the door.

The girls were not asleep, for who could go to sleep after an evening like this? I told them about my wonderful new suitor and said, "Do you remember the pig who looked at me adoringly? He was nothing compared to what I managed to pick up just now." Most of the girls sat up in bed and I stood in the middle of the room and started imitating my Rumanian cavalier, exaggerating very badly. "Is he a cook?" they wanted to know. "No," I said, "he is not intelligent enough." And so, at last, we started giggling. "What does he look like?" I went on and on, trying to amuse them.

During the night, instead of sleeping, I decided that I would never again want to sit down to a Shabbat meal and try to remember the songs we sang. I would try to stop observing religion, not because of lack of faith but because remembering it all caused too much heartache. I thought I should like to observe all the laws of kashrut — we were still eating anything we were given but I had already tried to stop eating the non-kosher meat, if and when there was any — but I would stop keeping Shabbat and other holidays, which would remind me of things that were gone and would never be again.

The following morning, a girl came in excitedly and told us there was a truck going down to the lake near Hannover, and there was plenty of room for us as well. I decided to go, although it was the Shabbat and this was not something I was forced to do.

I got into the back of the truck and tried not to think of

my deliberately breaking Shabbat. We arrived at the lake and everybody descended and went into the water. Except for the Rumanians, nobody had swimsuits, so we swam fully dressed. I waded into the water for a few minutes and then went and sat under a tree, away from them all, to do some thinking.

It was obvious that I was crazier than ever and that, in my opinion, I was also a complete emotional cripple. During the last year I had tried not to have too many friends. Those I had were soon killed. I had Judith and Dori but we were not close enough to stay together after the war. They went back in search of their families and I was trying to go to Palestine. In fact, my only love or passion was for my future country and for my people, who had suffered so much. I had not met a single boy or man who I was interested in. Though I had seen two or three girls who were in love with someone for a few days, it didn't last. My diagnosis was that we were all crazy, not fit to lead normal lives — besides our physical shortcomings, we were most definitely emotionally finished.

One thing was certain: my trip to the lake was not a success because however hard I tried, I could not run away from myself. Therefore, even if I decided not to keep Shabbat, I should be less happy and totally without an anchor.

I lay down under the tree and must have dozed off to sleep because when I woke up, I found a very good looking blond young man sitting not far from me. He was well fed and well groomed and obviously not a Holocaust survivor. He greeted me in Rumanian. I nodded, stood up, and thought, "Dear me, even here one cannot be alone with one's Creator."

On our way back to the camp, the girls started pulling my leg and claimed they found it incredible that I could not keep up my record of attracting only pigs and idiots. They said,

"You should have seen how that good looking boy was watching you."

We were terribly restless, neither well nor sick and not doing anything. Survivors kept coming from other towns and camps, looking for relatives and bringing news, most of the time false. One of the most terrible things was the rumors. These had started already in Auschwitz, when people came to say that they themselves had seen or heard from someone who heard from someone, who had seen a husband, mother, sister, or other relative of one of the girls. Ninety-five percent or more of these rumors had no foundation and no one knew who started them.

On Sunday at about noon, three girls arrived and one of them knew the tall woman with the big nose (I cannot remember her name). She told her that she had seen her husband at some other camp and that he had been asking about her, that he had moved on, and that she had no idea where he had gone. His wife could not understand why he had not put his name on any list and why he had not seen her name on the lists. "Was he with my son? He was a big boy, already twelve, and he went with his father..." The girl said she had not seen him, but he had had someone with him. So she went off to the camp where she was told there were several people from her town, to ask them where they thought her husband might be heading. She did not know how to get there but left immediately, without money, without food, and just the crazy hope in her heart. The new arrivals did not find anyone they were looking for and soon left.

On Monday morning I went to look for a job, not an easy task. They needed people who spoke Polish, which I did not, to work in Uelzen, where they were all Poles, Hungarians, Estonians, and other collaborators. About that time, we heard that Yehudi Menuhin was in Germany and had traveled to Uelzen to give those "poor people" a concert. The hall was packed out — it was free music — but when those Poles heard him play, they got up and left. This was not the kind of music those crude uneducated people were expecting to hear. Yehudi Menuhin was left at the end with scarcely thirty people. What a pity that someone had not advised him to travel another twenty minutes to Bergen-Belsen, where he would have had the most enthusiastic, grateful, and applauding audiences.

On Tuesday evening the lady who had gone to look for her husband came back, completely downcast. She had not found anyone from her town and, in fact, very few survivors at all. She had gone on to another camp, not far from Uelzen, and no one knew her husband or anything about him. Poor thing, this went on all the time. There was no telephone service, no postal service, and no permanent address for anyone. The only way was to go and look for the person.

Some other girls arrived who had met up with girls from my town. I kept asking about my sister and cousin, and unfortunately I heard from three different sources the same story about the ship blowing up with the girls, including my cousin, on it. I still had not heard about my sister, but I found one cousin on the list together with his fifteen-year-old son and that was all.

Every other day, several girls went into Hannover. We were on the outskirts and that is why the school was still standing and not in ruins. I do not know what we did all day. We just sat and talked. There was nothing to read and even if we had had books, we could not concentrate. We had no radio. We were young people living like zombies and just waiting for better times.

At lunchtime, when we went to take our food back to our rooms, the tall, blond, and too-well-groomed young man came up to me and introduced himself as Yonel. In order to make conversation, he asked me in good German if I had any books he could exchange with me. I looked at him in amazement and told him that all the libraries and bookshops were empty in Auschwitz. He went red and said, "Of course, how stupid of me." I said, "It is," and left him. Toward evening there was a knock on the door and he came in carrying two books. One of the girls asked him in German, "Who are you looking for?" and he was in trouble because he did not know my name. He said, "Your friend will enjoy these books. Please give them to her when she comes back." I was on my bed but he could not see me. The following day I took the books with me to the kitchen in order to leave them there, but I saw him and thanked him and said I did not want to read modern German writers but if he had or could get me a book of poems of Heinrich Heine, I should like that. He promised to try to get me a copy and obviously did not know that Heine was taboo with the Germans.

Toward evening two girls I knew appeared; I had been together with them from Reichenbach until after our liberation. They were sisters and were looking for family and friends before returning to Budapest. We were glad to see each other, and they told me that the previous week they had been in Braunschweig and that my father was in hospital there, and they wanted to know why I was not with him. I said, "Girls, you must be making a mistake. Even if my father had been taken to a camp, he could not have survived at his age." They were adamant so I made plans to go to Braunschweig straightaway. The two girls were expert travelers and told me that there were no trains at night. They advised me to get something in writing from someone in authority so that I could travel without paying. I did not bother about that, as it would have meant a further twenty-four-hour's delay. The experts told me that there was a train once a day to Braunschweig and Magdeburg.

I could not sleep that night and kept telling myself that this was just a rumor, like all the others, and that my father could not be alive. None of the girls or boys believed it either but I had to go and see for myself. I asked how to get to the station. It was rather time consuming if I wanted to go by bus. I rose at daybreak and without eating or having a hot drink, started walking into Hannover. *It amazes me now, as I write, that we were simply no longer afraid of the Germans. They could have killed me and dumped me somewhere, and it might have been weeks, if ever, before people started looking for me. The truth of it was that I was more afraid of life than of death. My only wish, which became a mania, was that I should be buried properly, according to Jewish rites.*

I went on shuffling in my football boots, as my Italian army boots were too heavy for long walks. It started drizzling and somehow, through the ruins of the town, I reached the bus stop for the railway station for Braunschweig. On the bus it was sufficient to show one's DP card, but I was most reluctant to do this. If I was asked for money for a ticket, I asked if it was not obvious enough what the Germans had done to me and usually added, "Even if I had money, I would not buy a ticket, because you people robbed me of everything."

At least I had a seat on the bus after my exhausting walk. I kept wondering how the poor footballers could run in those boots.

I arrived at the station. This was my first journey by train since liberation. There were hundreds of people waiting to board the train and two ticket collectors standing at the entrance to the platform. One was checking the tickets and the other was standing with a large sack and each passenger threw into it one, two, or three pieces of firewood log. They started to demand my ticket and said that if I wanted to go to Braunschweig, I had to bring, in addition, two logs. I repeated, loudly and clearly, that I had no tickets, no logs, no certificate from anyone, and that I had to get to Braunschweig by the first train. The wonderful, orderly, and civilized Germans all started to shout at me. I screamed, "Shut up, you *Schweinhunde!*" That was what we were called in the camps, amongst other things. There was a young woman who would not stop shouting at me to go home and not guzzle up all the German food and that they had had enough of us. I asked her where was her armband with the swastika, had she left it at home? After that I did not have to say a single word; the Germans screamed at each other, tearing each other to pieces.

There was a middle-aged man standing there with a violin. He shouted that the women had brought Hitler to power, that they had all been in love with him, and that he was now wandering about Germany, out of work. He had been in the Berlin Philharmonic Orchestra and now had no work, no home, and the German women were responsible for it. The ticket collector came back to me again and asked me for identification in order to be sure that I was a survivor. Some of the Germans tried not to laugh, and the violinist said, "*Menschenskind*, have you no eyes in your head. Has she got to prove it?" I was standing on the platform trying to edge nearer to the train. I let them shout and did not take any notice of them.

When the train doors were opened, the orderly Germans ran for it and started pushing. The train was packed to more than capacity, so much so that the doors could not be shut. I got as far as the second step of the train (these were old fashioned steam trains with several steps) and held on to the railings on either side of me, when the train started moving. I was hoping to get inside, but there was no possibility of that. All along the train there were people standing on the steps. As the train gathered speed, I found it was very windy and cold and I kept thinking that perhaps my father was alive and what would our meeting be like. Then I kept telling myself that it was certain that he was not alive. It started drizzling and then raining and I hung on to the train. I could not understand why, after I had cursed them, one of the Germans did not force my fingers open and just let me fall.

Luckily the train did not travel very fast, perhaps because it was burning wood instead of coal. The great German nation had no coal and so everybody had to buy a ticket and bring logs according to the length of their journey. The buses and trucks also ran on wood — since they had no fuel they replaced their engines with steam engines. I do not know how long the journey took. I thought we must have traveled about two hundred kilometers but in fact it is only about sixty-five or seventy kilometers between Hannover and Braunschweig. When the train stopped I could hardly release my hands from the bars which I had been holding onto. I had to sit down for a little while before I was even able to ask a German how to get to the hospital.

The town itself was not, as far as I could see, in ruins and had had little damage done to it. I met a few survivors at the station and asked them about the hospital and if, perhaps, they had heard of my father. "How old would he be?" asked one of them. "About sixty," I answered. They looked at each other and said nothing. They advised me to go to the displaced persons center where every survivor, either in hospital or living in the area, was registered. They told me how to get there and wished me luck. I went off, at first by bus and then on foot, and finally arrived at the office. I asked about my father, and they asked how old he was, and they thought I was crazy. I told them about the Hungarian sisters who came to Hannover and brought me the news about him. The man said, "Look, if you want to go back to Hannover today, there is a train in about an hour's time." I said I had to go to the hospital and see for myself. Perhaps my father had lost his memory and forgotten his name.

I went to the hospital, willing myself to hurry. At the hospital they had no one registered under the name of Fuchs. I asked if I could have a word with the matron or one of the doctors. The clerk told me they were busy people. I told him, "No they are not. I am a survivor of your brutal camps and when I want to see the matron, she will not be busy. Where is her room?" I shouted. A doctor stopped and asked me what the problem was, so I said, "All you damned Germans, you are the problem. I want to see the matron." He assured me she was not in the hospital but could anyone else help me? I told him that I was looking for my father, that I knew he was not registered in the name of Fuchs but perhaps he had lost his memory and could not remember his name and I wanted to go and look at the patients in order to be sure that he was not in the hospital.

He said, "If he is not here where else could he be? When did you see him last?"

"On the ramp of Auschwitz, a year and a half ago I saw him last, and if he is not here then your fine German compatriots have scattered his ashes with those of the rest of my family in Auschwitz."

After this loud, clear, and unhesitating speech, he could hardly refuse my request. He himself came with me and I looked at all the male patients. By the time we had finished our round, I was almost collapsing. The doctor said quietly, "I am so sorry." I turned round and almost ran out of the hospital. This was my father's final death, and this time I could cry for him.

Outside it was raining hard, a summer shower, and I walked and cried and realized that I had not shed a single tear for my whole family. How was that possible? I had lost my parents, grandfather, three sisters, a brother, two brothers-in-law, six children of my three sisters, cousins, aunts, uncles, and friends, my whole world had collapsed around me, and yet I had not and could not cry.

I do not know how long I walked and cried. I was wet and my clothes were dripping. I had a terrible looking brown coat and it was growing heavy with the water in it. I took it off and with all my strength wrung and shook it out and put it on again. I walked on, not thinking about anything except my family whom I had just lost, and mourning them.

As I walked on, all of a sudden I saw one of the most moving and beautiful things I have ever seen in my life. It was a large blue and white flag, with a blue shield of David in the middle of it — "My flag, my flag! These are my people." It was the clubhouse or headquarters of the Jewish Brigade. I could hardly believe my luck. Now I could find out how to get to Palestine and receive help from my own people.

I went inside. A lovely dark-haired girl in uniform was standing behind the desk, and she asked me in good German who I was looking for. Before I could answer, another uniformed girl came out and spoke to her in Hebrew. What music! There was an electric heater in a corner and she had a steaming cup of tea in front of her. I told the girl that I had found the place by chance but that my hope was to get to Eretz Yisrael to start a new life, and I was hoping they could help me. I was very embarrassed because my coat was dripping and making a puddle on the floor and I apologized. She said it did not matter and could I come back in an hour's time, when Sergeant So-and-So would be back and could talk to me. I thanked her and walked out into the rain again, shattered by my own people.

I did not cry anymore but thought I had almost reached the edge of the world and that this would be the end of me. I was sure that the young girl in uniform had not asked me to stay for a few minutes and dry off or offer me a cup of tea only out of lack of imagination, but it hurt terribly. She could have won her place in Heaven just by offering me a cup of tea and asking me to stay until the sergeant came back. I was certain that she was a very nice and decent girl, who simply did not think. *Today she is probably a highly respected grandmother somewhere in Israel and would be horrified to know what she did.*

I had no idea what the time was but had to make plans to stay somewhere. The curfew started at eight o'clock and any civilian found outside was picked up by the military police and handed over to the German authorities. In any case I could not walk around much longer; I was shivering with cold and could hardly walk from tiredness. I asked a German how to get to the survivors' office, but he shrugged and went on.

With my last strength I went to the German police station to ask for the whereabouts of the nearest DP camp where I could spend the night. I was directed to a sergeant who dealt with billeting people. There were thousands of refugees, mainly Germans, running away from the Russian zone of Germany, going west. Everybody was running to western Germany.

I entered a room. The sergeant was sitting behind a desk. He looked at me and I saw compassion in his eyes as he asked me how he could help me. I told him what I wanted and he said that there would be a train at six or seven in the morning, and that these days the trains in Germany did not run on a timetable, and that he would give me a place to stay, not far from the station. He gave me a card with the address of the shelter where I could stay and a card to a soup kitchen where I could get some hot food. I would not accept the card to the soup kitchen and told him I was not hungry. He said, "Look, you are so wet, take off your coat and get yourself warm near the fire, and I will bring you a glass of hot tea." I said, almost choking, trying not to cry, "Thank you, I am not cold or hungry." He explained how to reach the shelter and I left.

As I had no one to talk to and felt that I had reached the end of my tether, I spoke to my Creator and asked what else He had in store for me. Dear God, how could I possibly stand in a line in a soup kitchen with hundreds of Germans? "Please," I asked Him, "leave me my self-respect and just let me reach Palestine." The most difficult thing to bear was the behavior of the Jewish Brigade girl compared with that of the German sergeant, with his kindness and understanding that I was hungry, cold, and wet.

It took me a long time to reach the shelter but just when I thought I might have missed it, I saw hundreds of German refugees going the way I was going. It was growing dark and both they and I had to get off the streets. I saw the name of the street and then I saw a concrete building with an entrance in which hundreds of Germans were going with their bundles, whole families with babies and old people. This was the place where I was going to spend the night. "How many more bitter pills will I have to swallow?" I thought.

I started descending the stairs and there were ushers who said there was no room on the first two floors, so, together with the German refugees, I went slowly down into the bowels of that cursed country. The smell was terrible but I finally arrived, almost treading on people, and tried to find somewhere to sit down. There were concrete benches with back supports. Perhaps, during the war, people slept on these benches and could stretch out. On one of them sat a grandmother with her daughter and two granddaughters. I stood near them and they moved up to make room for me.

I looked around and there were only Germans and I thought that I, the only survivor and last spark of my family, instead of starting a new life, had survived in order to be murdered in this shelter. No one would know — they could simply dump me in one of those huge rubbish bins and who would care? What worried me was not so much being killed, but having survived so far, I wanted to be buried properly as a Jew.

I was giddy; the stench in the shelter made me feel sick and I was afraid I would faint. I took off my soaking coat but was afraid it might be stolen and put it on again; I was so cold that I thought that with the wet coat on me I should feel warmer.

The grandmother sitting next to me asked if I was all right, and I told her that I was fine, just a little tired. She started telling me how they had left everything behind and run away after she, her daughter, and her granddaughter of fourteen had been assaulted by Russian soldiers. She and her granddaughter were taken to hospital in a very bad way and she kept telling me how terrible the Russians were. I just listened and most of the time, dropped off to sleep. I could not imagine how I would know when to start walking to the station but luckily she told me that they were also taking the train to Hannover, so I thought I might go together with them. Then I thought I could not again travel standing on the stairs of the train because I felt too ill. She asked me where were my things. "What things?" I asked her. "Your luggage," she said. "Oh, that is in Auschwitz." But she did not know where or what that was. Luckily I had no strength to tell her, so I dropped off to sleep again.

I kept waking up, I could hardly breathe and my throat was hurting terribly. I was shivering and the woman next to me told me I was ill and had fever. I should tell the usher and I could go or be taken to hospital. I said no and that by morning I should be fine and that I had to get back to Hannover.

I kept waking, and merely looking around and seeing only Germans and hearing only German spoken was an absolute nightmare. The lights were very dim, and there were times when I woke up and was not sure if this was a dream or if I was really sitting there with all these Germans. I wanted to go to the toilet but was sure I would not have a place to sit down again so I thought I would wait until the station. I dropped off to sleep and woke when I heard everybody moving. I must have had a high fever because my face was burning; my glands were swollen and I could hardly swallow the saliva which accumulated in my mouth. When I stood up I fell back again. I pulled myself together and willed myself at least not to die here but upstairs, under the sky and decent air. I thought I could not start an argument again about tickets and logs, I just didn't have the strength. I asked my neighbor where were her logs for traveling, but she told me that refugees did not have to bring any and could travel free.

I do not remember how long it took us to reach the train, but I was very lucky because I found a seat and straightaway went off to sleep. I kept waking up and feeling terrible, and remembered that it was Saturday morning and that it was only twenty-four hours since I had left Hannover. It seemed almost a lifetime ago since I had been to the hospital, after which so many things had happened. I realized that I had recovered considerably since I had cried and was even now mourning my family as if I had buried them only yesterday. The train, or rather the wheels of the train, had a new song for me. They went on saying "Sha-bat, Sha-bat" all the time.

I slept some more and then the train stopped and I woke up. A lot of people were getting off and I heard the ticket collector saying "Hannover Station." I stood up and with the greatest difficulty climbed down the steps and onto the platform. My coat was damp but my clothes were nearly dry; it was drizzling again and the raindrops felt good on my burning face. I went to the bus stop and waited for the bus to take me into town.

How I managed to reach camp, I do not know because I had a fair amount of walking to do. I remember passing through streets where there was not a single house standing. I felt I had to sit down and have a rest so I sat down on what was left of a staircase, on two or three stairs, and thought that I was in ruins just like this house and street. I so much wanted to cry again for my father, whom I had lost the day before, and for my family, whom I had lost a year and a half ago, but the tears would not come. I wanted to cry for what had been and would never be again. I thought if this had been five or six years ago, when things were still normal, I should be in bed in my room, the doctor would come to see me and the maid would bring me a cup of hot tea, and my mother would make me fresh chicken soup and sit with me and coax me to drink it. She would also put cold water and alcohol compresses on my forehead and promise to buy me the biggest bunch of bananas for the time when I could swallow again, and there I would be lying, stretching in a warm bed with crisp sheets, knowing that everybody loved me and above all, feeling safe. "*Drágá Anyuká*, dear mummy, why oh why did you single me out to tell and command me to be all right? How can I go on? I get beaten down each time. Please forgive me, but life is too difficult. I do not know if I can go on much longer." By now it was raining rather hard. I do not know how long I sat there but I remember getting up, stumbling, and falling down. Both my knees and hands were bruised and dirty, but with no water to wash, I wiped them on my clothes.

Somehow, I do not know how or how long it took me, I arrived back to my "home" in the camp. The girls were very worried but did not ask any questions — they did not have to since it was written all over my face, or at any rate, part of it. I was put to bed with a cup of hot coffee. I wanted to drink only warm water and could hardly swallow. I had high fever but no one had even an aspirin. What heaven it was to be back amongst people who cared! I was asleep with at least one girl sitting near me, putting cold compresses on my forehead and wiping my face with cold water.

I woke up and there were two girls and the tall Rumanian standing near me. He held a stethoscope in his hand and said the girls had called him because they were worried about me, and although he was a children's doctor he hoped he could help me. He looked at my throat and asked if he could examine me. I said, "No thank you." He suggested I should go to a hospital for treatment as he could only give me aspirin. I tried to laugh but could not. "To a German hospital? Who is the doctor? Dr. Mengele?" But it was obvious that he had no idea who Dr. Mengele was. He said that this was dangerous and that I probably had pneumonia. "You mean I might die here amongst friends, rather than being treated by a German doctor and nurses? I choose my friends and my death," I said.

He tried to be patient and told me I had high fever and that was why I was talking this way. He gave me aspirin, and I started gargling with salt water and slept most of the time. The girls were wonderful. In the morning they said I had been saying something about being put into a rubbish bin and kept repeating it several times. The good doctor came to see me again and told me I was behaving like a spoiled child. He could not understand why I would not go to a hospital. "Good Lord," I thought, "the man has not the first idea."

After thirty-six hours, I started feeling better and had a little soup with bread in it but felt so weak that I could hardly stand on my feet. I had another visit from the doctor, but this time, instead of his stethoscope, he had a book in his hand. He brought a chair over to my bed and said he had brought me a book to read. "What, the poems of Heine?" I asked. He went red in the face and said, "That was not very nice, what you did to me. I went into a shop and asked for Heine's poems. I was told that it was not allowed to read him in Germany. You knew it, didn't you?" I said, "Of course I knew. He left Judaism, but in the eyes of the Germans he was a dirty Jew, like myself."

"Why do you punish yourself?" he asked. "Can't we be friends?" I said, "You have friends, a lot of them, the whole of Germany." He left, and when I woke again there were several people sitting round the table, including some British Jewish soldiers who had heard about the whereabouts of the survivors and had come to visit us.

I started to take an interest in life again and began eating and recovering, but found both the army and football boots too difficult to walk in as I was not yet strong enough for them.

I do not know who, but someone had discovered orchards, or rather small allotments, each with a wooden shed. Each allotment was owned by a different family, who grew vegetables and fruit trees as well. Whenever the British soldiers came to visit us, we all went for a walk to the orchards. We found German women and children cultivating their land, but of course there were very few men.

One particularly beautiful Sunday afternoon, we went to the orchards with two very pleasant British soldiers, who were in exceptionally high spirits because the war would be over in a matter of days. The reason was that the United States had dropped a nuclear bomb on Hiroshima and three days later, on Nagasaki. This was the first time we had heard of these towns in Japan and of this special bomb which, thank Heavens, neither the Germans nor the Japanese possessed. They told us about the enormous damage a bomb like that could do, and we all crowded round the sergeant who was doing his best to explain it to us. He also told us that the Germans thought that it was only American propaganda, and he laughed heartily.

It was time, I thought, to start working and through work, perhaps, manage to get to Palestine. The following day, on Monday morning, I went into Hannover to the military government to see if I could get a job. It was difficult, but I was promised that if there should be a vacancy, they would keep me in mind. No one could advise me about how to get to Palestine. "Patience," they all told me, "and meanwhile get back your strength."

On Wednesday, two days later, I went again in search of a job and met some people, typical wandering survivors, who came from Bergen-Belsen. One of them was originally from Kolozsvar, where two of my married sisters had lived. Both a girl and a boy said they had seen my brother-in-law, Dezso Deitel, whom they knew because they had lived not far from his furniture shop. However much I questioned them, they were certain that it had been he. They added to their description that I should hurry because they had heard that he was going back home to look for his wife, my sister.

Early on Thursday morning, I went off to the railway station again to travel the fifty or sixty kilometers to Bergen-Belsen. This was already August, four months after the liberation of the camp by the British army. There had been wonderful work done by the army and many volunteer doctors and nurses who came from Britain to deal with the terrible conditions of starvation, which had been further complicated by the raging of a dreadful typhus epidemic. That was the place where the enormous numbers of dead had to be buried by tractors in mass graves in order to stop the epidemic.

The original camp had been burnt down, and those who survived were put into a large, I think army camp, with proper facilities. It was the largest and best organized displaced person's camp I had seen. There were many volunteer organizations working in the camp. Amongst them was a cheerful little lady, in the uniform of her organization, smiling and greeting everyone and telling them not to forget to come to the dance in the evening. She was none other than the sister of the commander of the British army, Viscount Montgomery of El-Alamein. I saw her constantly running around trying to pour a little life into people. God bless her!

I finally reached the offices of the camp, after asking people on the way if they knew someone called Deitel from Kolozsvar. Unfortunately there were no signs of his having been there nor did he appear on any of the lists. I should have known better than hoping to find him alive. I sat down on a bench to rest and thought that if I was here, I might as well see if I could at least find any friends.

I found Judith and her two sisters and some other girls, who had stayed behind in Salzwedel rather than come with me to Hannover. They told me that when the British had handed the area over, the Russian army took all the girls from the place where they had been since the liberation, the barracks of the air cadets near the airfield, and put them into another camp with far worse conditions where they had been virtual prisoners, guarded by Russian women soldiers. They were not allowed to leave the camp and could not communicate with their guards. Finally they had had the chance of being transferred to Bergen-Belsen, in the British zone, and were delighted to do so.

We were very glad to see each other and Judith told me about Dori and her sisters, who had gone back to Yugoslavia to their home, hoping to find the rest of the family. The girls urged me to stay with them and even had a free bed in their room, where there were another ten to twelve beds. I told Judith about my trip to Braunschweig, where my father was supposed to have been in hospital. I did not tell her all the horrors which happened afterwards, my sleeping in the shelter with the Germans and being wet through and through.

I warned her of the difficulties they would have in trying to get back to Rakospalota, where they used to live, and told her that the whole of Europe seemed to be on the move from one place to another, without timetables and without ample room for the travelers. She was adamant to go "home."

On Friday morning, I went to the office of Rabbi Baumgarten and Rabbi Wilenski, who came to Bergen-Belsen together with Rabbi Munk at a time when typhus was raging there. These revered rabbis worked unstintingly for the survivors, helping in every way they could. Later, when people started recovering, Rabbi Baumgarten turned to the British authorities, demanding on humanitarian grounds that they open the gates of Palestine to these unfortunate, stateless survivors.

There were, unfortunately, a number of anti-religious, anti-Zionist people from Hungary who wanted to return to their "home country," which they had been thrown out of. They felt that Rabbi Baumgarten was weakening their chances of returning to their "homeland." On Saturday morning, some of them waited for him outside the synagogue and violently assaulted him. It was a shameful thing to have happened and even as I now write about it, I smart with shame for these fellow survivors.

I thought about staying until Monday morning so that I could find out more about Palestine and perhaps get some Hebrew books and a dictionary to start learning the language properly. I most definitely did not like the atmosphere in the camp but knew that it was probably the best place to be for getting to Palestine.

On Sunday, Zsuzsi, Judith's younger sister, took me to collect the breakfast rations for the girls in the room. We went to the central kitchen and brought back the food, which was much better both in quality and quantity than the rations in Hannover. By the time we came back, the girls were awake but still in bed. We handed each girl her breakfast and had our own breakfast in bed as well. As I was eating mine, I had a queer urgent feeling that I must get back to Hannover, the sooner the better. I asked the girls if anyone knew when there was a train to Hannover, and they said, "About ten o'clock." When we collected the breakfast rations from the kitchen I saw that it was already 8:30, so I said to Judith, "Please come with me for a few days at least. If we hurry we can get to the station in time for the Hannover train."

The girls kept telling me not to be silly and that Monday or Tuesday would do as well. I was possessed by a crazy urgency and begged Judith to hurry. I had nothing to carry, nor had Judith. As far as I remember, we had as yet not even a toothbrush, so that made our getting ready and hurrying to the train very simple. (I used to brush my teeth by wetting my index finger, putting salt on it, and rubbing it on my teeth and gums. I found that it cleaned them and I felt better for it, and slowly the painful gums started healing.)

We arrived at the station, both of us winded. The train had not yet come in and no one was sure if and when it would come. On the platform, which was fairly crowded, at least 70 to 80 percent of the people were survivors, while the rest were all sorts of different nationalities and were afraid to go back to their own countries.

After waiting for goodness knows how long, the train puffed its way into the station and there was enough room for everyone to get a seat. The train started off without much energy, like a ninety-year-old trying to drag some heavy things even if it would be the last thing he did. There was no question of tickets or wood, and the ticket collector stood by to keep order, I suppose, just in case. We traveled slowly and jerkily, and after a while the train stopped in the middle of nowhere, with fields on either side of the rails. The ticket collector went from carriage to carriage shouting, "*Alles auschteigen*" (Everyone out).

We asked him where we were and how long we would have to wait until the train would start again. He said the nearest town was Celle, about four kilometers away, and there would not be another train until the following day because of lack of wood. The whole trainload of people started walking along the railway lines toward Celle.

A Fateful Day

udith and I arrived in Celle with another few hundred people, amongst them several "experts," who knew their way around. They told us that there was a camp with some survivors from Hungary, although not many, and that we should ask around.

We asked in the camp for people from Hungary and Transylvania and were directed to a hut where there was a person from my town, Nagyvárad. I knocked on the door and someone with a melodious Hungarian accent told me to come in. We opened the door and there stood a young man from my town, Moshe Friedman. Although we did not know each other well, we were delighted to discover each other; neither of us knew that the other was alive. There was an instant bond between survivors from the same town. His parents had had a butcher's shop at home and Moshe used to work in the shop. He wanted to know how we had found him, and right away suggested that we should eat. Although it was way after lunchtime, he ran off and brought us some very well prepared food.

He, himself, was in charge of the kitchen.

When Moshe came back and was dishing out the food, he said to me that a British captain had been looking for him on Thursday in order to inquire about the Normand and Fuchs families, because he had heard that he was from the same town. He had not been in Celle on Thursday, he told me, but the captain had left a message for Moshe with Rabbi Munk, saying he would return sometime during the week. "Did he leave his name?" I asked. Before he could answer, there was a knock on the door and a tall captain came in, together with a girl in the uniform of the English Jewish Relief Unit. The girl spoke to Moshe and introduced him to the captain, after which she excused herself and left. The captain, in grammatically correct but not fluent German, asked Moshe if he knew of any member of the Normand or the Fuchs families. Moshe pointed to me and said, "Here is one member of the Fuchs family, why not ask her?"

When the captain turned to me with a smile and introduced himself, I was most impressed with him. He wanted to know exactly who I was and what did I know about Lea, to whom he had been engaged. He had heard the same thing as I had, that she had been killed. He asked me to finish my meal but by then I was not hungry, so he asked if I would come out with him to the officers' club where we could talk quietly. I started laughing and said, "Are you sure? Like this?" looking at my enormous Italian army boots and the jacket from the Yugoslav partisans. My blouse was pure silk from a US air force parachute, sewn by hand, and I had a navy skirt which was also handsewn. I do not think that my clothes were a very good fit because I never learned to sew. Our clothes, of course, were also badly creased because we had no irons but that did not worry us. It struck me as very funny that this charming captain was asking me out the way I was dressed, but when I said, "Are you sure?" he answered, "But why not?" as if what I was wearing was the latest fashion in London. I told him they would not let me in like this. Again he said, "But why not?" and I saw he really meant it. He didn't realize that, in any case, civilians were not allowed into the officers' club.

The boys and girls in the room said, "Why don't you want to go with him?" and Judith said, "Can't you see he is embarrassed with all of us listening when he wants to talk to you?" Meanwhile, while we were all talking in Hungarian, he took from the front pocket of his battledress trousers an oblong tin filled with "Senior Service" cigarettes and went round offering them to everyone. When he finished the round, he snapped it shut and put it away. This was the first time that someone offering cigarettes did not urge us to take all of them because he had or could get more. I was rather impressed by his behavior because he treated us as equals and not as unfortunates. I said good-bye, that I should soon be back, and left Judith with the people she had just met.

As we walked out of the room, I saw that there was a car waiting, with an officer and a driver. When we entered the car, I was introduced as Miss Fuchs and the officer as Dr. Gale. Later I heard he was a radiologist, and the two officers were rather friendly as they shared a room at the hospital.

The driver had to ask the way to the officers' club, and Celle being a small town, we soon arrived there. They arranged that the car would be back for us at six o'clock, which was in nearly three hours' time. We were left near the club and the car drove off with Dr. Gale. I felt rather silly and embarrassed to go into an army club dressed as I was and did not want to embarrass the most charming captain either. We approached the club door and on it we found the chart for the opening hours. On Sundays they opened only at five o'clock. I was rather relieved, but the captain thought the most important thing he had to do was to give me a cup of tea.

It was a nice sunny August afternoon and I suggested that we just walk around the town. "No," he said, "I have just thought of something. Why don't we go to the headquarters of the Jewish relief team and scrounge tea from them? I am sure that they will love to give us tea." We walked around a little and I saw that the good captain was not very well orientated. Although he assured me that he knew where the place was because he had been there only an hour ago, it took us some time before we found the Jewish relief unit's headquarters.

We went in and at a desk at the entrance sat a uniformed Jewish girl from England. She said, "Good afternoon, sir, can I help you?" The captain answered, "This is Miss Fuchs, and I was wondering if we could get a cup of tea from you people, as the officers' club only opens at five and I have to get back to Luneburg, the hospital where I am stationed."

We were taken upstairs to a medium-sized room with a large table and chairs around it. At the head of the table sat a very distinguished lady, reading a newspaper. The girl who took us upstairs said, "Lady Henriques, the captain was asking if he could get a cup of tea for himself and his friend." We introduced ourselves and Lady Henriques invited us to sit down, and soon a plate of very thinly cut bread and butter appeared, and a tray with a teapot together with a cosy (it was the first time I ever saw one), and a milk jug, sugar, and teacups. Meanwhile the captain, whose name was Mark, told our hostess that he had just met me by chance at the DP camp, and I happened to be his missing fiancée's first cousin.

I do not know how our conversation turned to music and

the influence of the country on the composer. We were discussing Chopin and if his music was more Polish than French.
I kept insisting that it was more French simply because I could
not bear the idea of a lovely composer like Chopin being a
Pole.

I had had English tea before but not served as it should
be, pouring first the milk and then the tea, and making a social event of it. I almost pinched myself to make myself realize
that I was not dreaming and that the company, the conversation, and the surroundings were real. We finished our tea,
thanked Lady Henriques for her kind hospitality, went downstairs, and started walking. We still had two hours. Mark told
me that he wanted to find out more about Lea, the family, and
myself. We came to a small park and poor Mark had to answer
the salute of every soldier who went past.

His first question was about Lea: what had I heard about
her since the liberation? I told him that, unfortunately, I had
heard the same story from three different sources, that she
had been killed near Studhof. He said he had heard the same
thing and wanted to know how I was related to Lea and who
else was alive from the family. I told him, possibly Lea's
brother, who had been in a Hungarian forced labor group and
not in the camps, and that perhaps a sister of mine might be
alive, although I had not heard from her until now.

Then we spoke about where I was heading, and he had
heard that most people were going back to their homes. I told
him I could not bear to go back and that I knew that apart
from my eldest sister, there could not be anyone alive. As for
claiming back property or belongings, I preferred not to, and
all I wanted was to go to Palestine as soon as possible and start
a new life. "What would you do there?" he asked me. "I would
go into a religious kibbutz and work at anything needed, and

in that way the kibbutz would be my family." He said it sounded like an excellent idea and that he could even tell me about kibbutzim, because in 1941 he had been stationed in Palestine for six weeks and then in Iraq, Syria, and Persia, after which he had been stationed in Palestine again for six months before going up to the Western Desert. He had had wonderful friends in Palestine who had opened their homes to him, first and foremost Chief Rabbi Herzog and his charming wife, who had been wonderful to him after he had been wounded. He had also received marvellous hospitality from the Wolfsberg and Breuer families.

Mark asked me when I would be going, and I told him that as I had no one to worry about me and no one to whom I was responsible, I could go any time the opportunity arose. He said it was a bad idea just to go off without people knowing when I left and where I went. "But," I argued, "what difference does it make? I have no one."

He started to do conjuring tricks. At first I thought he was a little retarded, but he went on and on and finally said, "Please, couldn't you at least smile? I am working so hard to make you laugh."

"Poor man," I thought, "doesn't he know that laughing has to be learned again?"

He asked me what I was doing now, and I told him that I hoped to be getting an interpreter's job in Hannover. He said, "Please, as a special favor for me, could you collect the few things you have from the camp in Hannover and go back with your friend to Bergen-Belsen, where I could be in touch with you?" He told me that, in addition to being an army anaesthetist, he was also in charge of a DP hospital in Luneburg because of his knowledge of German and that they needed an interpreter. "So please," he said, "promise me that by Wednesday you will be back in Bergen-Belsen and on Thursday I shall come to visit you and by that time I hope to arrange a job for you at the Displaced Persons' Hospital."

I promised I would go back to Bergen-Belsen because he assured me that he himself would help me go to Palestine and because one was more likely to hear of groups going there in a large place like Bergen-Belsen.

I asked him what those colored ribbons were on his uniform, and he explained one after the other. I asked him about the first one, which was white, dark lilac, and white. He said it was a Military Cross, which he had received for fighting with his syringe at El-Alamein. I told him that my father had also received an award for bravery as an officer, a gold cross in the First World War. Then he explained that the other ribbons were for other fronts he had been in but I could see that he was most proud of two of them: the Military Cross and another of the Eighth Army.

He kept making me promise that I would go back to Bergen-Belsen because in a crazy country like Germany it was very hard to find people if one did not know where they were. He said again that on Thursday he would come and see me and hoped that by that time he would have the job arranged for me. I promised to come back to Bergen-Belsen. He offered me his cigarettes and after I had taken one, he lit it for me and put the rest back into his pocket. I was most impressed.

He asked, "Tell me, have you anything to read?"

I thought he had asked if I had enough to eat and snapped at him, "Of course I have enough to eat."

"But of course you have! No, I was asking you about reading." I gave him a watery smile and he said, "Well. At last! That's better."

It was time to walk back to the officers' club. Somehow,

although I didn't know why, the world looked a nicer place. The trees were greener, the sky was bluer, and even my Italian boots were not so heavy anymore. The car was already waiting near the corner of the club; we got in and the car took me back to the camp. Mark stepped out of the car and I said good-bye to Dr. Gale and thank you to Mark, but he said, "On the contrary, I am so delighted that we met and could spend the afternoon together. Thank you so much." He reminded me again that he would come and see me on Thursday afternoon. Unfortunately, he could not get away before. I stood there and watched the car pull away, turned round, and, with a small song in my heart, knocked on the door and entered the room where I had met Mark only a few hours ago.

Judith was the first person I saw. She came up to me and said, "You will marry him. I have never seen two people made for each other as you two are."

"Don't be silly," I said. "Judith, do you realize that he treated me as if I had walked out of my parents' home and was returning me to it? He needs an interpreter at the DP hospital in Luneburg and made me promise to return with you to your place, since today in Germany it is so difficult to find people without a proper address."

Judith asked, "What did you say?"

"I promised him to go back with you. He also told me to go back later to the house of the Jewish Relief Unit, where they have a club and get-togethers for survivors, and to look for Rabbi Munk, whom he knows from England, to give him his regards and say how sorry he was to have missed him." Rabbi Munk had come out with the Relief Unit and worked day and night to help and ease the lives of the survivors.

We told Moshe Friedman that we would walk over to the survivors' club and would come back later to sleep. He was very nice to us and told us that our supper would be waiting for us on the table and showed us which beds we could have. Judith and I walked down to the Jewish Relief Unit, where they had arranged a club room with music, dancing, or just meeting one another, and had even tried to arrange lectures and lessons in Hebrew — but unless it was something extremely interesting and short, it was too much effort to concentrate. At first, when I could not remember my address at home or my sister's married name or her address, I was sure that I had permanent brain damage, either from the beatings or from the starvation or both. To read or concentrate on something for more than a short time was very difficult.

There was a lot of noise at the club and the relief people encouraged us to talk and dance in order to help people return to life rather than mere existence. In the midst of that hubbub, I found Rabbi Munk talking to the people. I went up to the rabbi, introduced myself, and gave him Mark's message. He asked me where I was staying and what were my plans. When he heard that I wanted to go to Palestine, he said, "It might take some time but we are working on it."

We spoke to several people but neither Judith nor I knew anyone there. Toward evening, we went back to the camp. It had certainly been a fateful day, never to be forgotten, a day packed full of so many things that had tired and yet excited me so that sleep would not come. Judith and I spoke for some time until we finally dropped off to sleep.

In the morning we rose early, had something to eat, thanked our host, and went off to the station, hoping that this time we might even reach Hannover. There was a long wait but finally the train came. There were many survivors traveling and there was no question of tickets or logs either. We arrived at Hannover and somehow the town looked more pleasant and the ruins more picturesque than before. We watched how three generations of women, with a grandfather here and there, were clearing away the ruins of their homes, stacking the bricks. Where there was even a square meter of earth, they would plant it with beans, rhubarb, or any other vegetable.

Another phenomenon, seen in Germany after the war, was the sight of young men on crutches without artificial legs, or sometimes a man without an arm and with no artificial arm. By August the streets started filling up with one-armed and one-legged people.

We arrived at my camp in Hannover and I introduced Judith to the people. I also told them that I had met the fiancé of my cousin and that I should be going back to Bergen-Belsen with Judith.

Amongst the men in the camp was a jeweler, who must have been about twenty-seven or twenty-eight years old. This jeweller was afraid that he had forgotten his craft because his fingers were frozen and swollen. In order to regain his skills, he began to make rings and discs with people's names and prisoners' numbers engraved on them, finding pieces of tin, aluminum pipes, or anything else he could use as material. When he heard I was leaving, he hurried and made me a disc and a very stylish signet ring engraved with my number. The disc was just a small round thing with my number on it, and I wore it round my neck hanging from some cotton thread.

It seems incredible to me now but I wore that disc for at least two years inside my clothes in order not to forget my family, my people, and the suffering. I also wore the signet ring but for less time. I did not realize then what I know now, that what we have gone through has become part of us. I feel that the suffering has made me into a better human being and I learned to love my people with desperation. It is not that I do not see our faults, but they hurt me and make me feel responsible to do something about them and improve things.

The following day I went into Hannover together with Judith, and there was great excitement going on at the DP offices. There was a man in torn old clothes who came into the office to take out a DP card. He looked too well fed and did not have that terrible haunted look of the survivor. There were several boys present and they started chatting with him, asking about the camps he had been in and the people who had been with him. His answers were suspicious and so they undressed him and found, under his armpit, his tattooed SS number still in place. Many of these people had had their numbers surgically removed and were caught in the hospital. If they were suspected or arrested, the authorities always looked for a scar or number under the armpit.

Judith looked at the Red Cross lists all the time, as we all did. We talked that evening at length with all the survivors present and I told them that, in my opinion, one should try to go either to a larger camp or else to places where the survivors were better organized and were getting much more outside professional help from Jewish institutions. There were people living in Hannover itself, in apartments. Where they received their rations I do not know. There were survivors who originally came from Hannover, who even recovered their businesses.

There was one street where the damage was not so great, and as I walked through it I saw a blue and white flag made of paper in a shop window, and a notice: "Aryans not wanted and not served in this shop." It was a leather shop, belonging to a Jewish family. One of their sons survived and he claimed and got the shop back. There was not a lot of merchandise left for him to sell, but he was better dressed than the rest of us.

We all went into the shop, delighted, and congratulated him. There were always many survivors around the shop and near the DP office, but no one knew where they were staying or if they were just wandering types.

In the morning I started packing my belongings, which consisted of two thin blankets, a shirt, underwear, a Yugoslav army jacket, one pair of football boots, and my horrible brown coat, which I had been given in Salzwedel by a girl who had taken two coats from a shop and given me one. I had nothing in which to carry them so I simply rolled them up in one of the blankets. Someone brought me a piece of string and I tied it up. Judith and I said good-bye and au revoir and left for the railway station to travel to Bergen-Belsen. The screaming and demands for tickets which I had suffered the first time I traveled did not recur. I suppose that traveling to Bergen-Belsen was a legitimate thing, even in the eyes of the Germans.

When I had said good-bye to the people at the camp, I did not realize that I should be meeting most of them on my later visits to Bergen-Belsen. After they felt that they needed a far better organized place in order to be able to make plans for the future, most of them simply moved over to Bergen, while some of the others went to other places.

The day after we arrived back in Bergen-Belsen, Mark was supposed to come in the afternoon. I was looking forward to it but tried, without much success, to dampen my enthusiasm for his visit, telling myself that perhaps he would not come at all. Perhaps he had forgotten his promise to look for work for me, or perhaps he had other things on his mind. Earlier than I expected, there was a knock on the door of the room which I shared with twelve other girls. Instead of Mark, there entered a tall, slightly built, bespectacled , middle-aged man with a large hooked nose, who introduced himself as Dr. Kutz. He told me that Captain Chayen could not get away and had asked him to bring me this book and letter, with his apologies for not coming. I thanked him warmly and he left. I did not know what to make of Dr. Kuc, whose official story was that he had been a political prisoner in Auschwitz and other camps, and that he was not Jewish. He looked better and was far better dressed than any of the survivors.

I took the book and letter and went to the window, where the sun was shining into the room, and opened his letter. He wrote, "Dear Lea, I was so disappointed that I could not get away today as I promised you. I was so much looking forward to meeting you again. If you can still put up with me, I should like to come on Sunday and we could go out and have a picnic at a nice spot." He also mentioned that he hoped to have my job fixed up by Sunday. I cannot remember if Dr. Kutz came back for my reply or whether Mark was sure that I would not say no to the picnic.

I took the book and on the flyleaf I saw Mark's signature for the first time: M.S. Chayen. I did not know what the S stood for. I looked again at the book, which was from a book club, and its title was "Being Met Together." I looked out of the window, smiled, and thought, "Mark is either an idiot who does not understand that I need good food, soap, a toothbrush, and hundreds of other things, or he treats me as he would have treated me if I were still in my parents' house. I wanted to believe and really did believe that he was such a highly civilized person that he could not possibly send me anything except a book.

I opened the book. Inside was written again, "Being Met Together — by Vaughan Wilkins." Underneath the name of the author was written the oath of allegiance of George Washington in 1778, and underneath that was the following: "The

President of the United States and the Prime Minister, Mr. Churchill, representing His Majesty's Government in the United Kingdom, being met together, deem it right to make known certain common principles in the national policies of their respective countries in which they base their hopes for a better future for the world." The Atlantic Charter 1941. I read it and was moved to tears to realize that not the whole world was barbarian.

I tried to read the book. I read the first page again and again, but it was far too difficult to concentrate. To be honest, I was very worried about my lack of concentration but tried hard not to deal with it at this stage. "What if Mark asks how I enjoyed the book," I thought. I decided to tell him about my lack of concentration and even about not being able to speak for a few hours after being liberated and not remembering my address at home or the names of people. The addresses and names of people came back slowly, but the lack of concentration and my not remembering good times at home persisted.

During those few days in Bergen-Belsen, I met several people from my hometown, most of them waiting to go home. There were already rumors of so-called illegal immigration to Palestine but there was yet nothing organized. Judith still had that grayish complection and her favorite pastime was being cooped up in bed.

Sunday arrived and I wished I had something to prepare for the picnic, but there was nothing. Mark arrived in the early afternoon and suggested that we drive out to somewhere pleasant. He asked his driver, a German prisoner of war, if there was a good place to go for a picnic and he took us to the Luneburger Heide, the Luneburg Heath, which was almost back at the place they had started from. It was a very pleasant spot but on principle I did not want to enjoy anything German. The Heath was covered in heather; we stopped in the middle of it and sat down and had our picnic.

He apologized about not having been able to come on the previous Thursday, and had therefore asked Dr. Kutz to take the book and letter to me and had sent him off with his car and his driver. He asked me how I liked the book, and I told him of my problem of lack of concentration and not remembering names of my family, but added that things were slowly getting better. He said not to worry, that it was a normal thing.

He told me that he had wonderful news, that there was a job waiting for me but that he would have to get a room requisitioned for me through the Town Major. At any rate, until that was ready I could sleep for a few nights on a collapsible bed in one of his offices at the DP hospital. He was very keen for me to come to Luneburg because, as he put it, "People get lost so easily in Europe today and it is so difficult to find them afterwards." When we drove back toward Bergen-Belsen he made me promise again that even if I decided to go back to Hungary or to try to go with an "illegal" group to Palestine, I would let him know and talk to him first. I promised and told him that more people from my town had arrived and perhaps they might know more about my cousin.

When we arrived back to the camp, I took Mark to meet some girls from my town. The oldest one present, probably thirty-five years old, was Zissy, who had lost her husband and only son. *She later married my cousin and became a wonderful mother to his two teenage boys.* I think there was another young woman called Trude, and last but not least, Edith Robitsek. *She later married another cousin of mine.* I think there were some other girls but I cannot remember them. We did not stay long because Mark had to return to his hospital.

He told me that there was no camp near Luneburg but

there were sixty to eighty survivors who lived in rooms in town and a most devoted man, called Goldstoff, who originally came from Kraków, who was trying to build up a community and a communal kosher kitchen, which was like a restaurant and club at the same time. This was the place where the survivors met and had one hot meal a day, the rations being brought over from Bergen-Belsen. Mark said there were some very nice people among the survivors in Luneburg and of course he met many of them at the DP hospital. He said he would be coming back for me on Tuesday and could I please be ready as he would be able to get off for only about three hours altogether.

On Tuesday morning, I rolled up my few belongings in one of my blankets, tied it up with string, said good-bye to the girls, and, with a heavy heart, left Judith behind.

Luneburg

Mark arrived, said hello and good-bye to Judith, and we set off for Luneburg, with the German driver driving. Mark said that Germany was not for any decent person to stay in and that, if I was agreeable, he would very much like to get me to England. He was sure that both his brother and sister-in-law would be delighted to have me. His sister-in-law's parents were the people who had brought out and employed Bertl, who had been my governess and later the governess of my cousin at home. I said that I would like to go from Germany to Palestine, but he argued that it should be easier to arrange from England. I did not at all like the idea of going to people and being a millstone round their necks, but Mark urged me to let him apply for permission to go to England and if that came through and I did not want to go, I would not have to. He also told me that he had not had the time to arrange a room for me and so, for another two or three days, I might have to sleep in one of his offices, which was used by his corporal, Greg, during the day only.

When we arrived at the DP hospital, which had been set up in the building of a high school, Mittelschule, Mark took me to the office, where there was already a folding bed in a corner, and introduced me to Corporal Greg, who came from Glasgow and had retained a really thick Glaswegian accent. There were also another two soldiers whose duty was to collect rations for the hospital from the Town Major's office.

The following morning I rose early, folded up my bed and put it in a corner, and started going round to find out with whom I was to work. First I met Dr. Kuc, who was the head of the hospital, then I met the matron, Schwester Elizabeth, a most charming lady, who was a trained nurse and had worked in the Jewish Hospital in Berlin. She could not have been very young because she had a grown-up daughter who had also survived with her. There was a Dr. Friedlander, also from Berlin, who had also worked in the Jewish Hospital in Berlin and was a skin specialist.

Then there was an Estonian, an overdressed and overfed surgeon, and he had a Lithuanian assistant and many Estonian nurses, who were beautiful but nasty. Besides Dr. Kuc, I cannot remember any Polish doctors amongst the motley crew who made up the staff of the hospital.

There was also an overly elegant and overly smooth smarmy Hungarian doctor who was in Luneburg with his overly elegant wife and daughter of seventeen. These were paid volunteers, who had come to Germany to assist the Germans, either from ideology or for the good money they earned, or maybe for both. The Hungarian doctor welcomed me as a brother would a sister far from home, until I asked him why, now that the war was over, was he not going back. I knew the answer and he knew that I knew it. And this put an end to his friendliness.

There were also two nurses from Holland, who were terrified of going home as they would have been questioned and sent to jail.

There was also a pharmacist, a Holocaust survivor, called Kaufman, from Warsaw. He was always very polite and perfectly behaved, and although he must have gone through several years of hell, he never talked about it.

Amongst the patients there were many survivors, some from Hungary. It was Schwester Elizabeth who took me round to see the survivors. These were people who were beyond help, either mentally or physically. It was not pleasant that most of the time I was dealing with collaborators, who did not know any English and were in the most lucrative jobs, namely working in the kitchen. The kitchens were in the cellars and so were the storerooms. By the time the food reached the first or second floor, the patients received a minimum to eat. Schwester Elizabeth complained and said that this was no sort of nourishment for tuberculous patients and other undernourished people.

The first evening after we arrived, Mark had to hurry back to his hospital, which was the 74th British General Hospital, an army hospital. The following day, he had no time to come to the DP hospital and, in fact, did not come every day but only when he managed to get a few hours free. In the evening he rang me at the hospital and asked me if I was listening to the concert on the radio and told me what station it was on. I thanked him and we chatted a little. Later on he called me again and wanted to know if I had enjoyed the concert. I told him that in the whole hospital I had been unable to find a single radio.

The following day, Mark went to the Town Major and arranged a room for me. It was in a pleasant neighborhood and was a large, airy, nicely furnished sitting room, with a sofa bed, a few comfortable chairs, one very large armchair, and a largeish round table. The table and chairs were in a bay window and there was another large window as well. The room itself was the first door as one entered the apartment.

The name of the owners was Hosang. The woman was not too bad as far as Germans go. They had no children and he was out of work. He had been an important official in the town but apparently now the job was obsolete. She was most obliging and would have been willing to do anything. Luneburg and the whole area had been an absolute black spot and a hotbed of Nazis, and that is probably why Mr. Hosang hardly ever moved out of his room. Mrs. Hosang told me that he had been questioned and she was willing to offer him up to anyone willing to take him away.

Mark used to come and see me even if it was only for an hour and we would go for walks in a lovely park nearby, which was on a little hillock with a lot of trees. During the month of August, in the evenings, children would walk about with lanterns and sing special songs. It could have looked pretty but how could I enjoy children singing when I knew that all our children were ashes thrown into the River Vistula, put in a heap in Maidanek, or just scattered in Belsec, Sobibor, Auschwitz, and Birkenau? That is why I could not bear to see them enjoying life as if nothing had happened.

Mark told me that, after four and a half years of service, he would be going back to England for twenty-eight days of home leave. I started panicking and was sure that I should never see him again. Two nights later he came to me with a small bundle and asked if I could do him a great favor as he had nowhere to leave a few books and his small radio. Would I be kind enough to look after them for him until he came back?

I realized that he wanted me to use the radio, which was a small Philips set that he had bought from the factory itself in Eindhoven, Holland, after the liberation.

I told Mark that I should be very happy to use the radio as long as it was understood that as soon as he returned I would give it back to him. We spent a lovely evening walking around. When it was time for him to go, I could not believe that I was going to lose someone again. He asked me to write to him regularly and gave me his parents' and brother's addresses, and he requested that under no circumstances should I leave for Palestine or any other place before contacting him. I wished him a happy new year, as he was going to reach home the day before Rosh HaShanah and would be staying at home for Yom Kippur and Sukkot as well. He promised to write to me and asked me again if I would write or at least answer his letters. He said that I could ask any of the soldiers or officers working at the hospital to send the letter for me, since there was no other way: all letters were sent "On Active Service."

The time came to really say good-bye. After he left, I went completely to pieces. Here was someone I loved so dearly and because of that, who knew what would happen to him? I started running down the stairs and into the empty street, just to have a last look by which I could remember him. I could not see him as he must have walked very fast. I felt desperate and blamed myself for all the terrible things that would happen to him. I should have warned him about the curse that was on me.

I kept running round the room until I was exhausted and then I lay down, fully dressed, on my sofa bed. I must have had a fairly terrible nightmare with crying and shouting because I was woken by Mrs. Hosang, my landlady, who knocked hard on my door and asked if I was all right. I said that I was not and never would be.

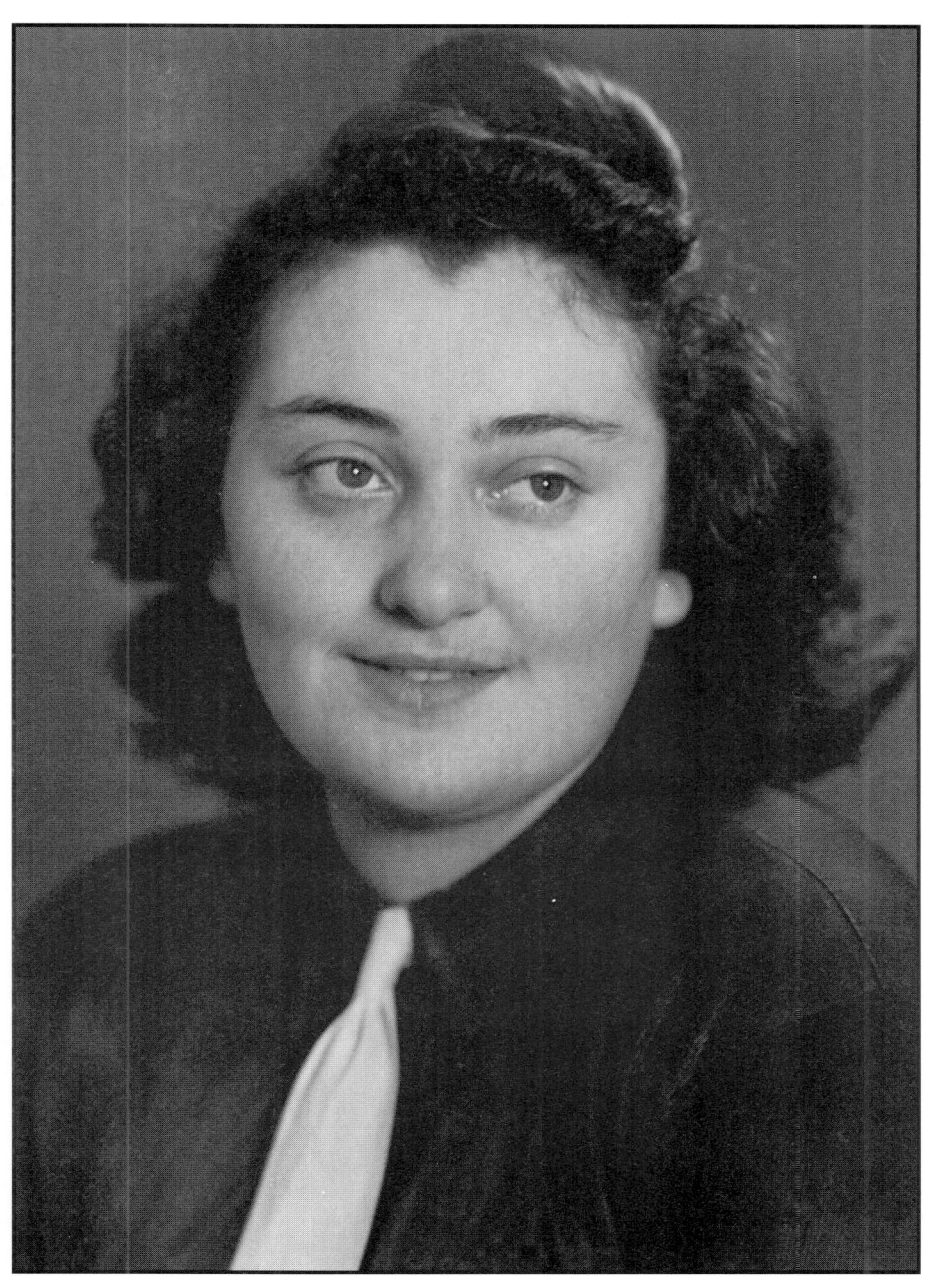

Me in Luneburg, 1946.

A drawing of myself by a British soldier, April 25, 1946 .

Captain M.S. Chayen, M.C., 1944.

Mr. Jehoshua Goldstoff, z"l, the head of the community in Luneburg.

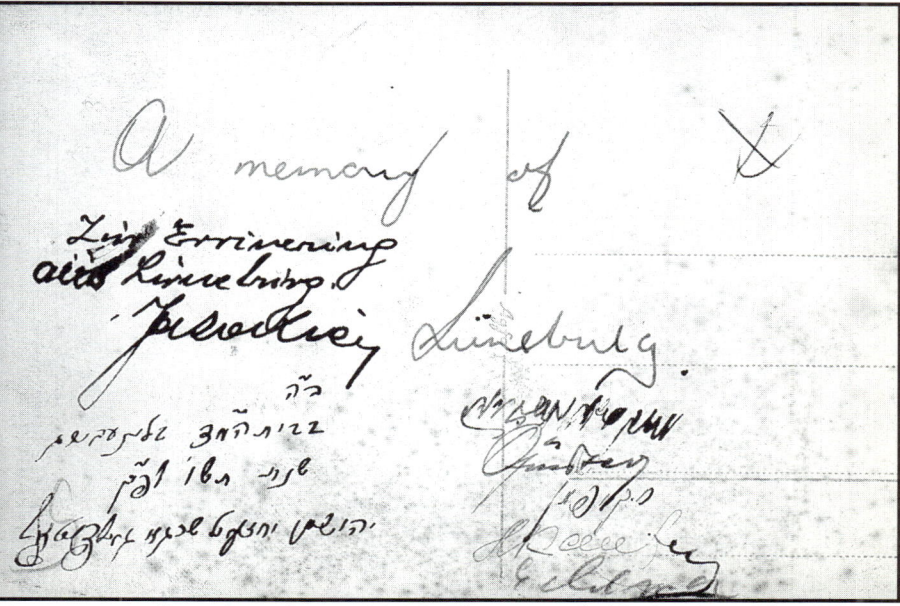

A momento from Luneburg, 1946. The second side is signed by fellow survivors.

"THE REGISTRATION OF BIRTHS, DEATHS AND MARRIAGES (ARMY) ACT, 1879" (42 Vict c. 8, Sec 2) and the "AIR FORCE (APPLICATION Army) In Lieu
OF ENACTMENTS (No. 2) ORDER 1918." Triplicate. of 4.42a.

Form to be used for notifying a Marriage for Registration in Army } Book 113 (Register of Marriages).

NOTE: This form is for use in accordance with paragraph 1741(c) of the King's Regulations, 1940, and paragraph 2369(3) of the King's Regulations (Royal Air Force) 1943, and must NOT be used for any other purpose or forwarded to the Registrar-General.

TO:— The Officer in Charge of the Register of Marriages (Army Air Force) Book 113) of the ....BRITISH ARMY.OF.THE.RHINE.

maintained at ....GHQ, 2nd ECHELON, BRITISH ARMY OF THE RHINE.

I, ...Aubrey FURNEAUX, Lieut-Colonel.
Here insert Name and Rank.

at ....LUNEBURG. GERMANY.........., and request that you will Register the same forthwith in the Register of Marriages (Army Air Force) Book 113)
maintained by you in accordance with the current Army and Air Force Orders and King's Regulations governing the Registration of Births, Marriages
and Deaths among Officers, Soldiers and Airmen and their families of H.M. Army and Air Force serving out of Great Britain and Northern Ireland.

Signature of Officer notifying } (A.Burnett), Lt.Col, A.DAG,
Marriage for Registration } 30 Corps District,
(Provident Officer).

Date ......7. Nov. 1946......

PARTICULARS OF MARRIAGE TO BE REGISTERED.

Date and Place of Marriage.	Name, Surname and Nationality.	Age.	Condition.	Rank or Profession.	Residence at the time of Marriage.	Father's name and Surname.	Rank or profession of Father.
May 19.46. at Luneburg, GERMANY.	Markham Sydney CHAYEN, English	30	Bachelor	No.169657 Captain R.A.C.	Active Service Abroad B.A.O.R	Samuel CHAYEN	Draper
	Lee Cirus FUCHS, Rumanian	22	Spinster	OF NO OCCUPATION	D.P. Hospital, Luneburg, Germany.	Salmon FUCHS	DECEASED, FORMERLY Merchant

This Marriage was solemnized in the Presence of us } (A. Burnett), Lt.Col, A.DAG, HQ, 30 Corps District. (Provident Officer).

Signature of Officer registering the Marriage......

Our Army Marriage Certificate.

PROFORMA IN ACCORDANCE WITH BRITISH ARMY OF THE RHINE
GENERAL ROUTINE ORDER 20??/45, para 3 (a)

(i)   I, LEA ~~CORN~~ CHAYEN........ (full names)

hereby declare that I will be able to reside at 14 LANCASTER -
GARDENS SOUTHEND-ON-SEA (full address)

on arrival in United King..... that I understand that on

entering UK I shall be s...... o the laws of the UK and

will only be able to leave it in accordance with current

regulations regarding civilian travel.

Signed L.a. Chayen...... Date MAY 9th 1946.

Wife of (No) 169657...... (Rank) CAPTAIN

(Name) M.S. CHAYEN..... (Unit) 106 MED COY

(ii)   authority is granted for Mrs. CHAYEN.
...... wife of

(No) 169657........ (Rank) Capt.

(Unit) CHAYEN (106) 106 Med Coy

to be m..............

........emergency passport .... t of an

emergency passport Mrs CHAYEN ...... should present

herself to R.T.O. LÜNEBURG ..... when movement

will be arranged on production of this authority and her

emergency passport.

Signed ...Bassst. RAMC   Date 9 May 1946.

for Lieut General
Comnd 30 Corps Dist.

Movement order of the British army of the Rhine, May 9, 1946.

In lieu of A.F.W 5133

Number ..... N/A .... Rank .... N/A ....

Name & Initials .... Chayen ....

Regiment or Corps (If N. state Branch).... Wife of Soldier

Authority for return .... 30 Cap In

Date of arrival overseas (present tour) ....

Reporting instructions on disemb. ....ing (if known by despatching unit if individual proceeding by air, date of emplaning if known, to be shown)
....
....
....

Signature of Individual ..... L. Chayen ....

Official Office Stamp
of despatching Unit

                                     Signature .... R.G. O'Canny ....
                                       Despatching Officer
                                       .... Sub A.T.S. ......

Date ... 23 May 46   Rank and Appointment
                                       Unit
                                         ....

FOR COMPLETION BY MOVEMENT CONTROL
AT PORT OF DISEMBARKATION

Date of Disembarkation ....

Individual will proceed direct to (state Unit) Hospital for period of leave
                                    granted)
....
....

Leave Address, ...
....

Certificate of movement control to Dover, May 23, 1946.

Since I had had the room at Mrs. Hosang's I had become civilized because there was a clock in my room. The clock now said four o'clock in the morning and I was still fully dressed. I took off my clothes, put on my brown coat, and walked up half a flight of stairs to the bathroom, which had a sitz bath but no shower. I used to clean it each time and fill it with enough water in which to be able to wash. During the eight and a half months that I stayed there, not once did I have hot or even warm water in the bathroom. When I felt cold in the winter, when the water in the glass would freeze in my room, I had to get tough with myself, fill the bath, sit in it, and wash. I felt warmer for it — maybe not warmer but certainly tougher — and did not feel sorry for myself.

I kept thinking of Mark and where he would be. It took two or more days to travel back by train and boat; I think that, in those days, flying was reserved for only the highest ranking officers.

It was our first Rosh HaShanah after the camps, the first Rosh HaShanah without family, and there was not a single person in the community whom I had known for more than ten days. I do not know how many Jews had lived in Luneburg before the war but there was a pleasant community house there which had become a pub and a kind of disco. Mr. Goldstoff reclaimed it in time to organize a synagogue in the largest room. There was a Torah scroll together with all the necessary prayer books, prayer shawls, and tefillin for those who wanted to pray with them.

During the High Holidays, we still ate in the community center — kosher food of course — where we had arranged a dining room near the kitchen. A little later, we took over a restaurant in the middle of the town in one of the better streets, and cooked our food with special rations we received from the British army, distributed in Bergen-Belsen. We found old prayer books under a pile of rubbish in the basement. I found a prayer book over a hundred years old and still in its original leather binding. *I am still using that prayer book today although, after a hundred and sixty years, its pages are rather frail. If only that prayer book could talk, we should hear many interesting things.*

All of us made an effort to put on our "best clothes." By Rosh HaShanah, one of my friends had given me an old pair of white tennis shoes and a pair of boots, several sizes smaller than those I already had. Of course there were people who were much better dressed, but somehow it did not worry me. I felt independent and not indebted to anyone. I was a free person.

There were a few Jewish servicemen stationed in Luneburg, who came and took part in the services and even stayed on to eat, to show complete identification with us. There were several regulars and one of them, an air force officer called Ansel, was very friendly and I wondered if he came in order to cheer us up or just because he enjoyed our company.

I thought a lot about Mark and wondered if he remembered me at all in his happiness at meeting his parents and his four brothers. He had told me that his younger brother, who was serving in the Middle East, would also be home on leave.

There were only a few people who believed that he had gone back to England for leave, but the others thought it was typical of the officer getting tired of his girl and leaving her.

In the evenings I started listening to the radio. I realized that I had to get used to concentrating again. I turned one corner of my room into a retreat. I took a largish box, which I turned upside down and covered with a piece of floral material. I put the books next to it and, in an ordinary jar, I made a Japanese Ikebana flower arrangement, mainly from twisted branches and a few leaves. Somehow that little corner was the place where I tried to start my new life. At first I listened to music, and after that, started reading and trying to concentrate. Very slowly, I started to remember what I read, and I also had my prayer book, so that I could pray not from memory but by reading the prayers. I asked Mr. Josef Stern to try to get me a Hebrew grammar book and some short stories. He was a fine gentleman who came from Budapest originally and worked with Mr. Goldstoff.

Mrs. Hosang was paid for my room by the Town Major and I received a separate salary. It was not a lot but there was almost nothing on which to spend it because there was nothing to buy.

There were few survivors passing through Luneburg because it was off the beaten track. One evening I walked into the restaurant and was told that there was someone in Luneburg from my hometown and that he would soon be coming back. No one remembered his name, but in the middle of supper the boy came back and we were both very glad to see each other.

I asked him where he was staying — I thought he had asked Goldstoff for accommodation — but he simply answered, "With you."

"Not with me," I said, "I have only one room." He assured me that that would be enough for us.

I was horrified that a boy who knew me still from home could suggest such a thing. Unfortunately, such was the atmosphere at the time. I told him he must be crazy, but he could not see anything wrong in it. But eventually he said something nice, which I really appreciated. He said, "You have not progressed with the times. You have stayed the same as you were at home." He did not mean it as a compliment, but I thanked him very much for saying such nice things about me.

At that time there was a lovely young girl, a survivor, who gave birth to a baby at the hospital. Who the father was, I did not know, nor did it matter because she left the baby behind in the hospital. Poor thing. What had the Germans done to us? How would we ever become normal people again?

Two weeks after Mark left, I received a letter from him complaining that he had not heard from me and hoping that all was well. He described his meeting with his family. The letter came addressed to Corporal Greg, in a double envelope, and he brought it to me, smiling. "There you are, lass, here is something to read." I read and reread it until I knew it word for word by heart. I was nevertheless worried that something would happen to him because of the curse I had on me. I wrote a short letter but had nothing much to write about. A week later I received another letter saying that he hoped to see me soon because his leave was drawing to its close.

One morning I went to work at the hospital and one of the Polish workers said that a boy had come the previous evening looking for me. He said he was a cousin of mine, and as he had nowhere to sleep he had slept in the basement, but where exactly he did not know. About an hour after hearing about my cousin's arrival and looking for him in vain, he came into the office. It was a ghost entering, a broken, middle-aged man, tired, unkempt, dirty, with rumpled clothes and a gray complection. He was only six weeks my senior — but perhaps I looked like that too. This was Lea's brother, Aron Normand. He had heard that I was in Luneburg and had traveled a long way to see me. He also wanted to go to Palestine to-

gether with friends from our town, who had gone to
Bergen-Belsen to meet their sister.

Ari looked dreadful. He had been in forced labor camps
with the Hungarian army, but the fact that no one of his family had survived shattered him completely. I went back to the
office and Miss Stevens, for whom I was interpreting, told me
straightaway to take the day off. "Probably you have a lot to
talk about after all this time that you have not seen each
other," she said. She was an extremely likeable and kindhearted person, a trained nurse who had come out to Germany with the Friends Ambulance Unit to help where she
could. I think that of all the volunteers, she was the only one
who had the training and understanding for running a hospital.

I took my cousin back to my room and arranged with my
landlady, against payment, that I should be able to sleep in another room. He had not eaten for nearly twenty-four hours,
but he was so tired that first he went to sleep, and I set off
quickly to the community offices to talk to Mr. Goldstoff
about getting things for him. Then I went to the community
kitchen and got him some food and something like coffee to
make him a hot drink. By the time I came back with the food
and a clean shirt for him, he had nearly three hours of sleep. I
woke him to eat and almost choked on my tears to see how
hungry he was, that carefully brought up, spoiled boy.

We started talking and he was the first person to tell me
that my eldest sister was alive, as were two of my brothers-in-law. He said my sister was still expecting her husband
and children to appear one day, that she knew I was alive and
was waiting for me to come home. He told me the difficulties
he and his friends had suffered on their travels to Germany.
They were intending to go on to either Italy or Belgium, from

whence they could get to Palestine. About his sister Lea, he had heard the same as I had and was very broken up about it. He was not sure how he would manage to carry on or for what reason to do so, as life was so very difficult and there seemed hardly any point to it. He wanted me to come to Palestine with them, but I told him that I was waiting for a more definite route to Palestine. I told him that Mark had been looking for our families, that I had met him and that was how I came to be in Luneburg. I asked him why he had not written to Mark. He was in a dreadful state of inertia and I felt that one had to push him to start living again.

In the afternoon we went to our communal kitchen-restaurant, where of course no one paid. I introduced him to the people there, we had our meal, and then we went back to catch up on what had happened to us during the last year and a half. Aron stayed another day and then I asked for two days off so that, with Saturday and Sunday, I had four days to go with him to Bergen-Belsen. Aron had brought me a watch, with which I was delighted. He asked me how it was that other people had almost normal clothes while I looked as if I was wearing clothes that had been left behind by others. I told him that I did not mind, that a great deal of clothing was being handed out by various organizations but that I was not willing to accept things like a beggar. He said that the world had changed, standards had changed, and that I was swimming against the current.

I spent a few days with Ari and his friends: Nashu Schwalb, whom I had known only by sight, his brother Mendu, whom I did know, and their sister Zipporah, with whom I had been friendly and who had also been a friend of Lea. They were all going on to Belgium, from where the Jewish Brigade smuggled people out of Europe with false papers and then into Palestine. As it turned out, they stayed in Belgium for well over a year.

I went back to Luneburg, to my work and my loneliness, trying to fight against depression. I spent the evening at the community center, but the nights were too long and often I woke up with my pillow wet, not knowing what I had dreamt but just waking up depressed. A wash down in cold water, getting dressed, saying my prayers, and hurrying off to work did wonders for my mood. I had to prove to myself that I could and must go on doing the normal things of life.

One evening, after returning from supper at the center, it was raining and I was wearing my brown coat and tennis shoes, which had become rather wet. I was just taking off my soaking shoes and shaking out my coat, spreading it out to dry, when I heard the doorbell and Mrs. Hosang opening the door. I heard her saying, *"Guten Abend, Herr Kapitan."* I stopped breathing and did not believe it. After a knock on my door, there stood Mark, in his wet trenchcoat, larger than life itself. I could not believe that this could happen to me, that I was actually seeing him again. He also seemed very pleased to see me and immediately noticed how wet my feet and clothes were. He said, "Look, dear, luckily I have brought you a decent pair of shoes and some clothes. I hope you will like them and use them." He took out a pair of sturdy black shoes, a warm navy skirt, a white sweater, and a pale blue one. I thanked him and tried on the shoes, which fit, and was so happy to receive them from him. He said, "Look, my dear, I went out with Mama to buy these things and she said that what you needed at the moment were warm clothes rather than fancy ones."

I was sure Mark was hungry but I had nothing to give him to eat, and I apologized that I could not even make him a warm drink. The room was very cold, there was no heating at all. It was the beginning of October, but I knew that there would be no heating in December or January either. Mark said he did not feel the cold and did not want to eat because he was feeling rather sick after the channel crossing and traveling by train for another fourteen hours to Luneburg, reporting at the hospital, and coming straight to me. At about eleven o'clock he stood up and said that it was sad but he had to go and that he hoped, if not the following evening, then the evening after he would come and see me. He thought it a shame that we could not even talk to each other on the telephone. Before he left, I told him about Lea's brother's visit but that meanwhile they had left for Belgium.

Mark said it was not very nice of me to have written to him only once and then only a few cold lines, but he hoped I was as pleased to see him as he was to see me. He left and I unpacked all those lovely new, warm, and normal clothes and arranged them in the sideboard, where I kept whatever clothes I had. Life seemed to be much more pleasant again, but like a crazy person I was still afraid for him because of the curse I was convinced I had on me.

The following morning it was still raining. I put on my new warm things, my proper shoes, and my wet brown coat and went to the hospital. The nice people there wanted to know if Mark had come back and had brought me all those lovely things, while there were others there who just looked at me and sniggered. Who cared?

In the evening I hurried home because he had said that if he could get away, he would not be able to come before nine o'clock so that he would not come to the community center. I waited but he did not come. The following evening he came earlier but said he had only one hour because he was on duty, but he did not want to miss seeing me. When he had to go, I suggested that as it was about forty minutes' walk to his hospital, I would come with him and we could talk on the way, but he would not hear of my going back alone.

Two evenings later he came and said, "Look, dear, I have some not so good news. I have been posted. As long as I am in the army, we just have to accept things and make the best of them. Let's not spoil our evening by being sad. We shall have to write to each other every day so that we can keep in touch. Do you promise?" he asked. I said I would, but how could I send or receive his letters? He promised to arrange all that before leaving. He was being posted to a base hospital in Bremen.

The following afternoon, while I was still working, Mark came in to say good-bye. A patient had to be taken to the Bremen hospital and was being sent by ambulance. Mark was to be the doctor accompanying him and would be taking up his new job the following day. As he had promised, he had arranged with one of the girls in the Jewish Relief Unit to send on my letters, and she was willing to receive his letters for me.

That evening as soon as I returned to my room I sat down and wrote him an honest letter, telling him how much I should miss him. The letters took several days to reach their destination and sometimes two or more would arrive together, but we both wrote every day! I remember the writing paper and envelopes, which were impossible to buy. I think the Relief Unit gave me some, and some were given to me by Mr. Goldstoff, who thoroughly approved of Mark.

I remember some remarkable people living in Luneburg at the time. There were several girls who lodged together, amongst them a Rozsi Tabak, and there was a Mr. Tuchman, with a grown-up son and a young boy of thirteen or fourteen whom he had adopted and looked after. There were also several girls and boys from Saloniki, whom I admired very much because they spoke Hebrew. There was a very likeable and serious girl from Poland, who spoke a good Hebrew as well, and I took lessons from her, insisting on either paying for them or doing so by knitting pullovers for her. It was still very difficult to concentrate.

Some time toward the end of October or beginning of November, the hospital moved further out of town. Schwester Elizabeth left and went back to her hometown of Berlin, and we were given a real German hard-faced sister as head nurse.

There was talk of bringing out Jewish children who had somehow managed to stay in hiding in Berlin, or somewhere else in Germany, and had gone back to Berlin after the war. The children, we were told, needed feeding because they had suffered so much during the war. There was a lady in the Jewish Relief Unit who had managed to escape in time to England, but she herself came from Berlin. She had relatives there after the war and she was one of the main movers in starting a *Kindersheim,* a children's home, or as most of us understood it, an orphanage. Three very pleasant and able girls came to Luneburg from the Jewish Relief Unit in order to organize the place, which was a large house in its own grounds, commandeered by the army for the children's home. One of them was Mabel, a very likeable brunette, and then there was Milly, a more serious girl. The third was Bertha Smith, who came later.

One day, Bertha came to me and said, "Are you Lea Fuchs? How do you know Dr. Mark Chayen?" I explained to her and she could not believe that Mark would be coming to Luneburg soon. She told me that she had been working at the London Jewish Hospital, when Mark had done a six-month house appointment before joining the army. She had been a nurse on his ward, and I should imagine a pretty efficient one.

After that, I sent my letters through Bertha, and she added a note to the first one, which more than surprised Mark. She was an efficient, dynamic nurse type and of a cheerful disposition.

Meanwhile, it was growing colder and damper by the day, but not having any heating did not worry me very much because I kept telling myself that the previous year I had had far fewer warm clothes, and that I must not start feeling sorry for myself.

There was a girl who had a lot of knitting wool in gray and navy blue, but she did not know how to knit. She was, however, a seamstress and had managed to get herself a sewing machine. I told her that I would knit pullovers for her and she could pay me with knitting wool or by making me a dress. My trouble was that there were no materials to be had. I had a hard, heavy, green silk curtain, I cannot remember from where, and the dressmaker made me a horrible dress out of it. I knitted for her in lieu of payment and then I started knitting for anyone who could pay me with knitting wool or some kind of material. I used to get into bed in the evenings, put on anything I had to keep warm, and would knit well into the night with frozen, swollen hands and fingers.

The frostbite on my feet and hands became most painful with the colder weather. I used to have two bowls, one with cold water and one with hot, and I used to put my feet in them alternately in order to improve the circulation. When I finished with my feet, I would start on my hands. The trouble was how to get hot water. I was sure that I should never have decent looking hands again. Mark promised that things would improve and heal within a year or two. I wondered, but did not ask him, whether my soul would heal as well as my sores and frostbite. My hands and legs, when cold, would ooze blood and I used to feel embarrassed in the presence of people who did not realize that this came from frostbite and damage to the capillaries. I could not change my stockings several times a day, so the only thing I could do was to wipe my legs with a wet cloth. When my legs were wet they hurt more and bled more, and it became a vicious circle. It was a blessing to be working at the hospital, where it was reasonably warm all day.

One evening when I came to the community center, there were survivors and youngsters whom I could not place. I was told that the children had arrived a few days earlier than expected and the children's home was neither ready nor warm enough for them to sleep there. It was suggested that whoever could possibly do so should take one or two children home to sleep, and that during the day they could stay at the community center, where the people there would occupy them with something.

I took two girls home with me. I must say that it was difficult to imagine that these children had been hiding or starving more than the German population. On the way back to my room I helped carry their necessary baggage for a few nights, and this was the normal baggage that youngsters have in normal circumstances: pajamas, toothbrushes, and change of clothes, which had been put into a small, not new but very good leather bag. The two youngsters put on their warm winter coats, gloves, and knitted hats, took their bags, and even had a handbag each. One thing was sure: they looked neither physically nor mentally like haunted, starved children.

I asked them what they knew of Judaism. They looked at each other and then, like children who have not forgotten what they have learnt by heart, said together, "Not much, we were not religious at home." I asked them about schooling, about how many school years they had missed, and the answer was, "During the fighting and the bombing of Berlin, of course, we could not go to school, but otherwise, the war permitting, most of the time we did not miss much." I had a terrible feeling that I had taken into my room, which was my home, German children.

By the time we arrived at my room, the children were tired and I asked Mrs. Hosang, my landlady, if I could have two extra beds for my guests from Berlin. She came into the room to arrange a mattress on the floor and change the bedclothes and spoke to the children, aged twelve and ten. When she arranged my bed in the other room, I saw she could not understand how or why these children had been brought out of Berlin to be looked after by us. The girls were very well behaved; they undressed, put on warm pajamas (who had anything like that?) and asked if they could read for a little while. I told them I would come back in half an hour to switch off the lights.

We said goodnight to each other and I took their books to put them on the table. As one of the girls finished reading just one more line, my eyes caught an illustration and I could have died, realizing that I had horrible little Nazis in my room. I switched off the light and took the two books into another room with me in order to read them. The first book I took up had a typical Sturmer illustration, showing a big fat Jew with an enormous hooked nose and huge feet, holding a small sack of dollars and running after children to catch them with his claw-like talons. The book was full of similar pictures, and the second one also had terrible stories of the impure race of people, with pictures of Jews with the Magen David burnt into their bodies, with the German soldier standing on their throats and the Jews dying.

My first reaction was to go to the girls and, if not to throw them out into the cold night and the rain, at least to ask them who on earth they were. Unfortunately, I had been badly brought up and could not bring myself to do it. I was in a terrible mood. I tried writing to Mark but could not. I undressed, put on not warm pajamas but a sort of summer dress, long and very large, which was my nightdress. I locked both doors against the Germans — one against the Hosangs and the other against those girls with their terrible background.

In the morning, I woke them about an hour before I should have done, at six o'clock. It was still dark outside and very cold in the rooms. I had no hot drink, neither for myself nor for the girls, but I had my wash down with ice cold water in the sitz bath, which was half a flight up, about twelve steps. As I had no dressing gown, I used my damp brown coat instead. When I was fully dressed, I told the girls not to get out of bed yet because it was very cold, but I had woken them because I wanted to talk to them and ask them some questions. I told them that I had looked at their books and I was shocked because they were meant for Hitler *Jugend*, with the stories and pictures. They sat up in bed and I asked, "Who are you? What are you? Where were you and your parents during the war?" They said in unison, "We are Jewish." I asked, "Were you Jewish during the war as well?" and they answered, "No, it was dangerous. We could have been killed."

Gradually I asked them about their fathers. One of them said she had never seen her father, and the elder one said her father had been in the army but not the SS and he had not been a Nazi. "What about your mother?" I asked. "No, she is Aryan," they both answered. "And your grandparents?" The girl who had never seen her father said that her grandfather had been taken away to the ghetto with the Jews because he had had one Jewish grandparent. The older one shook her head and had no idea of where they were and what had happened to them. "Have you family in Berlin or in other places in Germany?"

"Yes" was the answer.

"Well," I said, "I have not, nor have the other people you met last night at the community center, like Herr Goldstoff, Herr Stern, and all the others. How did you dare bring books like these with you? Isn't it lucky that I do not behave as the filthy Germans did?"

The girls said, "But we could not bring any other books. All our books are like that."

"It was terrible in Berlin," the older one said. "We did not have enough food or medicine and there was all the fighting and bombing. So when my mother's cousin, who had run away to England and now drives an ambulance for the British, came to Berlin, she said that some Jewish organization was opening a *Kindersheim* with good food and that we could get clothes as well. My mother was happy to send me." I told the children to get dressed, took them to the community center, and went off to the hospital.

At lunchtime I went back to the community restaurant and found Mr. Goldstoff and Mr. Stern who were fuming about the so-called "poor starving Jewish children from Berlin." I am afraid I poured oil on the flames by telling them about the books the children were reading and of my conversation with them. I asked them what had gone wrong and was told that the excuse given by the lady who organized the transportation of the children — the British army ambulance driver — was that there were no other Jewish children survivors. *This was not true but the several hundred children who had been hidden in double walls, or had been brought up in cellars, not seeing the light of day for years, or who had lived in the woods, were found only some months later when either their families or the Jewish organizations started to look for children who might have survived.*

A few weeks later, one of the men living in Luneburg went back to Poland and found his son, Avremele. He brought back a little boy of five or more, but I never dared ask his age. He had been brought up in a double wall by some Polish gentiles, who were humane enough to feed him and keep him alive at the risk of their own lives. *Even now as I write about Avremele, my heart aches for a child who did not know his mother, whose legs were twisted, who could not talk, and had only a few teeth. That poor child received so much love from his father and all of us that after a week, he would stretch out his hands and smile as soon as he saw any of us. I wonder where he is now, if he managed to overcome the wickedness of the Germans, if he is leading a full and happy life. He should be a grandfather by now, I hope.*

It was growing very cold and there was no heating in my room. I never complained because it was senseless to do so. I knitted a lot and in exchange received knitting yarn for myself. Sometimes I was even paid. I received enough yarn to knit myself a gray cardigan and a navy sweater and made both short sleeved so as to stay tough and not mind the cold. I received a salary from the hospital, but there was very little one could buy, anyway.

One Sunday afternoon Mark dropped in just for an hour. He had come down from Bremen with a patient in an ambulance and dashed in to see me. Of course, we continued to write to each other every day. I had to stop frequently in the middle of writing in order to rub my fingers and hands, which became stiff from the cold.

How lovely it was to see him and spend that heavenly

hour together with him. As soon as he left, I wrote him a letter. About two weeks later, he appeared in my room in the evening and said that he had been posted back to the 74th General Hospital in Luneburg, for one week, in place of another anesthetist who had gone off on leave. This was certainly a piece of luck we had not expected. Mark joined me whenever he could for supper at the community's restaurant. The people there knew him and liked him very much. One of the things that was most impressive about him was his obvious feeling that "just by the grace of God, I could have been in the same spot as you." That is why he joined the army as soon as he qualified, in order to help stop the Nation of Darkness from spreading its destruction.

Mark warned me that the following day he could not leave the hospital, but the evening after he hoped to be able to come, although it would be rather late. It was obvious to me that he had forgotten that this would be the first night of Chanukah. The following day I managed to obtain two candles, one to be lit and one with which to light it, and I started to plan what to put them in so that they should burn for at least half an hour. I could not find anything appropriate so I stuck the candles onto a saucer, which I had to borrow from my landlady, and when they were firm I put water at the bottom in case the candle should fall down.

Mark was taken by surprise because he had totally forgotten that it was already Chanukah. He lit the candle and said the blessings, and at the third blessing, *Shehecheyanu*, thanking the Lord for preserving us, we both felt very moved. After lighting the candle we sang the customary *Ma'oz Tzur*.

Nowadays, when we light the Chanukah candles for the fifty-fourth time together, with our own tribe of our children, their spouses, grandchildren, with the husband of one grandchild and

the fiancés of two others, and with our new great-grandchild, we are
more than twenty people. Each year I thank the Almighty and offer
a thanksgiving prayer in my own words.

A few days later Mark had to return to Bremen. I knew he
was due for home leave in December and he warned me that
we might not be seeing each other for some time. When he
left, I tried not to panic. Having seen that he had come back
once already unharmed, I was beginning to hope and think
that the curse on me had lifted.

One evening after Mark had left for Bremen, Mr.
Kaufman, the pharmacist, walked up to my table at the restaurant, bowed to me in the accepted European fashion, and
asked me if he might have the pleasure of my company at one
of the Sunday afternoon concerts. These were excellent concerts, performed by survivors of all nations. I accepted his in-
vitation as long as Mark would not be in Luneburg. He asked if
he should ask for permission from Mark to take me out. I assured him that it was not necessary. The girls and boys at my
table started pulling his leg about asking me out. He said that
the following Sunday he would be on duty at the hospital but
he hoped we could go on the Sunday after that.

When the appointed Sunday arrived, there was a lot of
snow and the streets were terribly slippery. Mr. Kaufman
wanted to pick me up but I insisted on his not coming because
the poor man had a terrible limp. One of the boys told me that
a German political prisoner, who was a *Kapo*, had deliberately
broken his leg as a punishment instead of giving him
twenty-five lashes. How he managed to stay alive, walking on
a broken leg on top of everything else, is amazing.

During the last few weeks, when the weather had turned
so terribly cold, I used to walk to the hospital on Sunday
afternoons after lunching at the community restaurant. I

would spend a few hours in the warm deserted office and write my letter to Mark, knit, and later on go back to the restaurant to eat.

That Sunday I walked to the hospital so that later on I could meet Mr. Kaufman near the hall where the concert was to be given. I was walking slowly because the road was slippery and it was snowing hard, and I walked with my head bent, watching my steps. When I lifted my eyes, I thought I was hallucinating. Mark was hurrying toward me.

We were both overjoyed to see each other because the following week he was going back to England on seven days' leave. He told me that Major Beaver had offered to drive him down on the icy autobahn from Bremen because he enjoyed driving under difficult conditions. Before the war he used to race for Bentleys. Mark was full of admiration for Dr. Beaver both as an anesthetist and as a driver who could control his skids at seventy miles an hour.

"I am looking forward to seeing you again," Mark said to me, "because I am going to discuss some important things with my parents and my oldest brother." After about an hour and a half, he had to leave to go back to 74th General Hospital, where Major Beaver was waiting for him. How nice it must be to be looking forward to seeing one's family in another week's time and being spoiled!

I stayed on for a little longer in the office, without any light, enjoying the peace and absence of a crowd. I sometimes found it difficult to appear jolly and smiling, when I would have loved to sit down and have a good cry.

The boys of the Jewish Brigade started to come to Luneburg and we loved seeing them in their uniforms. I spoke to them about going to Palestine and when they saw how much I longed for and loved the country, one of the boys asked me, "Do you think one can win a war without arms?" I answered, "Of course not, but what can I do?" It was obvious they wanted me to do something minimal. I told them about Mark, that he was a British officer through and through, with complete allegiance to his country. Therefore, whatever they wanted me to do would have to be something that on no account would I tell him about, but neither would I have to lie to him. He explained to me that I would be used as a contact and would have to talk to people, Germans, who would contact me, mainly with messages about selling their own or other people's jewelry for coffee, cigarettes, or cocoa. He said that sometimes he or his colleagues might perhaps leave something in my room for half a day or a whole day.

I was very happy to be doing something useful. I took two boys back with me and introduced them to Mrs. Hosang, one as yet another cousin but this time from Palestine, and the second one as his friend. I told Mrs. Hosang that when they had a little time they would come in during the day either to leave their things or to rest up for a while, because they were posted beyond Hamburg. I gave them one key between the two of them, and that was all for the time being.

The following Sunday morning, Mrs. Hosang announced a German woman, who was very elegantly dressed and looked as if she had never had to go without anything either during the war or now. She opened a large black crocodile-skin bag and showed me some exquisite jewelry — sapphires with complete sets of diamonds — and said would I please tell my friends that she had what they were asking for. She gave me a list of how many thousands of cigarettes, and of what brands, and how many kilograms of coffee and cocoa she would want for them. One of the boys came to the community center in the evening and I passed the list on to him.

On another occasion, I received a small sack of Swiss watches, which stayed in my room for two days. I did not like the responsibility of it. Later on, on two or three occasions, the boys came and said they had bought some lovely things, but would have to leave them with me during the night and would come to fetch them in the morning. The two boys arrived with a small bag, as if they were coming from a game of tennis. They were all very bright and cheerful, and when Mrs. Hosang saw them come in, they even stood and chatted with her.

I realized at once that what the boys were carrying was neither jewelry nor Swiss watches. They said, "We don't want to leave these things in the bag. If you don't mind we shall have to do some reorganization of this lovely deep upholstered armchair so that we can put these things inside, alongside the springs." They did a wonderful job and hid a few smaller parts behind one of the sideboards. They said it might be better for the upholstery not to sit on it. They hid firearms, taken to pieces, pistols, and I think grenades as well. I never asked them; I preferred not to know exactly what the hidden things were.

They left, and I continued my letter though I was not sure if Mark would get it before going on leave, but at least he would read it when he came back. It is queer that I never had any pangs about keeping the secret of the Jewish Brigade, because I was sure that when Mark was out of Germany and out of the army he would approve of my helping the Brigade — which was working for our side, for our suffering people to get back to our country, which was ours by Divine right.

One night there was a storm and so I did not hear the front doorbell. There was an energetic knock on my door and before I could answer, Mark came in, absolutely soaked. Oh! What a lovely reunion that was. The poor man had come to Luneburg instead of going to Bremen, but he had to leave in another hour's time to catch a train to his hospital and report for duty. He had landed at Cuxhaven on his way back from leave, but the crossing had been very rough and he felt terribly sick. I did not have anything to give him so I asked Mrs. Hosang if she could please make a cup of tea for him, and she did so with zest.

Three or four minutes after his arrival, Mark simply said, "Look, my darling, do you think it would be a good idea to get married?" I thought it was a funny way of asking for a girl's hand and I started laughing. Mark said, "I am proposing to you, don't you understand?" I tried not to laugh but it was funny. "Well," he said, "do you think it is a good idea? You have not answered me." I replied, "But of course, how could it be otherwise?" I was in seventh heaven. Mark said, "i suppose, in Hungary, a chap gets down on his knees and if the girl does not accept him, he shoots himself."

We were terrifically happy. Mark had discussed his intention to marry me with his parents and elder brother, and they also thought it a good idea. In between sipping Mrs. Hosang's tasteless but at least hot tea, we made plans. First of all, Mark would have to obtain permission from the commander in chief to marry me, since I was technically an enemy alien. He warned me that the moment permission came through, he would like us to undergo the civil marriage, which had to be in Germany, and would then like to send me to England to be out of this accursed country.

It was time for him to leave, and though it was hailing he had to go on foot to the station. We promised each other always to be as happy in each other's company as on that evening and, thank Heaven, we have both kept that promise.

After Mark had left, I was truly in the seventh heaven, but as soon as I remembered I had no one with whom to share my happiness, I became deeply depressed. I remembered when my sister Gili became engaged, I must have been a little girl of seven or eight. It was after twelve o'clock at night and they woke my parents, sisters, and even my brother, and I dressed quickly to wish them *mazal tov*. The engaged couple went off with my parents to wake my grandparents to tell them the good news because they could not wait until the morning. What a happy couple they had been, with what a happy marriage, but my sister and her son of ten and that lovely little smiling Noemi finished their lives so very prematurely in one of the gas chambers of Birkenau.

I thought of my other sisters and how happy they would be for me, and my parents with both their worry and happiness. How my mother would start planning the engagement party, how clothes would be ordered for the occasion, and how friends and our very large family would participate in the celebration. All that was gone forever. Nevertheless, I felt I had to talk to my parents and ask for their blessing, but then I suddenly smelled gas and felt I was going to choke. I opened the window and the blast of cold air and rain brought me back to my senses.

From now on I knew that Mark would be my friend, husband, and family forever. I sat down and wrote him a long letter, telling him how happy I was and omitting the sad things. I thought about his parents and what fine people they must be for not even trying to persuade Mark not to marry a girl who had gone through such a lot. I am sure they must have been worried. Yet, though it was taking a chance, they had given their blessing.

The following day I told Miss Stevens that Mark had come back and that we were going to be married as soon as permission came through. She congratulated me and seemed genuinely happy for me. I also told Dr. Kuc about our engagement, and he very correctly congratulated me and wished us all happiness. When I went to the communal restaurant in the evening, I first of all told Mr. Goldstoff and Mr. Stern and they were tremendously happy for both of us.

At their table sat Mr. Tuchman, a middle-aged man who, after several years of hell, had survived together with his son, aged twenty. His wife had been murdered, and he never mentioned if he had had any other children before the war. His son's name was Matsek and he had started studying medicine in Germany. He had a girlfriend, Shoshana, of whom I was very jealous because she spoke a fluent Hebrew. She had gone to one of the few, perhaps the only Hebrew high school in Hungary. As far as I remember, Tuchman had been a lawyer in Poland before the war and to start something new in a new country must have been very difficult even to think about. He did one very nice thing: he adopted a fourteen-year-old boy with whom he and his son had lived together in the camps. I cannot remember the boy's name but he was very quiet and depressed and obviously living with his memories. I sat with him on several occasions and tried to start a conversation but was not successful.

My good news spread from table to table and people came to congratulate me. In the evenings there were always more people at the restaurant, which was a warm meeting spot as well as the only place where one could obtain something to eat.

At the table where Hilda was sitting there was a new man, and he rose to wish me all the best and introduced himself as

Marek. Hilda was the secretary of the community, working for Goldstoff, and even before the war she must have been an expert and fast stenographer, in Polish, German, and English. She must have been over forty; I was sure that she had been married with children before the war but she never spoke about it, at any rate not to me.

I went to sit with Rozsi Tabak, who was with her friend, a very pretty girl, and two boys, survivors from Saloniki, and perhaps one or two others. There were few survivors from Saloniki but they were pleasant and tough and spoke fluent Hebrew. They told me that before the war, the ports in Saloniki were closed down during the Jewish holidays because all the porters were Jewish. Rozsi Tabak was a solid, serious person who had not changed during the war. I had great respect for her and for anyone else who managed to swim against the existing strong tide.

Later in the evening, Marek joined our table. He was an extrovert and looked better than most of us. He had been a lawyer in Warsaw and had served as an officer in the Polish army. On the second day of the war he had been taken prisoner together with his fellow officers, and had stayed with them and suffered from them more than from the Germans because he was a Jew. He wandered round Germany looking for his wife, after having gone back to Warsaw where he had been unable to find her. He had been married for two years. Like thousands of others, he was wandering from place to place in Germany in the hope of finding someone who could tell him something about her.

In the evenings, some of the Jewish soldiers and officers stationed in Luneburg would join us and it made a big difference to our feelings. There were several boys who came regularly. One of them, Nathy, whose parents had a grocery shop in Stamford Hill in London, stood up and said, "I want you all to know, I am going to be at her wedding." *Nathy was indeed at our wedding in London and I was delighted that he could come. He was one of two people who knew me before coming to England. The other was Bertl, who had not seen me since I was eleven years old. She had been my governess and later had looked after my cousins, Lea and Ari. Bertl was the only person who could vouch for my having had a background and family in another world — perhaps in another planet.*

Mark spent the train journey to Bremen writing me a long letter, brimming with happiness, and another to his parents and brothers, telling them our good news. He wrote that he was going to put in the request to marry me and that Germany was no place for decent and normal human beings to be.

I am trying very hard to describe Germany after the war. I think the nearest description would be to imagine a large beehive with every bee running about, coming and going, crazed, each speaking a different language, and seeking something different.

I was hoping that permission would not come through too soon because on no account did I want to go to England without Mark. The rough date for his demobilization was about April or May and he hoped very much that we could manage to get through our civil marriage before then, though it would not be effective for us personally without the religious ceremony of *chuppah* and *kiddushin*. He was hoping to have a proper wedding in London with friends and family, such as I would have had at home in my parents' house.

I thought about going to England on my own and staying with my sister and brother-in-law, and I knew that I could not stand it. However good an actress I was, I was not good enough to survive even twenty-four hours in England without

Mark. I realized how terrified I was of starting a normal life amongst normal people who, though they had gone through a great deal during the war, would find me totally strange and crazy. We could talk to each other for hours at the club in Luneburg, but it was not normal polite chatting — we were always discussing something important and sometimes making decisions which were beyond our capacity to take.

I thought of how life would be in England and started getting cold feet, realizing more and more that it was unfair to burden Mark with my problems, as I was sure that I could not again lead a normal life as I had before the war. It seemed to me incredible how much time we had spent at the dressmakers, tailors, and choosing other items of clothing. I had lived in an atmosphere of life and death for several years, and that other life was too long ago. Even as it was, it was sometimes difficult to smile and go on living.

When I think back about people I knew, whose stories I knew, and I remember them smiling and laughing sometimes, I think that they were, and I am sure stayed, first-class actors — each of them should have received an Oscar prize for acting. When one comes into a room, even after thirty, forty, or fifty years, and is reminded of something terrible but stretches out one's hand in greeting and smiles because that is what society expects of a normal person, one feels schizophrenic. One goes on talking, drinking, and smiling and then remembers the ladies' room, where one can escape for a few minutes to straighten one's mind and put on more lipstick.

Somehow Palestine and a kibbutz seemed different because there would be many more mentally wounded like myself. Mark wrote me that his parents were trying to vacate the tenants from their three-bedroom house so that we could live there to start with. I was growing panicky and was trying to imagine Mark going to work in the morning and my having to wait ten, twelve, or even, when he would be on duty, twenty-four or more hours for him to come back, when he was my only anchor to a normal life. Was it fair to him? Should I tell him now and let us part because he deserved something much better?

I continued having nightmares but now Mark and England were involved. I decided I was crazy and probably worse than most of the other survivors.

I went on knitting and had enough money to buy Mark a present. There was a secondhand shop in the middle of the town where one could either buy or exchange things. I went there one afternoon and found a good silver cigarette case and knew I had to get it. I bought it, remembering the long flat tin box, formerly of a transfusion set, in which Mark kept his Senior Service cigarettes. He also smoked a pipe but I hoped he would use my present all the time. I asked Mrs. Hosang where I could have a silver cigarette case engraved, she told me, and as soon as I could, I went to the engraver. Although I hated giving any livelihood to Germans or having any dealings with them, I had no choice while I was still living in Germany. On the lid I had engraved the entwined letters "MC," Mark's initials, then in one corner "Celle 19-8-1945," and in another corner, "From Lea, Luneburg, 26-11-1945," the date when we were first unofficially engaged. I wanted it done so that next time Mark came down for a few hours, it would be ready for him.

Meanwhile he was posted even further away, to Nijmegen, in Holland, and he wrote that instead of coming nearer to me and obtaining permission to marry, he was posted further away. What Mark was worried about was that his demobilization order would come through and he would have to go back to England, and then, as a civilian, he would not be able to return to Germany to marry me. *I do not know how long the military governments of Britain, the USA, and Russia stayed in Germany, but it was a long time before order and normal life returned to that country. As far as I am concerned, it came too soon and they did not deserve it.*

More and more of the survivors asked me to knit for them and they paid me. Most of them did not work officially so I do not know from where their money came.

Mrs. Hosang told me about a salon where a dressmaker and an artist who made lovely things worked together, but they were rather expensive and very busy and one had to wait weeks for something to be made up. I went to see the place, in an old beautiful house, standing in its own grounds. It was furnished with period furniture and was full of German women.

I did not have to wait long before one of the owners came to me and asked how she could help. She said in advance that if I could pay her in cigarettes or coffee, she could manage to get me material for clothes or anything I wanted. Needless to say, compared to the other women present I looked an absolute beggar the way I was dressed. I told her I would pay her in her own money, that I had neither coffee nor cigarettes, and I asked her if she could make me a nightdress. She told me the price and said she also had some red silk with white polka dots and could make me a blouse. I ordered the nightdress and a blouse made of light material because being tough in the face of the cold was my mania. She asked me which one I wanted first and I said the nightdress. The material was thick and pale blue and she made it up into an attractive looking nighty, my first since leaving home, long, going right down to the floor. What luxury! These two things and Mark's cigarette case rather depleted my savings.

Mark wrote every day and so did I. He wrote that he and the surgeon attached to the field ambulance unit had started a fitness campaign and the whole unit did cross-country running every morning. One morning, he said, he tried to jump across a large puddle and fell backwards into the middle of it. He added, "Please, darling, don't laugh at me."

Meanwhile the Friends Ambulance Unit was posted somewhere else and other volunteers came instead of them. I missed Miss Stevens, but she came back to visit us several times. Miss Faulkner, who came with the other volunteers, assured her that she was looking after me and sending and receiving letters for me. As we were talking, one of the men came in distributing mail and there was a registered letter for Miss Faulkner. She said, "This is Captain Chayen's handwriting."

She opened the envelope and sure enough, there was another one inside, sealed and rather bulky. She handed it to me; I could not wait to open it and inside was my engagement ring, wrapped in cotton wool, and an appropriate letter with it. It was a lovely sapphire, set in white gold. Everybody admired it and Miss Stevens said the sapphire was supposed to bring luck. I put it on my left hand as they wear it in England. In Hungary, both wedding and engagement rings are worn on the right. Everybody noticed it at once, perhaps because I kept looking at it all the time. But a person like Miss Faulkner could see through my forced smile and said, "Don't you worry about the future, with a lovely man like the Captain," all this delivered in a broad Lancashire accent. She was a good sort, who could feel with other people, a rare gift.

One morning, an officer came to the hospital from the legal department of the army to ask me some questions about the request Mark had made for permission to be married. He had Mark's request before him and was checking on a number of points. What the army usually did was lose the request for a few months and by that time the soldier or officer had, in most cases, changed his mind.

The visit of the officer worried me. On the one hand, I wanted more than anything in life to go with Mark to England and to be married to him. On the other hand, I grew scared when thinking of living with people who had led a steady and quiet life compared to mine. We had decided that we would not stay in England for more than five years, but Mark wanted to go back to earn enough money, after five and a half years in the army, to buy furniture and other basic things with which to start our new life in Palestine.

Within five years we indeed settled in what was no longer Palestine but Israel, where we now live, together with our children and grandchildren. I did not realize that wherever in the world I would have started a normal life, it would be difficult, and that wherever I went, my past life would be with me.

It must have been the beginning of February when I finally decided to write to Mark and tell him that I should always love him but I could not marry him because I was not capable of leading a normal life again. I asked him to please understand and forgive me and said that I would try to slip away and that in the end we should both be better off for it. I looked at the cigarette case I had bought him and had not had the chance to give him.

There was one more important thing to do, which was to go to Porta, the village near the camp where we buried my friend Oli, and put up some sort of memorial on her grave. A few weeks previously, I had gone to Bergen-Belsen in order to find someone in authority to order a headstone which would be light enough for me to be able to handle. I was told I should ask Rabbi Wilenski, who had come from Manchester, England, to help.

His problem was how to transport it. I said I did not know, because it was a few kilometers from the train station down to the village, unless there was another way of reaching the village and the cemetery. "How many of you would be going?" he asked. "Only me," I answered, "there is no one here, that I know of, who was with us or who would be interested in coming." He said, "You could not drag it five meters. I'll get the headstone ready and in two or three weeks' time, on a suitable day, I shall send you down with my car and driver." He looked at the map and spoke to his driver, who said it was not so far and it could be done provided we started during the morning so as to get to the cemetery while there was still daylight. I gave the Rabbi Oli's name, but did not know her family name or date of birth — only that she was born in Budapest, was an only child, and that she had been buried by a few friends exactly two weeks before the liberation.

On a Sunday morning, Goldstoff was going to Bergen-Belsen and coming back in the afternoon. I went with him and waited a long time for the Rabbi, who finally came back to his office and showed me the headstone in blue with deep, white lettering and large shield of David at the top. It was well made, of heavy wood, and I could not have budged it even two meters. I asked when it would be possible to take it to Porta, and he said he could not promise any definite date but that I should come back to Bergen-Belsen for a few days and then he would try and release his driver for half a day.

I sent off the letter to Mark and spent a terrible day, regretting that I was ever born. The Brigade boys had not been for some time; I wanted to ask them to get me out of Germany.

It was freezing outside, with ice on the roads. I waited an

extra day in Luneburg for the weather to improve. In my clothes it would not be easy to go to the station in Luneburg, or from the station in Bergen-Belsen to the camp. I was really stewing in my misery. I did not have anyone to whom to write, so I just sat. I must have dropped off to sleep in the large armchair, and I woke up with something sticking into me. I realized that the boys must have been while I was gone and hidden their supplies in the armchair. *All these were used by Haganah — the underground army of the pre-Israel state. I only wish I could have done more for the boys.*

It was only nine o' clock so I went to see if Mrs. Hosang was around. As I came near the kitchen door, Mr. Hosang came out, greeting me in a most servile fashion. Every time I saw him I wanted to vomit. He was very tall with a bent back, on top of which was a death's head with thick glasses and nasty small eyes peering at you. Mrs. Hosang rose and invited me into her reasonably warm kitchen. She said, "I was just coming to you, Miss Fuchs, to give you regards from your cousin. He will be back tomorrow morning and hopes to see you either here or at the hospital."

I wanted to wait for my "cousin" and then go to Bergen-Belsen to take the headstone to Oli's grave, and after that to leave Germany, never to set foot again in that blood-drenched country again. I was going to talk to the boys and tell them I wanted to leave in about three days' time. There were illegal transports leaving Germany all the time and it was very cleverly done. I do not know from where they collected all those uniforms on which they put the badges of the Jewish Brigade. With specially printed movement orders, the boys and girls traveled on British troop trains and two Brigade girls or boys traveled with them to see that things went off smoothly. They took them either to Belgium or Italy. During the winter months, there were virtually no ships going to Palestine because of the choppy seas and the unseaworthiness of the little, so-called "illegal" boats.

I went to bed, resigned to my future, whatever it would be. If I should have to wait in Italy it would be at least one step nearer to reaching my country.

I woke up to a lot of shouting going on in the street. Someone was banging on the door of the house, which was locked after ten or eleven at night. People were calling from their windows, "Who is making all that noise in the middle of the night?"

It struck me like a bolt of lightning that it was Mark — but, I thought, he could hardly have received my letter and obtained leave to come. Someone must have opened the door downstairs, the doorbell to the Hosang apartment sounded, and Mrs. Hosang opened the door. I sat up in bed and sure enough, after knocking, Mark appeared looking worried and said, "Thank God you are still here." He had been traveling for sixteen hours from Nijmegen. The letter had reached him rather fast and the moment he read it he had gone to the officer in charge of the unit and simply told him the truth: that I was going to slip away, and in the madness of Germany and Europe he would never find me and therefore he needed two days of compassionate leave. This was granted immediately, and he caught the first train to Luneburg.

We both looked awful and were both miserable. We spent the rest of the night talking and Mark admonished me for doing silly things. Finally he promised me that if after coming to England and giving me a chance to get used to things I still felt I could not lead a normal life, he would give me my freedom. In any case, within five years, we should leave for Palestine — Eretz Yisrael.

He opened his bag and took out some things he had brought me. There was a lovely, too elegant, more housecoat than dressing gown, in pale blue taffeta, and a pale blue silk nightdress. I gave him the cigarette case, which I had managed to fill with Senior Service cigarettes. We were both happy again, but Mark kept telling me never to do a thing like that again and asked me always to talk things over with him. Luckily I had some bread, jam, and margarine because I had wanted to take the train to Bergen-Belsen and intended to prepare some sandwiches, so we shared the bread and jam.

I was getting ready to take Mark out for a walk because I had to get him out of the way before the Brigade boys came back. He could not understand why I would not let him sit in the large armchair. I kept telling him that it was broken and "Please let us go out into the fresh air, it will do my headache a world of good." The poor man kept telling me that we should get wet, but I said it was only drizzling. It was not cold and I took Mark as far away as possible from my apartment.

He said he was going to nag the legal department of the army until they granted permission for our civil marriage. I argued that I wanted to stay in Germany until the date of his demobilization and then go to England together with him.

For lunch we went to the community center and then back to my room. Mark had to leave at eight o'clock in order to catch his train back to Hannover and from there on to Nijmegen.

The hospital was closing down and the patients were being divided between two hospitals, one in Uelzen and the other further away. I was given a very kind offer to continue working for the British volunteers, but I declined. Nevertheless they were worried about how I could keep my room and pay for it. An officer from the military government came to the hospital and offered me a job with them as interpreter, but I preferred not to be mixed up with their jolly crowd. I was told there should be no problem in keeping my room, that the military government would go on paying for it as they did for all DPs living in town and not in camps.

Once I had stopped working at the hospital every day, I received more and more orders for cardigans and sweaters. I was knitting all day and had lots of time for thinking and being depressed. I would listen to Mark's radio, which he refused to take back on any account, but even listening to music needed some degree of concentration. When I felt I was running toward the edge of the world, from which one falls down, down into deep misery, I would get up and go to the community center to talk to people and reassure myself that I had not been left alone amongst the Germans.

Mark's birthday was only a few weeks off so I knitted him a sleeveless navy blue sweater. I managed to buy a few fresh eggs, a small tin of golden syrup, and some baking flour, and with Mrs. Hosang's help I made a cake for Mark and sent off both the cake and the sweater to reach him by his birthday. The parcel reached him in time and luckily the cake did not go mouldy. He was very happy with the presents and I do not think that I have ever given anybody a present which needed as much planning and effort in order to have it ready and sent off in time.

There was a tailor in town, apparently the best, who during the war years used to make only officers' uniforms. A few months after the war the British shut down his workshop, but after a year he was allowed to start work again with several assistants, but only for the military government. He had a great deal of suiting, which he was allowed to make up only for people with permits from the military government. Goldstoff had a suit made early on, for everyday use, from American khaki blankets, and later on he had a different one made for Shabbat and holidays. Many girls had skirts and warm coats made out of blankets. Everybody in the community received a permit to have either a suit or a skirt and jacket made by the tailor. I think it cost a hundred German marks but if one did not have the money, payment was arranged through the Town Major's office.

I had the money, otherwise I would not have ordered the skirt and jacket. I went to the tailor to choose the cloth and have my measurements taken. There were two kinds of cloth from which to choose. One was a brown herringbone and the other a gray herringbone. Besides these, he had a lot of German army clothes, stacked in a corner of his large salon. I chose the gray herringbone and thought how lucky it was that I was going to England and not staying on in Luneburg. I could imagine, in about two months' time, how all our people would wear this uniform of herringbone, made in exactly the same way by the same person.

The cloth itself was a proper German war product and so was the lining. This skirt and jacket were going to be my first new and normal looking clothes, made to measure for me. I bought several second hand summer dresses — there were no new ones to be found. There was a black dress made of very thin material, embroidered with small white flowers, and I wore that for my first two years in England, in summer on a hot day. I even bought myself a pair of high heeled shoes, second hand of course. They were not what I wanted, but they had high heels and were gray suede and to be able to put on a pair of normal shoes almost made me feel a young girl again. I looked for a coat or raincoat I could buy, but without any success.

One sunny morning I decided to retrace my steps to the courthouse where the Bergen-Belsen trials had been held in Luneburg by a British military court. They had tried J. Kramer and Dr. Fritz Klein, with altogether fifty-two SS, amongst them Irma Graese. I had a personal interest in her trial because I had myself suffered from her beatings and had seen her daily in Birkenau with her whip and pistol.

I went back to see the place where she and the others had been tried. I wanted to leave behind me their cursed memories in that cursed land. Their trials had started on Sept. 17, 1945. It was our Yom Kippur, our Day of Atonement, just a year after her going from one hut to another in Birkenau and telling us, with a demonic smile, that we must eat, that the food was better than ever before and we could have second helpings as well. I heard about the trial several weeks after it had started, as we had no newspapers or any official news. I went to the trial but it did not make me happy; all I wanted was for all of them to be dead and to be rid of them and their memories.

At the time I could not sort things out: I felt it was good that "justice" would be done — that they would be tried and punished — but somehow that wasn't ultimately "right," it wasn't enough. Hanging was too good for them, but who could or wanted to get down to their level of cruelty to give them the death they deserved? By all rights, they should have rotted alive as we did, and even that would not have made me happy.

As I walked into the courtroom, I realized that I should always hate them, their country, and their people, but I preferred to have nothing to do with them.

I stood outside the former courtroom, remembering how I had been taken into a small room and the military police girl had done a thorough body search on me, and how I was told to leave my bag, which was a large boxlike shoulder bag I had received from my cousin, Ari. I thought they should have taken my shoes as well, because in order to express one's feelings, one should have taken off a shoe and hurled it at those horrors sitting down below. I remembered how the military police had been standing along the walls, watching all our movements. The people present, who were not very many, were constantly on the move, trying to obtain a better view of the SS from whom they had suffered. It is strange that the place had not been full and that the survivors, rather than watch the trial, tried to get on with their lives.

I tried to edge my way to the right side of the gallery where I would be opposite Irma Graese. I looked at her with hate; she was no longer beautiful but looked sulky and unkempt. She was talking to her lawyer and had a handkerchief in her hand. This impressed and infuriated me most. I thought bitterly, "Probably she has toilet paper as well, and hot water for showering, and soap. She should be left to rot as we rotted away," but that could not be done by civilized nations.

The proceedings were interrupted and the judge announced that Irma Graese would be taken to the dentist because she had toothache and would be cross-examined only on the following day. The moment this was announced, we all started running down the stairs. I only wanted literally to spit in her eyes but there was no chance. She came out of the courthouse led by two jailers, between two massive walls of military police, and straightaway was put into a military transporter. Her hair, which used to be shining and smooth, was frizzy. We were all screaming things at her. I was exhausted and disgusted and went back to the courtroom, retrieved my handbag, and went away.

I did not talk about it much. I was so consumed with hatred that I just wanted not to remember that farce called the Bergen-Belsen trials. I never went back to the trials, and it was much later that I found out that the SS guards were mainly found not guilty and went free. Eleven of them, including Kramer, Dr. Klein, Irma Graese, and some others, were hanged on December 12, 1945. Twenty-seven received prison sentences ranging from one to fifteen years, but by 1954 all of them were out of jail. As I stood there, remembering the trials only a few months previously, I could see before my eyes Irma Graese still wearing better fitting clothes and better shoes than I did. I turned round and went back to my room, hoping never to see the place again or to set foot in a country which could produce people like the local inhabitants.

It was interesting how little I knew Luneburg, although I had lived there for nine months. I was not interested in the place and hated the people, so I went from my room to the hospital and the community center, and very little else.

On Saturday, Goldstoff told me that there was a Hungarian survivor, a girl, in the local mental hospital and would I like to walk out and visit her and possibly interpret for him? It was a pleasant day, not so cold anymore, and several people attached themselves to us as we walked.

There was a fairly new arrival, a tall man with sunken, sad eyes, a hollow cough, and, I was sure, a high fever. As we walked he started to tell me about his wife and *"kinderlach."* "They are all gone," he said, "and I am going too. When we went onto the transport from the ghetto, my oldest son of seven years old begged me, *'Tatte,* take me with you.' I tried not to hear him and the child jumped onto me and clung to me crying, *'Tatte,* take me with you, I want to live!' I also wanted to live and I knew that if I took him with me we should both die, so I threw him off and ran away from him. And now," he said, "I am going to die because I have no lungs left. I could have died with my children and not have suffered for four years and not deserted my children."

What can one say to a man with such a story? I did not know what to say and kept quiet. He said, "And my son, my own flesh and blood, hated me when he died because I would not take him with me. Now that I am soon going to die, I am going to hate myself for wanting to live when I knew that neither my wife, who was pregnant, nor my children could go on living. I am telling you this because I have to talk and I cannot talk about anything else. Forgive me," he said, "forgive me." I still did not say anything because I did not know what to say. I felt like crying, just sitting down and crying for hours for all the wasted lives, for the misery, for the pain, for the memories, and for the people who are gone, millions of them, without even a grave. I told myself one has to be tough and has to take in one's stride conversations like this one.

We arrived at the mental hospital, a very large building, but not big enough to hold all the Germans inside it. Mr. Goldstoff and I went into the office to inquire about the Jewish Hungarian girl survivor. A nurse took us down a long corridor, unlocked a door, and then, after we had entered, relocked it, telling us all to sit down and that she would bring the patient. It was a very large airy room, and we realized that we were in a closed ward. The nurse returned with a woman of about thirty to thirty-five who spoke only Hungarian. I started talking to her; she knew her name and where she was from, which was my hometown, and she said to me, "I think I know you."

She spoke perfectly normally. I asked her why she was still in the hospital and she told me that everybody had decided she was crazy because she did not want to live. Her husband, she said, had died in 1942 and left her with two small boys, whom she could not manage to support. She herself had grown up without parents or family, and she said to me, "Am I not right that I do not want to go on living, now that I have not even got my children?" She spoke a little Yiddish and talked awhile with Goldstoff. She said to me that there had been a gentleman called Salamon Fuchs who had arranged for her children to be taken into an orphanage. She said she had gone to his house and he had been so kind to her; it had been lunchtime and Mrs. Fuchs had invited her to sit down with the family to eat. I was shaken — she was talking about my father and mother. I asked her if she wanted to stay on in the hospital, and she said it did not matter to her because she would not know where to start living if she were outside. To me, this sounded perfectly normal. If she took her own life I think she would have been far better off than being stuck in a German mental hospital.

Mark received his demobilization date, which was May 21. His letters were more worried every day and he kept telephoning the legal department of the army to find out if they had not lost the application. The officer he spoke to said, "Of course we lose each application for a few months for the good of the applicants, but if you still want to marry that girl, old boy, we'll see what we can do. Most applicants are cured after a few months of waiting to marry a foreign girl, and we save them a lot of trouble."

I had to go for my second fitting at the tailor's on May 7. It was a warm sunny day and a long walk, but I felt rather beaten down by all the rotten, smiling Germans around me. Just one year after liberation and they were trying to lead a normal life. There were few young men in the street except for those with one leg or one arm — or those with no legs in a wheelchair. For some reason they did not have artificial limbs fitted and they looked grotesque, these people hobbling down the road.

I had my fitting and was told by the tailor that everything should be ready in four days' time. It was lunchtime and I cut across the park on the hill near where I lived and sat down to rest and cool off in the shade of a large chestnut tree with its lovely pink flowers. It reminded me of the two chestnut trees we had had in our garden, with the hammock hanging between them, and of my family and of things which would never be again. I heard laughter and children came running through the park on their way back from school. I rose, I did not want the shade, I did not want to hear the laughter of German children. I thought, "If only I could have a good cry, just to sit down and let go and have a good sobbing session!"

I started to climb the stairs, slowly, like an old woman, but when I was on the first floor, I could hear someone moving on the landing above me. After a few more stairs, I looked up and Mark was standing there waiting for me in his service dress, complete with Sam Browne belt. I ran upstairs, and with a huge smile he asked me, "Have you time, this afternoon, to come and get married?"

He had been waiting for me in my room for over an hour and did not know where and how to look for me. He had received official permission to marry on May 4 and later on the same day had received a posting to 106 Medical Company. This was more than he could stand, to be posted again, perhaps still further from me, and just prior to leaving the army. He went to his commanding officer and asked him to send a signal contesting the posting. This he was ready to do. "But," he said, "let us first look on my map to see where 106 Medical Company is." It turned out to be at Celle, about fifty miles from Luneburg, and it must have been planned by someone rather kindhearted to send him nearer to his bride. Mark had packed up in the middle of the morning and sent a message to 106 warning them of his expected arrival the same evening.

The following morning he had rung the Judge Advocate General's office to ask whether he could marry us, and the answer was, "Yes, either today in Luneburg before 4:00 P.M., or in six months' time, because I am off to take part in the Nuremberg trials."

Mark told me how he had gone to the Town Major in Celle to ask for transport. The Town Major wanted to know why he needed transport and when he was told it was for getting married, he congratulated Mark, but he said, "You know, I need a doctor for five minutes to be present at the execution of a Polish soldier." Mark agreed and after the execution had come straight to Luneburg, to my room, but I was not at home.

We had to hurry and also to decide on witnesses. Mark said, "You choose the witnesses, my darling. If you want to have them all from the community it's fine with me, after all we are the same people." I almost cried with happiness to be marrying such an understanding man as Mark. We walked to the community restaurant to have lunch and, above all, to ask some of my friends to be witnesses at our lay marriage. There was great excitement, and after lunch two cars started off to take us to our civil ceremony. Mark and I sat in the army's Volkswagen and leading us was the old but large car of the engineer Furst — it was packed to overcapacity, but being an old car it had running boards, and so on both sides there were boys standing on them, waving at us all the time.

On the way our car broke down but luckily the driver was also a mechanic and so he managed to repair it on the spot. Meanwhile three of the boys disappeared into the garden of one of the lovely homes, to look for flowers for the bride. They said, "Who has seen a bride without flowers?" Just before our car was mended and we were ready to continue on our way, they reappeared, dragging a small lilac tree with them. They had been trying to break off a few branches when the tree broke, and they were happy to bring it out whole. They tied it to their car and said, "Now everyone will know that this is a wedding procession."

We arrived at the last half hour of office hours and entered what must have once been the home of very wealthy people, which had been taken over by the legal department of the British army. As our witnesses we took Mr. Goldstoff and Rozsi Tabak. The Judge Advocate General came into the room with another officer and started the lay marriage ceremony, saying that he had been invested with the power of performing marriages by Viscount Field Marshal Montgomery and then asked us if we had a wedding ring, which we had not, so we used my engagement ring. The witnesses signed our wedding certificate, as did the judge, after which he congratulated us and our ceremony was over. We did not consider ourselves a married couple, since we had not yet undergone the religious ceremony, which we were going to have in London.

We came out into the street and, of course, everyone fell on us with their best wishes. As the driver was holding the car door open for us to get in, he turned to me and said in German, "May I wish you all the very best for the future?" I said, "No, you may not. I do not want any good wishes from Germans. I don't want to have anything to do with you." Poor Mark felt very awkward and did not know what to do or say. I said, "Sorry, darling, I hope in future we won't have anything to do with Germans."

Mrs. Hosang, with whom I had to have reasonably "normal" contact because she was my landlady, was already waiting to congratulate us and she offered to make some tea, which she served in her best china cup. Mark asked me if I would mind very much if he gave the driver a cup of tea, "After all, he is a human being and I can't let myself down to their level." I told him as long as he gave it himself, it was none of my business, but I simply couldn't and wouldn't give him even a drop of water. Mark asked Mrs. Hosang for another cup of tea and he himself took it down to the driver, who was waiting for him in the car. I wondered if the driver appreciated Mark's bringing him the cup of tea or if he wished the outcome of the war reversed, so that he could kick him and all other British officers around. Of one thing I am certain and that is that no British prisoner of war ever had a cup of tea brought to him by a German officer.

We had only an hour to make plans. Now that I was married to a British subject, I could obtain a British passport, but we had to go to Bad Oeynhausen with photographs and the marriage certificate in order to receive it. Bad Oeynhausen was about a hundred and twenty miles away. Mark did not know how much work there was at his new position or when he could take a day off and obtain transport again. Another problem was how to communicate with each other, because letters could take from one to six days to arrive. Mark also told me that Rabbi Dr. Brodie, who was the Chief Rabbi of the army and later of Britain and the Commonwealth countries, had promised him that when he married he would come from anywhere to perform the ceremony. He asked if I liked the idea, and it was agreed that he would write to Rabbi Brodie as soon as we had a definite date for our wedding. We were both very happy about the arrangements, as it looked as if we would be able to go to England together. On May 22 Mark had to be in Liege, in Belgium, for demobilization formalities, and we wanted to meet in or near Calais so as to cross the Channel together.

On Sunday morning, May 12, Mark appeared again and said he had been posted to Luneburg until May 22. There was no work for him in Celle and probably there would not be any at the field ambulance in Luneburg either, except for emergencies. His billet was just down the road from where I lived and we would be able to spend a few days together preparing to leave.

The following day he again went to the Town Major to ask for transport to Bad Oeynhausen. On Tuesday I prepared a few sandwiches of whatever little I had so that we would be able to have a picnic lunch on our way back to Luneburg. We were again given a Volkswagen but this time with a middle-aged, intelligent, and educated looking German driver. I could see the hatred in his eyes and commented on it to Mark. He said, "Nonsense, he seems a nice chap."

They started a conversation and Mark told him about the terrible camps in which I had been and that I had lost my whole family. He listened but never said a word; he just said nothing. Mark asked him, "Are you not sorry for all these things you Germans have done?"

He answered, "I am sorry — you have no idea, sir, how sorry I am — that we lost the war." This was the only honest German I met, who did not deny anything that had happened.

It was an overcast day. We arrived in Bad Oeynhausen, went straight to military government, and within half an hour received my temporary passport. What followed was most fantastically organized: Mark had to go to Liege for demobilization and I received a movement order, with which I had to report to the RTO at Luneburg about two days before leaving for 30 Corps. I was even told what time I was to be at the station.

We spent a few lovely days together. Early in the morning, Mark would come over from his billet and say his morning prayers in my room, in which he left his phylacteries so that he would not have to bring them over each day. Occasionally he had a few hours of work and then I used the time to make inquiries about buying some sort of a suitcase. Finally a Polish boy, a collaborator, with whom I used to work in the hospital office, came to my rescue.

He asked me, when we met, how was the "Mr. Captain," and I said he was fine and that we were both leaving for England. I asked him if he knew where I could buy a small suitcase. He asked, "New?" A new one would cost a kilogram of coffee and about one thousand cigarettes. I told him I had no coffee nor cigarettes, so he told me he had a friend, who lived exactly opposite the Hamburger Heim, where the DP hospital used to be, and that he was hard up and would be willing to sell one of his suitcases.

I went to the house and it was horrible. I must have been completely crazy to go there alone. I was taken into a very large room, in which there must have been living ten or twelve couples. Most of them, I am sure, were hiding from the authorities and I was hoping to get out of there alive. None of them worked and they started to offer me various things to buy. I began moving backwards and said, "This must be a mistake," and only when I stood near the front door, which was locked, did the man bring the suitcase that he was willing to sell. It was old and battered and made of cardboard, and had to be tied up with string. I gave him the money he asked for and thanked my lucky stars when I found myself in the street again. I thought, "Dear God, I am counting not the days but the hours that I have to stay amongst these cursed people," and I was rather shaken at how I had walked into that house without thinking.

When Mark came back in the evening, he asked me if this was the so-called suitcase and I said that it was. "But, darling..." he started to say but I told him that I would not go into any more German houses to buy a suitcase — there were none to be bought anyway.

The people of the community were very happy for us and we spent part of the evenings with them and sometimes went out for walks with them during the day. On Shabbat, Mark was called up to read the Haftorah. I was happy beyond belief but still apprehensive as to how I would get used to normal life and fit in with Mark's family and friends. I decided, without knowing them, that I would get on well with all of them and like them because they were Mark's family.

During that last Shabbat, I was scared about how the following Shabbat would be. Our program had been worked out by the army. On Tuesday afternoon, Mark was leaving Luneburg with all his kit en route for Liege, where he was due on Wednesday. There he would arrange his demobilization papers, spend the night in Liege, and on Thursday morning catch a train to Calais. I would leave Luneburg on Wednesday, travel all night and the following morning, and arrive in Calais just before Mark.

On Tuesday, after he had left, I felt really depressed. He had warned me not to forget for one second that soon I should be out of Germany, never to return again, and we would be married forever and ever after. Many of my friends came to my room for the last evening, and some of them took me to the station with my disgusting so-called suitcase. Mr. Goldstoff was very angry with me for not telling him that I needed a suitcase and wondered how I could go to England and Mark's family with a horrible-looking thing like that.

I handed in my suitcase and was told I should receive it back again at Calais. We said our good-byes and the train started puffing its way toward my new life. Because of Mark's rank I was put into a first-class carriage, together with some ATS officers, members of the auxilary women's service. They obviously knew each other and ignored me, for which I was rather grateful. I could think and hope. I had had a letter some weeks previously from Coralie, the wife of Mark's elder brother. It was a sweet letter and she wrote, "My dear little sister." I had been really touched by that.

I thought how lucky I was to be leaving Germany behind, to be marrying such a wonderful person as Mark, and above all, I thanked the Almighty that I had managed to cling to the principles I had been taught to consider important. I was thinking of many girls and boys who were remaining in Germany, adrift without a rudder, not knowing what they wanted out of life in the long run, but just living for the present moment. I wondered if we should ever meet again. I had given Judith and Dori Mark's home address so that we could correspond, hoping to hear from them wherever they were. But as yet civilians could not send letters either to or from England since the civilian postal service was not working even in Germany itself.

The train stopped and the girl officers started to descend. One of them turned to me and said, "Won't you come down? We can get a bun and a cup of tea." It had all been arranged by the army that every so often the train stopped for tea, supper, breakfast, or lunch. I took a cup of tea and it was more than welcome. As far as I could see, I was the only civilian on the train. It seems funny to me how little I cared about my clothes as long as they were clean. I knew that I could not obtain better or more suitable garments, so I simply told myself not to worry about things which could not be changed.

I dozed off and must have slept rather a long time because the train was slowing down and the girls said we were coming in to Minden, where we should be given a hot meal. Ah yes, Minden! Do I not remember how twelve days before the liberation, we had been loaded into closed cattle trucks in Minden to be moved away from the Allied forces, who were closing the circle each day. How completely apathetic we had been! Or perhaps we could not spare any effort to talk or worry about other people. We had just sat on the floor of the boxcar, half lying because we were not crowded, and most of us did not care what was going to happen to us, provided it happened quickly. We were hungry, thirsty, and, above all, without a drop of strength. When they had started to march us out of the camp toward Minden, I was sure that none of us could drag herself more than a few hundred meters. All this had happened fifteen months ago and here I was getting off the train, a free person again — but, in all honesty, I knew that I was not, and never would be, free of the horrors and losses.

The army must have served thousands of dinners daily, and the children from Minden came to beg for food near the station. There was a tall fence dividing off the platform where the meals were served and the top of it was full of children reaching out for food or stretching out their hands with a container in which to put food. I went and looked to see what I could eat. I found that I could have only the bread and two apples, because for the last ten months I had already been eating only kosher food. An ATS officer came to me with a bowl of soup in her hands and said, "I see you are not taking out the cooked food so I took it in your name and, if you agree, I shall give it to those poor starving children." I put out my hand and said, "May I have my soup, please?" and walked out just outside the door, where there was a large container for throwing away disposable plates, poured away the soup, and threw the plate into the bin. I did not want to see the faces of the children, but how could I give food to them and be a traitor to the little ones who had been murdered by the fathers and uncles of these children? I hated the Germans for what they had made of me.

I climbed onto the train and was the first back in the compartment. I shut my eyes and tried hard to do two things: one, not to think and live in the past, and not to try to build a picture of Mark's family, friends, surroundings, and life in England in order not to be disappointed. I was sure of one thing, and that was that I should make every effort possible to get on well with all members of his family and friends. After all, the important and only person in my life was Mark and therefore all other things and people would be side issues. I was forcing myself not to think, yet I was wondering if those children on the fence were really hungry or were begging because they had been sent by their parents. I thought that in just another few hours I should be leaving Germany, never ever to return to it. "Oh dear God, will that cure me of my hatred?" I wanted to know. How could I ever repay them for what they had done to me?

The ATS officers started coming back and settling down with their lap blankets and completely ignored me. I thought when we pass the borders of Germany, what sort of blessing should I say? I went outside into the corridor to say my evening prayers. After that, I looked for a suitable psalm to say and I remembered that instead of the land of my forefathers, I was traveling to a strange, kind, and civilized country, and therefore I was afraid I might forget my longing for my own country and my duty to my people. I found psalm 136, "By the rivers of Babylon, there we sat down, yea we wept when we remembered Zion... If I forget thee, O Jerusalem, may my right hand forget her cunning. If I do not remember thee, let my tongue cleave to the roof of my mouth, if I prefer not Jerusalem above my chief joy." I said the psalm, meaning every word of it. *Even today during marriage ceremonies, under the special wedding canopy, we sing, "If I forget thee, O Jerusalem," and I am still moved to tears and feel so very privileged to be living in my own country.*

I went inside, sat down, and said a few polite words to the girls — and I suddenly realized why these nice girls kept their distance and none of them asked where I was traveling, where I came from, and who was I going to meet. I felt a surge of warmth toward them for respecting my privacy, which had been destroyed by the Germans. I realized that the girls were shy to start a conversation but were glad to exchange some words with me.

I counted the hours until I should meet Mark, my only anchor to life, so difficult to carry on. I thought it would be rather pleasant to be surrounded by neighbors who would not pry and want to know everything about me but would accept or not accept me for what I was. We all started dozing as the train traveled slowly, stopping and starting, not letting us forget for one moment that there had been a war brought on by maniacs who killed millions of people, destroying not only civilization and the souls of people but also the possibility of normal life in Europe for the time being.

Later on, one of the ATS officers opened a large thermos flask and offered tea to the girls and myself and I gratefully accepted. I dropped off to sleep and when I woke up, the surroundings looked as if we were out of Germany. I smiled and the girl opposite noticed that I was looking happier and said, "Yes, I think we left Germany just a little while ago." We were due to arrive in Calais at twelve o'clock and Mark was due to arrive from Liege at one thirty or two o'clock. I had no doubt that I should be met in Calais and that my miserable so-called suitcase, which I had booked through to Dover, would be waiting for me there. The organization was simply magnificent and everything went off smoothly.

We stopped again, early in the morning, for breakfast. This was the day I should be meeting Mark again, going with him to England and he would be taking me home with him to his parents' house. We all ate a hearty breakfast and I had hot porridge, a roll and butter, and lots of tea.

The train started moving. However much I wanted to make my mind blank and not think or worry, I nevertheless wondered how much my future parents-in-law would be disappointed in me. The girls began packing up their books and blankets, and started to make up their faces: pancake, rouge, powder, lipstick, eyebrow pencil, and a little perfume. They were all excited, ready to get off the train and go home on leave or to their new posting. I had it much easier because I had no makeup, not even lipstick. I was ready to leave the train hoping to meet, in two hours' time, the man I was going to love for the rest of my life.

The train pulled into a place not far from the sea. There were many large tents, streets of them, with army personnel busy about their jobs. The moment the train stopped, I heard the loudspeaker clearly saying, "Would Mrs. Lea Chayen, wife of Captain M.S. Chayen, please come to the meeting point on the platform?" With my brown coat on my arm and my over-large handbag, I went to the meeting point, where an ATS sergeant was waiting for me. She said, "I am sorry you have to share a tent with the wives of the other ranks, but the right hand side is for the officers' wives."

There were army cots along the walls of the tent, and on the right hand side was a very chic, obviously French girl, lying on the cot and reading. She greeted me in good English, with a heavy French accent, and said, "Hello, are you a wife as well?" I smiled and said I was. We started talking and she said, "You know, I was luckier than you. I was in the underground, fighting and taking escaped airmen and prisoners of war to safe houses. One of the houses was my parents' home, where we hid a wounded British officer. He is my husband now. He is not here, he is waiting for me in London."

I looked at the other side. There was a nice, dignified, grandmotherly type of French lady, and next to her a woman in her Sunday best, including a hat perched on the top of her head, looking like a peasant going on an outing. She had a little boy of about two and a half years old, a baby girl who was trying to walk, and another child on the way. A sergeant came in and the little boy ran to him, calling him "Papa," and the little girl wanted him to pick her up.

The French girl next to me said, "It makes you wonder how she will fit in and how his parents will like his choice." He must have been an escaped prisoner of war, hidden by this women, who became the mother of his children. The amazing thing was that she could speak no English and very little French; she spoke only Flemish, of which her husband knew only a few words. "Well," my new friend said, "the language of love is international. They can raise ten children and still never learn to talk to each other."

An ATS sergeant came and asked us to come to the hut where they were serving a hot lunch. I went with the French girl to the dining hall but could not eat anything except the bread and an apple. It was already one fifteen and every time I looked at my watch, my heart started racing. I prayed for Mark to reach Calais without any trouble or delay. I could not keep still and started walking up and down inside the tent and then I went out on to the platform but it was deserted.

It was an overcast day, with the sun trying to push its rays through. Then I saw the ATS sergeant going to the meeting point with a microphone and I knew that the train should arrive within a few minutes. I went and stood next to the sergeant, the train came in, and I searched the windows to get a glimpse of Mark. The train came to a stop and the sergeant next to me spoke into the loudspeaker, "Would Captain M.S. Chayen please come to the meeting point on the platform to collect his wife?"

Epilogue

"There'll be bluebirds over the white cliffs of Dover" goes the song. Instead of bluebirds, we had clear blue skies over the white cliffs of Dover, and the Channel was as smooth as a millpond for our crossing.

Mark and I stood on the deck watching the coast of England coming nearer. This was going to be my new country, the country which had fought and come out victorious over tyranny and barbarism, the country to which I owed such a lot. Mark was talking and explaining all the time, wanting me to love England as much as he did. I remembered as a child reading David Copperfield, in Hungarian translation, and how David was brought to his aunt in Dover.

We disembarked in Dover, followed a signposted route, and finally found ourselves opposite the train for London, with our luggage waiting for us. It was a fine sunny day in England, land of fog and rain, and I took it as good omen. We arrived in London and took a taxi to Fenchurch Street station, to travel to Southend-on-Sea, where Mark's parents lived. Before boarding the train, Mark took me into the station buffet and we had a "nice cup of tea." I liked the lady who poured the tea and said to me, "Here you are, dear, here's a nice cuppa."

We took the train and Mark explained everything on the way. When we reached Benfleet he said, "Thank Heaven the tide is in. Isn't it lovely, darling? You will love it here. We are going to buy ourselves another sailing dinghy — my old one is not seaworthy any more." We came to Leigh Old Town and he told me all about it. I loved all the sailing boats at their moorings, at least those I could see, because it was already dark.

The train pulled into Southend-on-Sea station and Mark said, "I hope you will love everybody at home, they are so anxious to meet you." I tried not to think, neither of the past nor of the future, but as long as Mark was at my side I was sure I could conquer anything.

We took a taxi and after a short ride, arrived at a detached double-fronted house. Mark said, "This is Timberscombe, my darling, this is where I grew up. Welcome home."

We rang the bell. It was about ten-thirty or eleven. Mark's mother came downstairs in her dressing gown and then his father came, and I was duly introduced. Mark's mother put on a kettle to make a cup of tea in true English fashion — at the time, I could not imagine that fifty years later I should still be making tea first thing in the morning and, of course, in the afternoon.

We had something to eat and had a cup of tea, and then we went to bed; I had been on the move for thirty-six hours and Mark was very tired, too. I went into the room prepared for me. I could not drop off to sleep although I was very tired. I thought, "The first hurdle is over. They are very nice people and I hope we will like each other."

The following morning I overslept. Mark was up in his dressing gown and knocked quietly on my door to see if I was awake. He said, "Would you like to come downstairs for a cup of tea, or would you rather I brought you one up?"

I said, no, I should be down in five minutes. I went downstairs and found a woman in the dining room cleaning, and later polishing the silver for the Friday evening table. I went into the morning room and greeted my future mother-in-law. I still had to grow used to calling her "Mama." She asked me if I had slept well, and after exchanging a few polite sentences, I drank up my tea and went upstairs to dress.

It was a lovely sunny day in late May but not at all warm. I came downstairs fairly quickly, choking back my tears when I saw the maid polishing the candlesticks and the silver goblet. There was a Friday morning smell of chicken soup, which I remembered from another world, gone forever. Mark was standing in the middle of the kitchen, in grey flannel trousers and a sports jacket. This was the first time I had ever seen him in civilian clothes.

We had breakfast. My mother-in-law was baking a cherry cake and I thought I should go crazy. I tried to smile, but I do not think it was convincing enough because Mama suggested that Mark take me out to show me the town and the sea. As we walked out of the house, Mark asked in a worried tone, "What is the matter, my dear, don't you like my parents?"

I answered, "Yes, I do, but I can't get used to living again."

We walked down Southchurch Road to Victoria Circus and turned left into the High Street. In front of a shoe shop there were standing three generations: a grandmother, her daughter, and a little girl of about two-and-a-half or three, wearing a red harness. I gaped at them. Somehow the Germans did not count; here people were still leading normal lives, while my world and the world around me had gone up in flames. I drew a little nearer to hear what they had been discussing for such a long time and was shaken that they were discussing what color sandals would be most suitable.

We walked down to the sea and sat on a bench, where we would not be observed. There I broke down and started sobbing. I begged Mark to understand and recognize his mistake in wanting to marry me, and please would he let me go? He again promised that if, after two years or even one year, I felt I could not lead a normal life, he would let me go.

We walked home, I with red swollen eyes and poor Mark, apprehensive.

We were married in London, three weeks later, with Mark's family and friends being so nice. Outstandingly so was my late sister-in-law Coralie, a fine, feeling person from whose house I was married, and her brother, Ronald, a dentist, who had just left the air force and was a great friend of Mark's and, later on, of mine as well. Unfortunately both of them passed on rather prematurely.

We bought a most cheerful house with a pleasant garden in Fairway, Leigh-on-Sea, near the golf course. We had two little boys, David and then Benjamin. We had many friends amongst our immediate neighbors, and also old friends of Mark. We bought a sailing dinghy, sailed, played tennis, and with Mark's love and help, I learned to live and laugh again.

My nightmares continued, up to and including this very day, but that is part of me and my life.

On the nineteenth of January, 1951, we left, with our two little boys, for Israel, where we had a girl, Michal, the first sabra (native-born Israeli) in our family. We live in Israel with our children, grandchildren, and a lovely great-granddaughter called Rina, and with the Almighty's help, we hope for many more. We take a very active part in the life of the country and find building the land of our forefathers a great privilege.

> "For Thou hast delivered my soul from death, my eyes from tears, my feet from falling. I shall walk before the Lord in the land of the living. I kept my faith..."
>
> (Psalms 116)